Barbershop

History and Antiques

Christian R. Jones

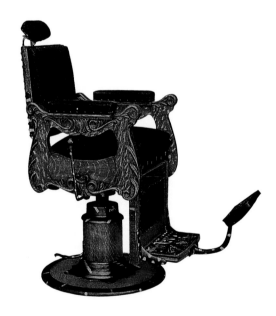

Schiffer Publishing Ltd

4880 Lower Valley Road, Atglen, PA 19310 USA

This book is dedicated to the memory of the late John D. Kamrad

----

As an 18-year old apprentice, I had the extreme good fortune to be taken under the wings of a true master barber. "Big" John, as he was affectionately known by *everybody* in the community, was a second generation barber of German ancestry. He epitomized the artisan barber who was dedicated to his work. As my master, Big John taught me barbering well. As my mentor, he taught me about life. He left us all much too soon, and before I adequately thanked him for sharing so much with me. He was a barber's barber; he was a man's man and I miss him dearly.

Library of Congress Cataloging-in-Publication Data

Jones, Christian R.
    Barbershop : history and antiques / Christian R. Jones.
      p. cm.
    Includes bibliographical references and index.
    ISBN 0-7643-0695-2 (hardcover)
      1. Barbershops--Equipment and supplies--Collectors and
collecting --Catalogs. I. Title.
TT979.J66   1999
646.7'24'075--dc21

                                                                98-41638
                                                                CIP

Designed by Bonnie M. Hensley
Type set in Americana Xbd BT/Humanist 521 BT

ISBN: 0-7643-0695-2
Printed in China
1 2 3 4

Published by Schiffer Publishing Ltd.
4880 Lower Valley Road
Atglen, PA 19310
Phone: (610) 593-1777; Fax: (610) 593-2002
E-mail: Schifferbk@aol.com
Please write for a free catalog.
This book may be purchased from the publisher.
Please include $3.95 for shipping.

In Europe, Schiffer books are distributed by
Bushwood Books
6 Marksbury Rd.
Kew Gardens
Surrey TW9 4JF England
Phone: 44 (0)181 392-8585; Fax: 44 (0)181 392-9876
E-mail: Bushwd@aol.com

Please try your bookstore first.

We are interested in hearing from authors
with book ideas on related subjects.

Contents

Acknowledgments

My gratitude is offered to the following people who offered their help in making this book a reality. Your time and efforts are sincerely appreciated.

Ben Powell, Columbus, New Jersey
Bill and Diane Wright, Pomfret, Maryland
Tony Gugliotti, Wolcott, Connecticut
Tom and Penny Nader, Allentown, Pennsylvania
Mike and Mary Sparks, Dallas, Texas
Phil Krumholz, Bartonsville, Illinois
Bernie Lucko, Granville, Ohio
Woody Lovell, Hollywood, California
Keith Estep, Old Lyme, Connecticut

Dave and Nancy Giese, Stafford, Virginia
Mitsuru Kajikawa, Misasa Onsen, Japan
Bill and Marlene Levin, Delran, New Jersey
Don Perkins, Indianapolis, Indiana
John Vaccaro, Mt. Kisco, New York
Mark and Connie Stellinga, Coralville, Iowa
Ray and Theresa Jones, Morristown, New Jersey

Together, we have been able to provide a book that should encourage a deeper understanding of *all* traditional barbershop antiques and collectibles. Hopefully, it will also serve to attract the interests of many new collectors to our enjoyable pastime.

By whose decrees, our sinful souls to save,
No Sunday tankards foam, no barber shave. -Byron

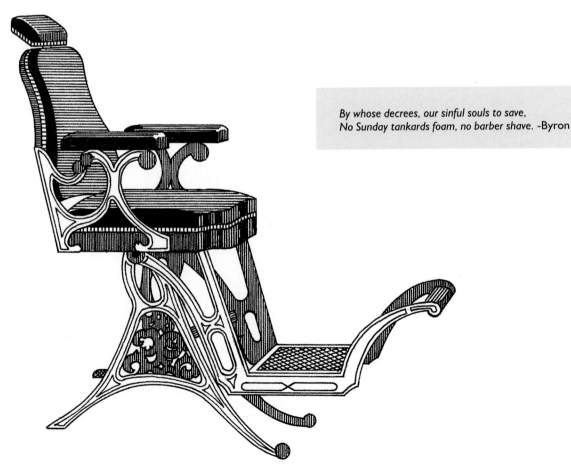

ARCHER'S PATENT
ADJUSTABLE BARBER CHAIR No. 5

Foreword

Within the antique and collectible world, the barbershop category has long provided many beautiful and interesting items. Until approximately ten years ago, the items that were most popular, and which also remain as the cornerstones of the barbershop collectible spectrum, include shaving mugs, straight razors, barber bottles, and striped barber poles. While poles have always been purchased by a general antique buying audience, razors, mugs, and bottles have had hotbeds of organized collectors who clamor for every item that finds its way to the marketplace. One would only have to see the prices realized from recent auction sales to understand just *how* sought after these articles really have become. The demand for them continues to spearhead the market, however in recent years there has been a rapidly growing interest from collectors who want to acquire more than just these "icon" pieces. Enthusiasts have become interested in exploring everything that recalls the old time barbershop experience: furniture, tools, advertising, photos, catalogs, post cards, and more; simply everything!

Change at the barbershop

The underlying thrust behind the broad range of interest in barbershop collectibles seems to be the universal consensus that barbershop experiences of old are fading fast. It appears that traditional barbers are joining an expanding line of occupations that have been eliminated as "progress" diminishes their usefulness. We're all aware of the historical passing of lamplighters, pony-express riders, and buggymakers. Traditional barbershops, as they were known in the slower paced time, seem now to be in their waning years as well. Now it is time to snare an article or two from barbering's proud occupational history.

A laundry list of social and economic changes has greatly impacted the traditional barber business so that the per-capita number of barber licensees is at an all time low. Since World War II, registered barbershops in America have dropped from nearly 123,000 to less than 60,000. This precipitous change has been duly noted by a recent spate of media attention, not to mention the average fellow who is having difficulty simply finding a good old fashioned barber! Change, as they say, is inevitable.

The Collectors

So, who are the barbershop history seekers? There are, and will continue to be, many established collectors of bottles, mugs, razors, and poles who are simply broadening their interests. There are occupational history buffs whose interests are in documenting and preserving the past. Many people have game rooms decorated like 100 year old, complete barber shops. Perhaps the fastest growing group of collectors are present-day owners of haircutting establishments who seem to have collectively discovered their occupational roots. The interest is global as evidenced by the shops of Mitsuru Kajikawa of Japan; Woody Lovell of Hollywood, California; John Vaccaro of New York; and many others in between. These modern-day practitioners choose to "retro"

decorate their current shops or salons with all of the barbershop antiques and collectibles they can find. All of them report that the resulting nostalgic ambiance is enthusiastically received by the public. No matter what reasons any of us have for collecting barbershop memorabilia, everybody seems keenly aware of the investment perspective on owning antiques and collectibles in general.

Who knows, if the trend of recapturing the old-time barbershop experience continues, maybe the traditional barbers' future will brighten once more. For me, there is enjoyment in collecting items which evoke such a long and interesting history. Those of you who have an appreciation for the past can read on and enjoy the journey!

At first glance, this photo appears to be from bygone days. Don't be fooled. Woody Lovell and Company of Hollywood, California have been at the forefront of contemporary barbers who are finding success with a nostalgic presentation and practical use of barbershop antiques. They are currently located at 6907 Melrose Avenue, Los Angeles, California 90038. Expansion plans include locations in Manhattan, New York and Europe.

Introduction

Much has been written about haircutting and shaving history, including documented information that takes the story back to the Stone Age. An attempt here to cover that entire time until the present would require this book to be little more than a long history lesson. While we *are* going to take look at many highlights of barbershop occupational history, the real focus of this book is to present barbershop antiques as bearers of information. There is an introduction to the broad scope so that beginning collectors can grasp the range of items available and specialty collectors can expand their awareness into other areas. It is also a detailed reference work for all collectors that will help to identify, price, and date their items. It promises to add provenance to articles you can add to your collections for years to come.

This book concentrates on the period of time that most collectors recognize as barbering's "golden years," from about 1880 to 1940. The events that contributed to the beginning and the end of the golden years are explained. You may be tempted to wonder, if there is really more than three millenniums of recorded history of haircutting and shaving, how a fleeting, sixty year period can have such a significant impact on today's collector. The answer is that there is now available a relative plethora of items from the most prosperous time in barbershop history. Let's face it, as collectors we need things to find. How much fun would it be if we only rarely found something to acquire when we went "antiquing?" In times prior to the golden years, barbers used little more than scissors and razors. They also performed medical and dental procedures for centuries, however the precious few articles that remain from that early history tend to be more archival than plentiful. Included here are items such as bleeding instruments, leeching and cupping utensils, and early tooth extractors that barbers may have used, but they are not plentiful or diverse enough to be easily found. Rather, items from the exclusive golden years era remain as the most desirable and *available* barbershop antiques and collectibles.

If a man have long hair, it is a shame unto him. But if a woman have long hair, it is a glory to her. -S. Paul

Practical Considerations
of Barbershop Collectibles

The Socio-economic Factor

The beauty and splendor that was obtainable in a barbershop during the golden years was not reached in *all* shops. Many of the barbershop items that were costly to manufacture and carried high price tags were not made or sold in large numbers. These items remain scarce in today's antique market. For every grand scale barbershop in the cities, there were many more counterpart shops in small towns making do with far less.

For example, an early 1900s grand shop in Los Angeles, California, may have had an iron sidewalk pole with whirling stripes; 20 work stations, each with wooden hydraulic chairs; central heating; electrified crystal chandeliers; custom carved wooden mirror cases with beautiful blown glass bottles on the marble counter; a 60 hole, tiger oak, rack filled with one of a kind, artist painted, china mugs; elaborate tile flooring; nickel plated, self righting spittoons; and flushing toilets. Conversely, just a 15-minute buggy ride into the country might bring you to the local barber's place with a hand painted wooden pole rotting at the base; 2 work stations with second-hand chairs; a pot-belly stove; oil lamps or bare electric bulbs for light; a mirror over a shelf containing a few clear glass bottles; no mug rack; plank wood floors; a bucket to spit your chew into; and an outhouse just down the dirt path. Obviously, most of the desirable items that are searched for today came from better financed shops in more populated areas. Therefore, there is a scarcity of better quality barbershop collectibles today. By the time the golden years were winding down in the 1940s, most of the big city barbershops had been scaled back and outlying shops had uniformly improved their establishments. There was then more parity in the barber business than at any time since the 1870s.

Catalogs and Photographs

There are no tools for compiling antique research material more definitive than catalogs and photographs which remain from the period being studied. Catalogs can determine in what year an item was available for sale and in how many styles, sizes, and colors it came as well as its original cost and manufacturer. Photographs, on the other hand, show the items as they appeared in the workplace and nearly always portray the ambiance of the shop and spirit of the barbers who posed stone-faced, but proud. If a collector finds an item that they *think* was used in a barbershop, nothing can confirm or prove wrong this suspicion better than a catalog or photograph of the item in use. Written and photographic evidence that validates an item is always desirable in a specialized collection because they make the articles more interesting and valuable.

In researching this book, 19 catalogs were utilized which represent 11 supply houses or manufacturers. They provide first hand, period documentation of the decades from 1880 to 1940. Also, hundreds of photographs were scrutinized, most with a magnifying glass. Therefore, nearly all of the items that appear in this book can be validated with catalog or photographic sources.

You Can't Get There From Here

Many people have visited my barbershop museum which exhibits nearly 3000 articles covering the full spectrum of barbershop occupational history. The most often asked question by these visitors is: "Where do you buy this barbershop stuff?" There are no

Calitype process color postcard of the elite Metropolitan barber shop in Los Angeles, California in 1910. Inset photo shows the owner, P.B. Roy who billed his 22 chair shop as "the largest and finest in the world." Postcard, $20.00.

Photo showing humble, but practical, rural shop of John Elgrim. Note the glowing pot-belly stove. 8" x 10", photo, $45.00.

auctions or antique outlets that deal *exclusively* in barbershop collectibles. To build a representative barbershop collection, a person would need to search a wide variety of specialty shops, shows, and flea markets. Many beautifully restored wooden barber chairs and whirling striped barber poles are placed in game rooms for their conversation value as well as comfort. Bottles may be found among antique glass, signs from antique advertising dealers and shows.

For shaving mugs, your best bet would be to join the National Shaving Mug Collectors Association, an organization of collectors who buy and sell shaving mugs continually. Organized in 1980, the group of 600 members worldwide preserve interest in shaving mugs and barbershop collectibles by maintaining 250 books and articles on barbershop collecting. They meet twice annually to buy, sell and trade items. To join, write to 1608 Mineral Spring Road, Reading, PA 19602.

For a barbershop reverse running clock, you could check with an antique clock specialist. For barbershop images on paper, price menus or postcards, attend rare paper or postcard specialty shows. Many of the smaller items, such as brushes, razors, and strops, will turn up at your local antique flea market. Collecting barbershop items in general can be complicated and requires patience.

The situation reminds me of a big city cabby who was asked for directions to a specific, but obscure, place across town. The cabby's face took on a perplexed look when he realized how difficult it would be to explain. Instead of trying, he simply looked up at the anxious pedestrian with a straight face and replied, "you can't get there from here."

To Restore or Not To Restore

Many discussions take place about restoring, reconditioning, or repairing antiques. Some people feel that all articles of age should be left in the condition as found. In barbershop collecting it would be a mistake to acquire a 125 year old wooden barber pole with *original* color remaining and paint over the old to brighten it up. The resulting "reconditioned" surface would confuse the age of the piece and probably lower the value. Other situations may be viewed differently but also carry significant ethical considerations. For example, if you have a great shaving mug with a chip on the rim, to make it appear complete you might elect to have it professionally repaired. Would this be right or wrong? Most collectors will agree that it is entirely appropriate to make the repair, as long as the repair is documented and the value appropriately adjusted when the mug is sold. Professionally repaired glass can be difficult to detect, but undamaged items always have more value.

Wooden barbershop furnishings and porcelain, mechanical poles almost always increase in value after a quality restoration because most people who own barbering items want to put them on display. If a 100 year old barber chair or sidewalk pole is found in the rough, it probably lacks eye appeal. Old chairs may have the original wood patina painted over, original upholstery is usually gone, and formerly nickel plated parts are often rusted or broken. Old poles may have the porcelain chipped, glass cylinders and globes cracked *or worse*, and motors or spring mechanisms frozen tight. These items most people want in their home in restored condition. Antiques like these usually can be accurately restored when materials consistent with the original are used. Nickled or chromed parts could be restored with either plating process, but you would not want to reupholster a 1910 barber chair with hot pink vinyl. Porcelain cracks and chips can have the porcelain re-fired or repaired with synthetic resins which offer as much durability as the originals. Restored items that retain their historic originality look better and are worth more to the next collector.

The antiques community in general is responsible about informing prospective buyers of any restoration work that has been done,

but selling ethics are not written in stone and you should ask questions if you have *any* concerns. Reputable sellers will welcome your scrutiny. A buyer would be foolish not to thoroughly inspect a piece for repairs. In addition to enjoying our antiques today, most of us expect their value to appreciate as time goes on. Nobody wants to find out after ten years that the shaving mug they paid $800 for has a whole bottom lip glued on; that would mean the mug was overpriced. *Stay awake.*

Price Guide Notes

Some books with price guides have left me scratching my head in wonderment. The values may seem too high or too low, or there are complex formulas that you must compute before reaching a "suggested" value. Formulas get so complex that they guy standing next to you can buy the piece and walk away before you have figured out even how much you should offer.

My goal with these values is to present only ballpark figures for a broad variety of barbershop items that exist in today's market; prices that you would realistically encounter on a current antique hunt or in an auction sale.

Here you will see photographs of original catalog pages and actual antiques as they appear today with prices in the photo captions or with the corresponding text. I am reluctant to place values on items appearing in catalogs pages, some of which are rarely, if ever, seen on the secondary market. Who truly knows what some of these wish-list items would sell for *if and when* they might turn up? However, when prices are put on catalog page items that are known to currently exist, they reflect a range that you could expect to pay if found in good to restored condition. The prices assigned to the actual antiques seen in this book approximate what you could expect to pay for them just as they appear in the photographs. Where a plus sign (+) appears after a price, it simply means that there are circumstances, such as auctions or an extraordinary example, where an item could be higher. There are *many* variables that enter into antique and collectible prices. To guard against overpaying, do your homework. **The more you know, the better informed your purchase decisions will be.** Be prepared for wild price swings that depend on different areas of the country, how common or rare the item is, the disposition of the seller, and *your willingness to pay based on how badly you want it!*

The values presented here are based on the author's activity for many years as a collector of *all* types of barbershop items. Attendance at flea markets, small and large shows, auctions, conventions, and business with specialty dealers, classified advertising in a broad variety of the antique trade publications, and recent absentee auction prices all have contributed to the indicators for some of the items seen on these pages. Prices from an auction are sometimes driven up by over exuberant bidders, yet auction prices *do* indicate the ultimate worth of an item, if only to one person. The key for you is to moderate and *decide your personal limits once you know the range.*

You may become interested in a particular area within barbershop collecting, such as mugs, razors, or bottles, and want to explore the well written books on those topics listed in the bibliography.

Reputable and experienced auction/clearing houses for razors, bottles, mugs, and more are mentioned in Chapter 2 under those headings.

This research is not expected to be the last word in the history of barbershop collectibles, which is not an exact science. The author and the publisher accept no responsibility for any loss that may incur through its use. When you can provide missing facts, hopefully you will let the author know by writing to him through the publisher. Above all, keep the hunt enjoyable. *Collecting should be fun!*

1894 Theo. A. Kochs barber supply catalogue. Heavily embossed and tinted. 90 pages in a 9.25" x 12.5" format. Lithographed, color illustrations of barber chairs, poles, mugs, and bottles. $350.00.

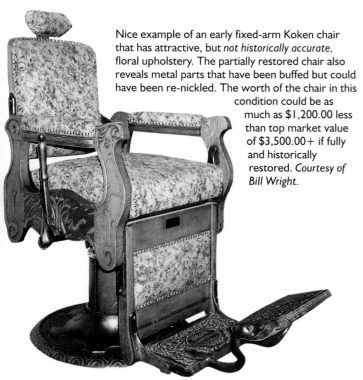

Nice example of an early fixed-arm Koken chair that has attractive, but *not historically accurate,* floral upholstery. The partially restored chair also reveals metal parts that have been buffed but could have been re-nickled. The worth of the chair in this condition could be as much as $1,200.00 less than top market value of $3,500.00+ if fully and historically restored. *Courtesy of Bill Wright.*

Koken manufactured chair that was labeled and marketed through Jones Bros. Barber Supply in Canada shows how a ragged, unfinished chair can appear. Round seat and back, brass trim, good working order, unfinished, $1500.00 to $2000.00. *Courtesy of Bill Wright.*

Chapter 1
The Golden Years Timeline

There are five primary reasons which contributed to the barbershop's Golden Years era between 1880 and 1940:

The Industrial Revolution

In the early to mid-1800s, a period of history began to unfold that would change not only the world in general, but also produced some of the most imaginative, beautiful, and plentiful items ever seen in barbershops. The Industrial Revolution began in England in the eighteenth century and it blossomed in America by the mid-1800s. Designs, machinery, and mass production expanded rapidly. It is amazing to consider that the very first United States patent was issued in 1836 and by 1911 more than a million more patents had been issued. Mass production brought about lower retail prices for most items. People were becoming accustomed to "store bought" items that had only been dreamt of previously. They could choose retail items in a dizzying array of sizes, materials, colors, and price ranges that reflected a good, better, and best quality. This was a period of innovation for barbershop related products. The Industrial Revolution brought a new era of commerce that was good not only for barbers, but for the industrialized world in general.

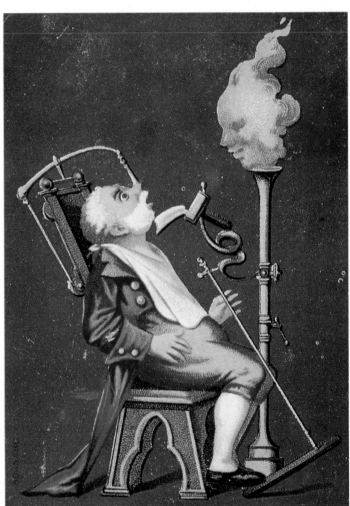

Victorian era card cleverly reinforces how imaginations were working with regard to the seemingly boundless products of the Industrial Revolution. Luckily for barbers, no machine was ever invented that could successfully wield a straight razor. 3" x 5" color-lithograph, giveaway card, $15.00.

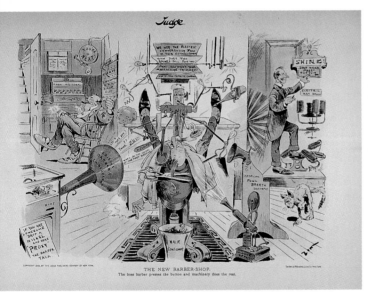

This lithograph cartoon appeared in *Judge* magazine in the 1800s. It was at a time when the Industrial Revolution was fresh in the minds of the public. People were fascinated by the emerging possibilities of mechanization and electricity. 10.5" x 13.5". $45.00.

Improved Transportation and Mail Delivery

Coinciding with the manufacturing boom were the great strides being made in transportation. Rail lines and steamship routes were being expanded dramatically. This made the previously relied upon horse and wagon transport modes seem more inefficient than ever. In fact, by 1869, the transcontinental railway had become fully operational and there were 50,000 miles of track being utilized throughout America at that time. Mail delivery service had improved so that most people could be reached by freight deliveries.

Hegener Barbers' Supply card from 1880s. Note the reference to "country" barbershop deliveries. 2.5" x 3.75". $40.00.

The Advent of Catalogs

Mail order catalogs developed in response to consumer demands for the new items that could be transported through the mail. Consequently, any barber with an order form and a one-cent stamp could purchase never before imagined items for his business. The widespread use of catalogs meant that anybody in any small town could shop almost as though they were spending a day in the city. Merchants experimented with the catalog idea in the early 1800s, but it met with little success. It wasn't until the 486-page *American Hardware Catalogue of 1865* was offered that America embraced catalog sales. By the early 1900s, some catalogs had reached epic proportions. Consider, for instance, the 1906 *E.C. Simmons* catalog which contained 4,200 pages and 21,000 illustrations. The 25,000 issues that were printed for distribution filled sixteen rail cars and had a cumulative weight of 500,000 pounds.

Letterhead in which the Kraut and Dohnal mail order barber supply company claims to have been the first in 1861. Letter size. $20.00.

While these catalogs did contain items for barbers, it was only in the 1870s and '80s that a variety of barber supply houses began to send out their own specialty catalogs. One of the earliest was Kraut and Dohnal of Cincinnati, Ohio, in 1861. Other prominent companies offering mail order supplies were the Archer Company, Berninghaus Supply, and the Kochs and Koken industry giants. Where barbers previously had gotten by with an old armchair and simple set of hand tools, they now could order an unbelievable array of furnishings and accessories. Better financed barbers purchased the best furnishings and supplies being offered and turned their shops into places of near opulence. There were: beautiful oak and black walnut chairs with hand carved embellishments and plush upholstery; thick, deeply beveled mirrors resting in elaborately carved cabinets; gleaming brass and nickel plating on towel steamers and spittoons; a rainbow of color from blown glass tonic bottles; one of a kind, artist painted, shaving mugs; ornately detailed advertising signs; Italian marble counters, and sometimes, marble flooring. If all of this wasn't enough, the "best of the best" shops had tray ceilings with artist painted frescos on them and crystal or stained glass chandeliers were not uncommon either. The innovative manufacturing techniques and trade catalogs had plenty to do with select barbershops becoming stunning places during the golden years.

Victorian Fashion Requisites

The reign of Queen Victoria in England, from 1837 through 1901, is commonly referred to as the Victorian Period. Her influence was felt in many diverse areas, not only in her homeland but in Europe and America as well. Queen Victoria was insistent upon strict morality that gave new meaning to being ladies and gentlemen and to displaying proper etiquette. In literature as well as the decorative arts and fashion her influence was felt. Victorian writers Tennyson, Kipling, Dickens, Darwin and Browning reflected the strict lifestyle of this era. Victorian furniture design, clothing, and grooming fashions all became fancy and ornate. Everything was done with a flourish: gilding, carvings, plating, etching, etcetera. Overall, this era is epitomized as "proper and fancy." Previously, barbers in America had served relatively unkempt patrons who had been fighting battles, building railroads, exploring uncharted territories, and generally laboring to build a new country. They could hardly be expected to be overly refined when it came to personal grooming. However, the pressures of Victorian attitudes and expectations ultimately influenced even the common man in America

Recommended hair style charts of all sizes and varieties were introduced during the Victorian period. Many were issued by hair product suppliers. The chart seen here is on a business trade card from the 1890s. 2.75" x 5". $25.00.

to develop regular shaving and hair grooming habits. By the late 1800s, product advertisers were posting charts of suggested hair and beard styles and were offering hundreds of tonics and scalp remedies for use in the tonsorial pursuit. By 1900, "proper" men everywhere were expected to be well groomed. The Victorian influence was undeniably responsible for the increase in barbershop revenues throughout the golden years.

Hair and beard style chart from Pinaud shows 40 different "proper" ways to be groomed in 1900. 21" x 14". $125.00

Barber Schools

In response to increased business, barber schools began to spring up in major cities in America soon after 1900. Many of these institutions belonged to A.B. Moler who devised a method of training which, to this day, remains applicable. His first school was established in 1893 and was loftily referred to as a Barber "College," as were most other barber schools for many years to come. Moler's idea developed in response to his dissatisfaction with the traditional apprenticeship training method in which barber "boys" swept floors and did menial tasks, sometimes for as long as two years, before they actually began to shave or cut hair. Moler's curriculum taught systems of sterilization and sanitation, how to make tonics and other toiletries, how to bottle them for resale and, further, *how to sell them* to the customers. Moler also taught ethics that should still be taught today. In short, Moler produced a more professional barber right out of school, one who would be able to walk through the front door of an established shop and begin working productively right away. While it was clear that Moler's schools were a better way of providing a labor

As evidenced by this creative magazine advertisement from the 1920s, Moler's initially humble course of instruction gained national prominence and success. 6" x 9" magazine advertisement, $12.00.

pool, surprisingly, the barber shop owners initially balked at his ideas primarily because barber schools usually had provided services for free or for a reduced price. Private shop owners feared that his teaching would cut into their own profits and that the students would not be capable practitioners. Both fears gradually were put to rest and barber colleges became generally established. The new training system greatly facilitated barbering's golden years.

> My hair is gray, but not with years;
>   Nor grew it white
>   In a single night,
> As men's have grown from sudden fears. -Shakespeare

The Golden Years: 1880 To 1940

If you had been a barber before 1880, you could have expected to earn a meager living at best. Working conditions of those times have been described by more than one writer as "squalid." Some barbers' stature in their communities was not reputable, since gamblers and drunkards idled away many hours at their establishments. Others were probably held in disdain for their never-ending attempts to sell customers quack hair remedies and cures for baldness.

Although contemporary, artist Lee Dubin's work entitled *"The Tonsorial Parlor"* captures the charm of a bygone time in exquisite fashion. This collotype print personifies the golden years and is available in 24" x 30" from the artist at Drury Lane Incorporated, 6442 Coldwater Canyon, N. Hollywood, California 91606. Phone: 1-818-509-2687. Current value, $60.00.

The social influences developing during the golden years, as explained above, changed this in most places. The shop furnishings were much improved. Emerging knowledge of sanitation became the order of the day. In keeping with proper Victorian attitudes of morality and behavior, drinking and gambling in barbershops was greatly reduced. As barbers' unions became organized, working conditions and pay improved immediately and dramatically. The unions also set codes of ethics and standards which included urging the barbers to refrain from selling quack hair and scalp remedies. That went a long way in helping them to be viewed as more professional.

Along with the industrialization of larger cities came immigrants seeking employment opportunities and swelling the population. This influx of people to metropolitan areas spawned a new kind of barbershop which often was found in the lobbies of hotels. Most were larger than barber shops had been previously, many with 15 or more work stations, and they were well appointed. No longer was the standard reply "a shave and a haircut," when the barber asked, "what will it be today, sir?" Price menus on the walls gave a long list of ancillary services that were being provided. Barbers were gaining respect as professionals and boss barbers were often considered pillars of the business community. Because barber schools were educating new barbers in

prolific numbers, the greater demand for services was easily met. Expansion and success came easy for city barbers during the golden years and, more importantly, they were accomplished in a dignified manner. Barbershops became gentlemen's grooming and social institutions where amiable, polite conversation was anticipated nearly as much as the services rendered. Bathing was often available and here a fellow could get a boot blacking and a good cigar.

The ambiance of these places was rounded out by their inviting aroma. Consider these facts: cigarette tobacco had no reduction of tar or nicotine. The resulting smoke produced a warm and mellow fragrance compared to today's harsh, almost acrid smoke. Pipe and chewing tobaccos often were flavored with different tastes or aromas including cherry, wintergreen, apple, and butternut. Hair singeing (the service of burning off hair) added to the room's aroma. One might think that singed hair would not smell pleasant, and that certainly would hold true today with our dry-look hair. However, during the early golden years, men's hair was almost always saturated with heavily scented pomades, oils, or tonics. The resulting scent blended right in with the others. Also, every customer got an atomized misting of bay rum or toilet water when they got up from the chair. Powders dusted on the patrons necks also were scented. Before electricity was available, shops used lamps fueled by kerosene or oil and these often were scented with pine oil. If you combine all of these scents and have them become embedded into the floors, the woodwork, and the fabrics of the shop, you would have a room with a memorable and inviting aroma: that was the barbershop aroma!

Barbershops of the golden years were wonderful places in an era that encouraged deep pride among barbers that was not experienced before, nor since. This era is chronicled and celebrated through the antiques it provided.

The Decline

In the previous paragraphs, we learned what *led up* to the golden years and what made them golden, beginning about 1880. To more fully understand the era, we also must learn why it ended in the 1940s.

Safety Razors
Mass production began on the safety razors designed by King Camp Gillette in 1904. While Gillette's safety razor was not the first one invented, it was the first one that was truly mass produced and mass marketed. Because of this, men by the millions began shaving at home rather than going to barbershops regularly. The safety razors' widespread popularity was bolstered by very effective national advertising campaigns that took aim directly at barbers. They urged an end to the expense and inconvenience of leaving their homes to be shaved by a barber. Barbers were defenseless to argue against the attack, in fact it *was* more economical and convenient to shave at home. Safety razors became so popular that the United States government issued them along with straight razors to the troops in World War I. Many soldiers saw for themselves how convenient safety razors were when they had a chance to compare them with straight razors, and continued using the safeties when they got home after the war. The loss of their shaving revenue posed an economic dilemma to barbers that forever changed "business as usual." While a man could still elect to get a straight razor shave at the barbershop in the latter golden years, it became more of an occasional, pampered event as opposed to a regular experience. Of the remaining traditional barbershops in business today, few offer straight razor shaves. Most contemporary barbers lament that straight razor shaving is a lost art.

This 1908 Gillette advertisement underscores how national ad campaigns were aimed at steering business away from barbershops. Color lithograph, 9" x 13", $35.00.

Artist's cartoon from 1911 historically reflects early public sentiment concerning barbershops' lost shaving revenue because of safety razors. 7" x 9" color lithograph. $45.00.

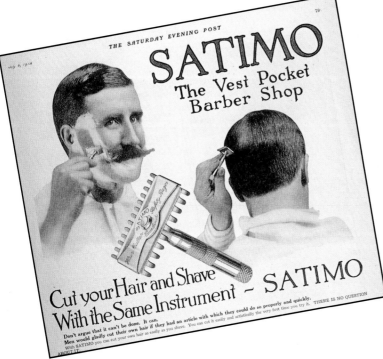

Black and white advertisement for Satimo razor is indicative of the hard-sell for "home" shaving, *and* haircut-ting. 11" x 14". $30.00.

The Depression Years

The beginning of the Great Depression was signaled by the stock market crash of 1929 and continued through most of the 1930s. During those years, much of the American population had little discretionary money and for them home haircuts and shaves became the *only* ones, in spite of well documented efforts barbers to roll back their prices during the hard times. Many barbers provided courtesy services for loyal customers during the Depression.

During this time, too, home haircutting kits were manufactured in volume and sold by major retailers such as Sears, Roebuck and Company. The kits were marketed as tools to give haircuts "just like the barber." Often, home users of these kits became skilled enough to remain the family barber for years to come and competition for career barbers.

Noted illustrator Harold Anderson produced this *Saturday Evening Post* cover for a 1933 edition. It graphically highlights exactly where many haircuts were being done during America's Great Depression. 11" x 14", $25.00.

Sears Roebuck and Company offered this logic in their late 1940s home haircutting kits. When fully opened in fold-out form, there are explicit instructions on how to cut hair at home. A portion of the directions read as follows: "visit the barber so that you will have a pattern to follow. By duplicating the barber in every respect, the haircut you give is bound to be right! *There's no chance to go wrong!*" Complete 1940s home barbering kit with this pamphlet, $35.00.

Shop Decor

Many of the largest and most beautiful barbershops were scaled down or had their appearances simplified through the late 1920s and '30s as the economic climate in America fell back. Cost effectiveness became a big factor in how things were manufactured by the 1940s. In the barbershop, hand carved wood was no longer affordable. Barber chair upholsterers switched from expensive leather and natural plush materials to synthetics. Mirror cases and countertops had less marble and more glass which cost less. Beautiful wallpaper and wainscoting was often covered with white paint, in keeping with the nation's growing preoccupation with sanitation. Some shops switched to white porcelain chairs, white cabinets and counter tops, white walls, white ceilings, and white furniture. In the 1930s and '40s, the white, sterile look ultimately prevailed and once-beautiful barbershops appeared like surgical theaters.

Middle-golden years barbershop shows use of carved wood, plush fabrics, marble, plantings, wainscoting, patterned flooring, and a generally "warm" ambiance. 5" x 7" sepia-tone photo, $35.00.

This photo, which was taken in 1939 of the Point Barber Shop in Hillsdale, Michigan, shows just *how* "white" barbershops had become as the golden years wound down. About the only things that weren't white or neutral colored in this shop, were the black chair seats, the floor, and the barber's pants. 6" x 8" photo, $30.00.

Right: You may recall this Donnelly Outdoor Advertising billboard that appeared throughout America in the late 1960s. It underscores not only a controversial issue of those times, but more importantly, the effect that long hair had on the decline of traditional barbers. 2.75" x 5.75". $10.00.

Population Change

When World War I ended in 1918, and again when World War II ended in 1945, America experienced a depletion of men who never came home. Only a handful of years later, in the 1950s, the Korean Conflict, and later the Viet Nam conflict, cost even more young men's' lives. The loss of lives in these actions was a poignant loss of the barbers' male clientele.

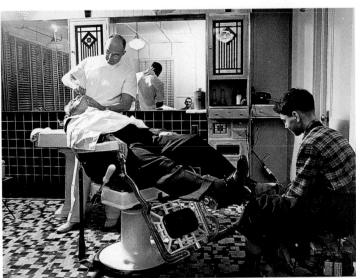

Lititz, Pennsylvania 1942. "Mr. Pennepacker, one of seven barbers in town, has 60 less haircuts a month since the boys left town." Caption and photo from the *American Library Of Congress* refers to the young men called to action in World War II. 8" x 10" print, $25.00.

Hair Fashions

Another downturn for barbers could not possibly have been anticipated, although its effect was swift and lasting. The British musical group *The Beatles* became popular in the mid-1960s wearing their now-famous, mop-top haircuts. Like no other time in modern history, a new men's hairstyle was completely embraced by the general public. Young men worldwide grew their hair long and barbers became little more than a memory to that generation. Long hair, in many variations, remained popular for the next 25 years and can be seen on some men today. The number of registered barbers continued to decrease during the long-hair craze.

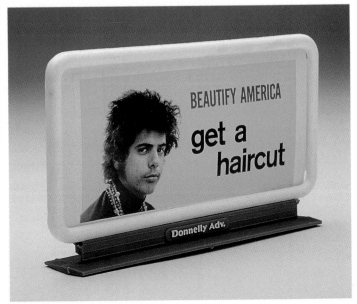

BEAUTIFY AMERICA
get a haircut

Donnelly Adv.

Cosmetologist/Hairstylist Licenses

More recently, and perhaps the most unkind cut of all (no pun intended), there is a shift among governing boards to channel the licensing of traditional barbers into the cosmetologist/hair stylist category. For example, in the state of New Jersey, there have been no new barber licenses issued since 1985. The state of New Jersey decided that year that all new hair cutting practitioners *must* become cosmetologist/hair stylists. There will be no more licensed barbers in New Jersey.

If you wonder incredulously "what...why?", the answer from the state licensing board was that the elimination of the barbering license would upgrade everyone to a more "professional" status that would be good for the industry in the future. Those who were already licensed as barbers prior to 1985 were given the choice to remain "grandfathered" and continue as barbers, or to pay for additional training and take the state board examination to become cosmetologist/hair stylists. Some barbers chose to seek a new license, while others did not. The result was that in 1998, the state of New Jersey had just over 800 traditional barbershops to serve a population of nearly 8 million people. The traditional barbers' future does not appear optimistic in the United States. This seems unfortunate because pride, heritage, and tradition suggest that barbers always have and could continue to accomplish a precision haircut in a minimum amount of time, in clean and congenial surroundings, and for a minimal price. *Long live traditional barbershops.*

The March 1966 *Elks Magazine* cover is one of those pictures that are "worth a thousand words." The barber observes (resignedly) as two teen aged boys walk by with hair covering their foreheads, ears, and necks. He knows it has been quite a while since their last haircut. Surely, he muses, because of all that "Beatles" nonsense. Little did he know on that day that their hair would grow even longer. Long enough, in fact, to threaten his very existence in business! 8.5" x 11", $25.00.

Unisex Salons

When men finally did begin to have their hair cut shorter again in the 1980s, many patronized "unisex" salons which sought the business of men and women alike. Not quite the "beauty parlor" of old for women or the "barbershop" of old for men, these styling shops gained popularity with the younger generation and, to this day, there are men who have *never* set foot in a traditional barbershop. The unisex salon concept remains popular and another issue in a line of events depleting the barbers' ranks.

This Antiseptic Age

Now in this age of fuss and flurry
When all the world is in a hurry,
And every one suspects his neighbor
And has a grouch against himself
And tries to hoard up all his pelf,
There comes into your shop some day
A man, and this he has to say:

"I want a shave and want it quick,
I have no time to burn;
I must have antisptic work,
And have it in my turn.
I do not want the kind of stuff
You fellows give to others,
Because I'm clean and up to snuff
And spurn my fellow brothers.

"There's germs upon the barber shears,
There's germs upon his chair,
There's germs upon the razor blade,
There's germs upon his hair.
There's germs upon his lather brush,

There's germs upon his feet,
There's germs upon his headrest,
And germs down in the seat.
There's germs upon the window pane,
There's germs upon the door,
There's germs upon the shaving soap,
Germs in the mug galore.
There's germs upon the looking glass,
And germs upon the floor."

You take a look into his eye,
And swell all up in front,
And tell him how to head about,
In language clear and blunt.
Tell him that where the microbes live,
There his remains will dwell,
When he winds up his little whine,
He'll find himself in H---
Happy land far, far away,
Where germs and microbes won't disturb
His never-ending day. -C.W. Wright,
Whitefish, Mont., 1915

Chapter 2

Furnishings

The main articles of furniture in nearly every barbershop were poles, chairs, mirror cases, and mug racks. We will also be looking at a reverse running barbershop clock, display cases, towel steamers, cash registers and stands, costumers (coat racks), and more. Our focus is on presenting the major style changes and periods of innovation as the Golden Years progressed. In this manner, the reader should be able to better approximate the ages of these antiques. There is information on the original materials, colors, and mechanisms used and tips on locating parts, maintenance, and transportation of heavier items.

Barber Poles

The barbers' poles are undoubtedly one of the most enduring and recognized trade signs ever known. They were whimsically referred to in an 1800s editorial appearing in *Harper's New Monthly Magazine* as "party colored poles that look like pieces of sugarstick wonderfully magnified." The electrified, mechanized poles we know today have evolved from bloodstained, white cloth dressings which hung to dry outside barbers' doorways centuries ago when barbers were referred to as "Chirurgens." In those times, academic physicians and barbers alike shared some medical duties and belonged to the same surgeons guild. It was routine for barber/medical practitioners to shave, cut hair, and perform surgical procedures, bloodletting, and tooth extractions as well. In the course of their work, they utilized notched metal basins for both shaving lather and receiving blood. The basins and bandages which hung outside their doorways gave the best indication that barbers' services were available within.

Over time, the barber pole evolved from a narrow, elongated, wooden staff that was painted with the same striped design we recognize today. Through the eighteenth century and into the nineteenth century, it was common to see two poles signifying a barbershop, one on each side of the doorway extending out from the building at a 45 degree angle. After King George II formally separated the surgeons' and barbers' guilds in England in 1745, barbers were required to display *only* blue and white striped poles, while surgeons displayed a solid red pole. It is unclear how long the blue and white barber pole was used, because red and white ones are most often described by early nineteenth century writers. The addition of a blue stripe to red and white barber poles became more common in the 1870s in America, apparently as a wave of patriotism which surrounded the Centennial of 1776 became influential to reflect the colors of the American flag. The addition of stars to late 1800s barber poles signaled an "anything goes" attitude concerning their styling and that period became the heyday of barber pole history.

Approximately between 1890 and 1915, barber poles were produced in an amazing variety of sizes, shapes, colors, and designs. There were geometric, diamond and wave designs, pin striping, opposing directional stripes, linked circles, and even designs with no traditional stripes at all, and the colors blossomed to include black, green, gold, yellow, and gray. Marbled blends at the bases of the poles were also popular. Over time, wooden poles were replaced with other materials such as rolled sheet metal and cast-iron. Sheet metal poles, although less expensive to produce, fell out of favor quickly because of their brief life span due to rusting. Bare cast-iron poles were much heavier but they were also susceptible to rust. To add longevity to cast-iron poles, manufacturers began to utilize fired-porcelain protective coatings and produced poles that became the standard of the industry for many years; many still exist in excellent condition today.

Victorian barber pole shows geometrical designs but *no traditional stripes*. 12" diameter wooden pole from late 1800s with representative original color. $2,000.00+. Condition and originality heavily influence prices on all wooden barber poles.

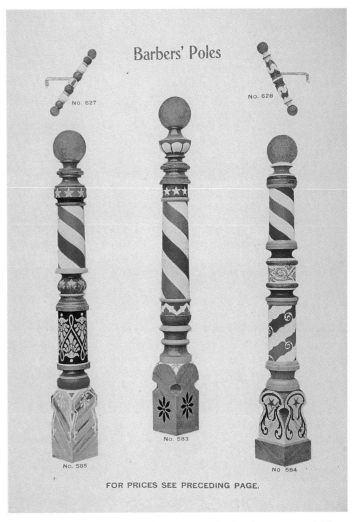

Ornate examples of pre-1900, cedar wood poles that were available in 10" 12" and 14" diameter by 8' tall. Notice Victorian influenced base designs. $2,200.00+ for column type with original coloring. $350.00+ for bracket type.

Less ornate, pre-1900, cedar wood poles. Bracket types were usually 3" diameter by 3' long. $250.00+. Column poles ranged from 6" to 14" in diameter and were from 6' to 9' out-of-ground height. $1,800.00+ with original coloring.

Furnishings

IRON BARBERS' POLES

No. 67
Height, 8 feet. Diameter, 12 inches. Fitted with 12-inch glass globe, rubber-covered electric feed wire and electric light socket.
Price $29.00

No. 71
WALL BRACKET POLE
Black and Gold.
Height, 56 inches. Diameter, 10 inches. Fitted with 10-inch glass globe with "burnt-in" lettering "Barber Shop" on two sides. Furnished complete with rubber-covered electric feed wire, flashlight electric light socket and wall brackets.
Price $23.50

No. 69
Height, 7 feet 6 inches. Diameter, 10 inches. Fitted with 10-inch glass globe, rubber-covered electric feed wire and electric light socket.
Price $25.00

No. 70
Same pole as No. 69, but striped red and white.
Price $25.00

No. 72
WALL BRACKET POLE
Height, 56 inches. Diameter, 10 inches. Fitted with 10-inch glass globe and furnished complete with rubber-covered feed wire, electric light socket and wall brackets.
Price $14.50

No. 73
Same pole as No. 72, but striped red and white.
Price $14.50

No. 68
Red and Gold.
Height, 8 feet. Diameter, 12 inches. The most attractive iron barbers' pole made. Fitted with 12-inch glass globe with "burnt-in" lettering "Barber Shop" on two sides. Furnished complete with rubber-covered electric feed wire and flash-light electric light socket.
Price $45.00

These poles are made completely of iron and steel. The bases and molded parts are made of hollow cast iron and the straight sections of steel tubing. They are painted with the finest and most durable colors and coated with extra quality exterior varnish. The gold stripes and decoration are not bronzed, but made of genuine gold-leaf and will not tarnish, but retain their luster. For the Nos. 68 and 71 poles globes lettered "Barber Shop" are carried in stock. Other lettering furnished on short notice.

Rolled, sheet-steel poles with hollow cast-iron bases are post-1900. Genuine gold leaf trim on select models and unusual diminishing stripe widths. Glass globes at the top were wired for light. Flashing top lights were available as an option. If found in good representative condition, large bracket poles $700.00+, column poles $1,500.00+.

Shear the locks excessive grief to show. -Fawkes

BARBERS' POLES

No. 30
Price, 10 in....$22.50
Price, 12 in.... 27.50
Fitted with glass globe with "burnt-in" lettering "Barber Shop" on two sides. Equipped with heavy rubber-covered feed wire and flashlight socket.

No. 20
Price, 6 in....$ 6.75
Price, 8 in.... 9.25
Price, 10 in.... 12.50
Price, 12 in.... 15.75
Price, 14 in.... 20.25

No. 31
Price, 10 in....$16.00
Price, 12 in.... 19.50

No. 32
Price, 10 in....$17.00
Price, 12 in.... 21.00

No. 26
Price, 8 in....
Price, 10 in....
Price, 12 in....
Fitted with glass globe, heavy rubber-covered feed wire and electric socket.

These poles are made of selected and well-seasoned cedar posts. They are painted with the finest and most durable colors and coated with best quality exterior varnish. Pure gold-leaf is used exclusively for the balls, gold stripes and other decoration.

Pre-1910 wooden poles still exhibited fancy influence with random symmetrical designs, *fleur de lis* designs, diminishing stripe widths, stars, and gold leaf. These poles are currently among the most desirable wooden examples. If found with original color, any one of these 8' tall beauties would be in the $2,500.00+ range depending on condition.

Early sidewalk poles were originally called "column" models and they remain as the ultimate in visual marketing for a barbershop. When the spinning stripe models were first offered in the late 1800s, the drive mechanisms were massive, weight driven movements which required hand cranking to operate. Later, the mechanisms became lighter with the advance to spring-wound drives, however they still required hand cranking. Once wound, some of these poles could spin the stripes for many hours. Electric powered motors to spin the stripes were gradually phased in from the late 1890s. As electric power became increasingly available, more of the previously popular hand cranked poles were replaced by the electric motor types. By 1900, barbers everywhere were buying models with spinning stripes. While there were still some painted wooden poles produced, by about 1915 they were most often the small, wall-hung variety. Large, wooden sidewalk poles were falling from favor as they were prone to rot at the bases; they were not competition for spinning striped poles.

By 1920, electric wall mounted poles, called bracket poles, also became popular. Not only were they smaller and more affordable, they were less prone to vandalism than the larger, sidewalk models. Sidewalk poles continued to be produced into the 1940s, but wall hung models surpassed them in popularity and sales by that time.

After the wild color variations previous to 1915, pole production once again settled into classic red, white, and blue colors. As the years progressed, there is little color variance to note except for pole bases which were produced in cream and blue and cream and mint green. Most manufacturers and some suppliers placed a small brass identification plate at the base of the globe or at the bottom of the stripes.

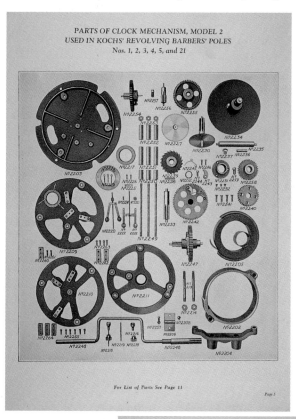

Examples of later golden years poles in the 1920s. They are all made of metal and are porcelain coated. On these particular models, the stripes were *non-revolving* but the tops did light up. As evidenced in the photo, the fancy designs from the Victorian era were absent by this time, although 4" wide stripes were still available. Unrestored but nice: $1,000.00. Complete restoration: $2,000.00.

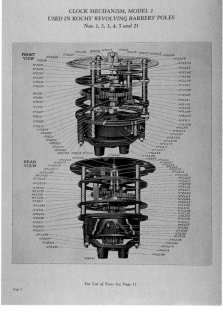

1920s examples of *electric, spinning stripe* models. Cast-iron bases with porcelain coating. Outer-glass cylinders to protect paper stripes. Bracket poles unrestored: $300.00+. Restored: $700.00+. Column poles unrestored: $1,200.00. Restored, $2,500.00. Pedestal or Boulevard models unrestored, $900.00. Restored, $1,800.00.

The standard, round globes at the top of the barber poles usually were opal or milk glass 8", 10", or 12" in diameter. Some pole top variations did exist, such as the desirable canteen style similar to the glass tops on old style gasoline pumps. Lettering on 12" diameter canteen models was usually sandblasted and painted red, blue, or black for contrast; beware of smooth, surface painted reproductions. The most popular words on canteen type globes were "Massage," "Hair Bobbing," and "Barber Shop."

Globe on the left is early and hand painted. 10" diameter. Value: $150.00+. Globe on the right is leaded glass art-type and was produced in 10" or 12" in diameter. These remain rare and can bring up to $1,500.00 in perfect condition. **Note:** Watch for leaded glass reproductions which are approximately 14"+ in diameter.

Original milk-white 12" canteen style. Black, paint-filled, etched-glass letters. $200.00+. *Courtesy of Tony Gugliotti.*

Original milk-white 12" canteen style. Hand painted letters include colored stripes. In condition as found: $150.00+. *Courtesy of Tony Gugliotti.*

Opposite page:
Bottom: To determine if a globe is a recent replacement or an original, closely examine the base. Old globes that have been exposed to the elements for decades will present a grayish etching in the recurved area. Unlike the convex top area, this etching doesn't usually come clean. Also, if you held one in each hand, replacement globes are noticeably lighter in weight than an early original. Plain white 10" originals: $100.00+. Current replacements: $28.95.

　　　　　　　　　　　　　　　　　　　　　Furnishings

Tiffany style, art-glass, leaded globes are a beautiful, hand made type intended to be illuminated and they are dazzling to view. Originals were made in *only* 10" and 12" diameters; beware of 14" or larger reproductions. Because originally they cost considerably more than their counterparts, not many were sold and they are rare today. Other interesting pole tops include pineapple-shaped opal glass models, hand lettered personalized globes, clear glass globes fully lined on the inside with gold leaf, and metal globes finished on the outside in gold leaf.

The striped cylinders that spun inside protective glass coverings were originally made of paper. Because of this, they were very susceptible to color-fade when exposed to direct sunlight. They needed to be changed fairly often and were the most requested replacement part for barber poles. Striped paper cylinders were available through most barber supply catalogs in three color combinations: red, white, and blue; plain red and white; and blue and white. The width of stripes painted on wooden poles prior to 1900 was usually 4" wide, however 2" wide stripes began to show up on cast-iron spinning type poles in the 1890s. Paper stripes were originally available in 4" widths, but the narrow 2" stripes became more popular and were used exclusively by the 1930s. Ultimately, paper stripes were replaced by a plastic derivative named butyrate, which is far more durable and color-fast than paper. When restoring poles today, plastic replacement stripes are the best choice for brightness and longevity. If, by chance, you have an original paper stripe that is still brightly colored, use it; they are rarely found in good condition and will add another dimension of authenticity to your pole. Custom made paper stripes can be ordered today through the Marvy Company for an historically accurate pole restoration.

Throughout the Golden Years, the Koken, Kochs, and Paidar companies were the leaders in barber pole sales. Not long after the end of the Golden Years, in 1950, William Marvy introduced his "Six Ways Better" poles at a barber supply trade show in Chicago. Made of non-rust aluminum and non-chip stainless steel, they had a non-rust plastic inner revolving cylinder and a non-breakable clear plastic outer cylinder. Marvy had rigged a mechanical hammer which repeatedly struck the wall-mounted pole, with no harm

Good example of original paper stripe cylinder. If found with remaining bright color: $150.00. Current plastic replacement: average price about $45.00.

done. At this time, barbers had been purchasing metal hoods to lock over their sidewalk poles at night to prevent vandalism. Suppliers liked Marvy's pole immediately and knew that their customers, the barbers, would too. The rest, as they say, is history. As the Marvy pole sales increased, the competition was eliminated until The William Marvy Company stood alone for years as the only American barber pole manufacturer. The company continues to prosper in St. Paul, Minnesota. In December of 1997, they put the finishing touches on their 75,000th pole which is specially trimmed in gold; this model "55" will go on display at the Smithsonian Institution in Washington, D.C., as a testament to the universal recognition and longevity of these trade signs. William Marvy's son Robert took over the business with the same enthusiasm possessed by his father. Robert's own sons, Scott and Dan, are now also employed by the company as the third generation of barber pole makers. As the decline in the barber business became obvious, so did barber pole sales. From their high production volume of about 5100 poles in 1967, sales dropped to 475 in 1987 and are currently at about 600 annually. The company has widely expanded their line of other barber supplies and continue to retain their prominence in the industry. Robert Marvy reports that a large part of the business today is servicing and supplying the antique and collectibles world. The company provides parts for a large variety of antique barber pole needs and rightfully claims ability to supply parts for almost any pole ever produced.

Pole Restoration and Practical Advise

For parts or information on pole restoration, you could contact The William Marvy Company, 1540 St. Clair Avenue, St. Paul, Minnesota, 1-800-874-2651. Scott Gohr is Marvy's resident barber pole technician who has become one of the world's leading authorities on barber pole parts and maintenance, both past and present. If he cannot answer your question, it's a good bet that nobody can!

To purchase fully restored poles, you could try attending Game Room or Advertising shows. Showpiece poles also turn up at better auctions and high profile shows, such as Atlantique City. Unrestored poles seem to pop up anywhere, from garage sales to your local antique co-op.

To move a cast iron pole, *take it apart* and move it in pieces. Too often, people have tried to move a 7' pole in one piece, and they have ended up with broken parts, *some of which are not replaceable*. If you buy replacement glass or other parts for your pole, store the cartons in which they were shipped, so that when you want to move the pole in the future, you can protect the parts with those specially designed cartons. For long distance moving, have the cast-iron pole sections crated in wood. The most practical way to ship them is by motor freight, insured for the current retail value *in restored condition*.

That ever since the fall, man, for his sin,
Has had a beard entailed upon his chin. -Byron

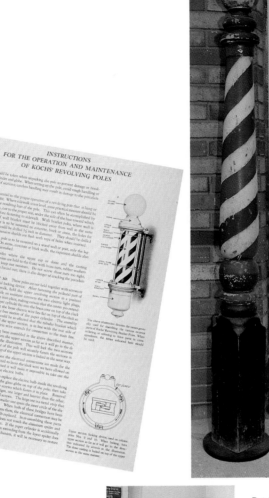

Pre-1900 wooden barber pole with early paint. Base has had repair work due to rotting as was common with wooden poles. Originally 6" diameter by 6' tall. As seen: $1,200.00+. Larger poles in same condition are correspondingly more expensive. *Courtesy of Tony Gugliotti.*

Paidar "pedestal" barber pole from the 1920s. Originally available as a windup or electric. Frames for this model all had the hole for hand cranks even if electric motor driven. Originally had brass rain cover that rotated aside to receive crank. 6' 6" tall. Completely restored "as new." $2,200.00+.

Original James Barker Foundry barber pole. Manufactured in Philadelphia, Pennsylvania to coincide with the American Revolution centennial. Pole is cast-iron and was made before porcelain coatings were used. Hollow brass tubes protected the outer glass cylinder. Surface was painted as seen and is believed to be one of the first iron poles to utilize stars *and* geometric designs for accents. Hand cranked, weight-driven, clock movement turns the stripes for up to five hours. Totally restored and running as original. Rare. $8,000+.
Note: Watch for recent reproductions made with lightweight aluminum castings and electric motors.

25

Furnishings

Kochs "pedestal" barber pole from the late 1920s. Sold as an electrified model. Cream and green in color. Unrestored but good working order. $1,700.00. *Courtesy of Tony Gugliotti.*

Paidar column model. Known today as a "sidewalk" pole. Built after 1920 and standing 7' tall. Electric motor and lights. Total restoration "as new." $2,500.00+. *Courtesy of Bill Wright.*

Paidar column model built in late 1920s has geometric ovals between upper and lower stripes. Electrified, 7' tall, and completely restored like new. $2,500.00+. *Courtesy of Bill Wright.*

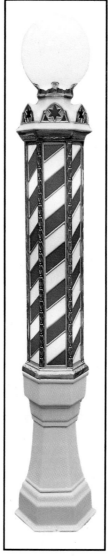

Cyclo model sidewalk pole from Atwater Manufacturing Chicago, Illinois. Made around 1910. Clear glass ball at top coated on the inside with gold leaf. Non-electric. Cast iron and sheet metal construction. Scarce pole. If fully restored, $4,000.00+. *Courtesy of Bill Wright.*

Art-Deco style column pole manufactured by Ideal. This style was popular in the 1920s and early 1930s. Six sided, geometric, colored glass panels. Unusual variant has blue glass stars in hooded porcelain top. Aluminum, glass framework. Porcelain over cast-iron base. Electrified for light. Total restoration "as new." Rare model. $6,500.00+. *Courtesy of Bill Wright.*

Koken model sidewalk pole. Porcelain over cast-iron base. Brass-tube glass protectors. Electrified. From before 1915. 7' tall. Completely restored. $2,500.00+. *Courtesy of Bill Wright.*

Koken wall model 36" pole from 1920s. Electrified with turning stripes. If completely restored. $600.00. *Courtesy of Bill Wright.*

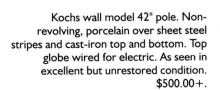

Kochs wall model 42" pole. Non-revolving, porcelain over sheet steel stripes and cast-iron top and bottom. Top globe wired for electric. As seen in excellent but unrestored condition. $500.00+.

Furnishings

Paidar 42" wall pole from 1920s. Porcelain over cast-iron. Offered as windup or electric. Complete restoration. $750.00+.

Deco-style, 1920s, Koken, wall pole. Colored glass geometric panels. Six-sided. Porcelain cap and base. Most of these had frames made of zinc or aluminum. More rare, are those cast in bronze as seen here. This style was made in regular and long wall models and also a freestanding column model. In condition as shown with bronze frame: $2,000.00. In zinc or aluminum frame: $1,200.00+. Matching sidewalk pole in zinc: $3,000.00+. In bronze: $4,000.00+

Deco-style, 1920s, manufacturer unknown, wall pole. Colored glass geometric panels. Six sided. Unusual variant top has hooded porcelain with blue glass stars. Rare, especially when matched with corresponding sidewalk model also seen in this book. Completely restored. $3,000.00+. *Courtesy of Bill Wright.*

Barbershop

Barber Chairs

There are few articles of contemporary seating furniture that offer more substantial construction and just plain whimsy than do old-fashioned barber chairs. Of the remaining chairs built before the 1950s, many are currently found in residential settings, not just in barbershops. Men will tell you that their barber chair is the most comfortable seat in the house. Women readily acknowledge the conversation value of them as unique interior decorating accents. A choice, early chair that has been carefully restored will receive "oohs" and "aahs" from *every* guest, and the cat won't go near the wooden or cast iron base.

If you've been thinking about getting a barber chair, you now have printed reasons to help you convince your spouse it's a good idea. But before you buy one, consider a few reasons why these relics aren't for everyone: 1) Old barber chairs are heavy! So heavy, that most barbershop patrons actually thought the chairs were bolted to the floor. Once it is in your home, you won't likely be moving it from spot to spot, nor will you be lightly nudging it aside to vacuum the carpet underneath. 2) Children approach them with mischievous glee. Most chairs go up and down, recline, and spin around. They have a big chrome joystick that attracts kids like a magnet and seems to make them believe they have found a "jungle gym" right in your home. This could be unsettling if you have thousands of dollars invested in this "appreciating" antique. 3) If you buy an old chair as a workshop project, you will need a strong back, plenty of patience, and probably more money than you *wanted* to spend.

The periods **Mid-1800s**, roughly 1850 to 1880; **Late Victorian**, 1880 to 1900; **Transitional**, about 1895 to 1915; and **20th Century**, 1915 to 1950, roughly correlate to major periods of innovation in American barber chair chronology. Style variations were virtually endless as new models were continuously introduced from the inception of mass-produced chairs. While all of them are not illustrated here, the four major types of construction are defined by their periods and materials.

Prior to 1850, most images that depict barbers at work show them using a chair not unlike a normal dining chair. Some of them appear to have legs that were a bit longer to provide added seat height, while others had a fixed position headrest. Chairs from about 1840 and earlier show no evidence of adjustable movements or upholstery. However, drawings from about 1850 on show mechanical chairs manufactured specifically for barbershop use.

Furnishings

Early "Edra" barber chair is not much larger or higher than an ordinary dining chair. It did provide a "flip" style padded bottom that insured each patron a fresh seat. Morris chair styled hardware allowed the back to be lowered into a shaving position. In walnut as seen: $500.00+. *Courtesy of Bill and Marlene Levin.*

Mid-1800s Period

When manufactured barber chairs began after 1850, sectional models were most popular. Available in a wide variety of styles, they consisted of two separate, but matching, pieces. The section that the patron sat in was wide and had a raised seat height. The frames were usually wooden (two notable cast iron exceptions were by Smith Brothers and Archer) and had comfortably padded upholstery. The earliest sectional chairs had a fixed seat position but the backrest reclined a few degrees which helped make the chairs more comfortable for the customer during shaving and haircutting. It was also much better for the barber's posture, considering it was not unusual for them to put in *12 hour days*. As time went on, the chairs became mechanized so they fully reclined, but they still didn't raise, lower, or swivel.

The footstool portion of mid-1800 sectionals was a multi-tiered unit providing leg support when the patron was in a prone, shaving position. Some footstools had two foot tiers, others had three, and usually the upper tier was upholstered while the bottom tiers were covered with brass or copper sheeting. Some manufacturers used wooden casters on two of the chair's feet, which allowed them to be moved about more easily.

By the 1870s, innovative manufacturers such as Archer and Berninghaus were experimenting with mechanized chairs and they began to develop more convenient designs. In 1878, Archer patented their first one-piece reclining chair with attached footrest, Archer's No. 5 model, which eliminated the need for a separate footstool. Archer quickly followed with their No. 9 model that not only reclined but also raised and lowered manually, all before the hydraulic mechanisms were used. Soon, the Berninghaus company invented and patented their first swiveling chair named the "Paragon" model which allowed the barber to turn the patron so he could "command the advantage of light." For that reason dentists also purchased the Paragon model. Reversible seat bottoms and cane seat bottoms, for warm climates or summer weather, were two more innovations of note in this period.

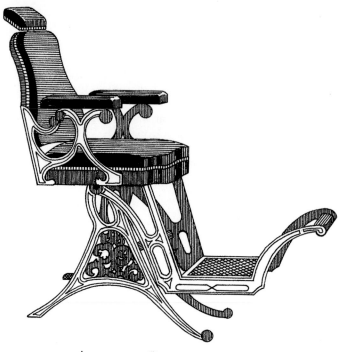

Archer's Patent
Adjustable Barber Chair No. 5

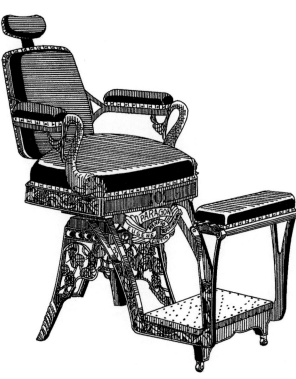

Eugene Berninghaus'
Revolving and Adjustable Barber Chair
"Paragon"

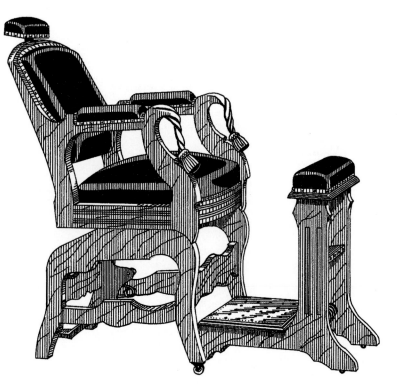

Kochs' Barbers' Chair, No. 21

Late Victorian Period

With so much experimenting going on, the manufacturers were challenged to incorporate the best ideas into a single, totally convenient, barber chair. The best of the one-piece chairs swiveled 360 degrees and fully reclined, had an attached footrest, and had hydraulics to raise and lower the chair. The materials they used were durable, heavy, and beautiful in appearance; these chairs would last for generations. The late Victorian chairs are characterized by a hydraulic pump nestled into an all wooden frame on four separate legs. They were plush covered and highly ornate with wood, fabric, and trim materials of a wide selection. Along with convenience and durability, style was important during this period as most chairs had fancy hand carvings or similar embellishments. More ornate chairs were sold than their plain counterparts.

mechanical functions into one lever. A paper dispensing headrest also was patented which provided a clean surface on which each patron could rest his head. Scalp conditions and lice were common in these times. Also patented were small-framed chairs for children that spiraled up and down, and sturdy folding chairs for military field grooming and hotel room service barbering.

Transitional Period

The transition from wooden chairs to heavier and more durable porcelain over cast-iron models marks this period from about 1895 to about 1915. Round, cast iron platform bases began to replace the four-legged style, some with wood veneers to match the ornate wooden upper portions of the chairs. Other base models were painted with black enamel, had japanned finishes, or were iron with fired-porcelain coating. Each of these is referred to as a transitional model that became the standard of the industry by offering the ultimate in stability over the previous four-legged models.

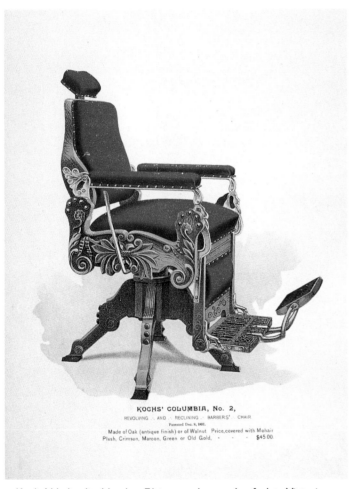

KOCHS' COLUMBIA, No. 2,
REVOLVING AND RECLINING BARBERS' CHAIR
Patented Dec. 8, 1901.
Made of Oak (antique finish) or of Walnut. Price, covered with Mohair
Plush, Crimson, Maroon, Green or Old Gold, - - - $45.00.

Kochs' Hydraulic, Number 71 is a good example of a late Victorian style chair. Most had four legs with a hydraulic unit. They raised, lowered, reclined, and spun around. Most had embellishments or hand-carving and plush upholstery. This chair, if completely restored as original, $3,000.00+. Carvings would add value.

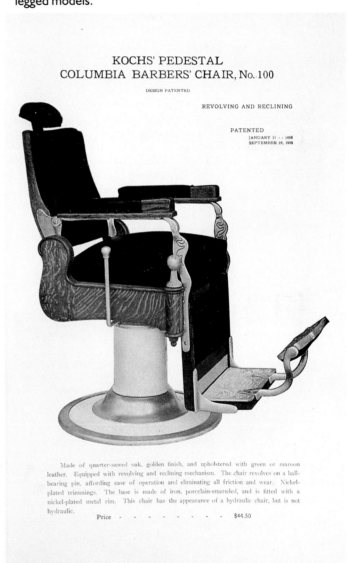

KOCHS' PEDESTAL
COLUMBIA BARBERS' CHAIR, No. 100
DESIGN PATENTED

REVOLVING AND RECLINING

PATENTED
JANUARY 11 - - 1898
SEPTEMBER 28, 1909

Made of quarter-sawed oak, golden finish, and upholstered with green or maroon leather. Equipped with revolving and reclining mechanism. The chair revolves on a ball-bearing pin, affording ease of operation and eliminating all friction and wear. Nickel-plated trimmings. The base is made of iron, porcelain-enameled, and is fitted with a nickel-plated metal rim. This chair has the appearance of a hydraulic chair, but is not hydraulic.
Price - - - - - - - - $44.50

The major development of this period was the widespread use of the hydraulic pump to enable barbers to adjust the chair's height. The chairs raised and lowered with an almost effortless pump of a foot treadle located on the base. Another convenient advancement came in the "joystick" side lever. This arm, which was patented by Koken, incorporated control of all of the chair's

Kochs' Number 100 shows the unmistakable look of a transitional model chair. Popular from the mid 1890s until approximately 1915, they are characterized by a cast-iron, pedestal base (iron bottom could be covered with wood veneers or porcelain) and a wooden upper-body. The stability made possible by the round iron base saw transitional models readily accepted. This no frills, non-hydraulic model when completely restored, $1,500.00+.

Furnishings

20th Century.

After experimenting with cast-iron bases on transitional models, manufacturers learned that they could produce chairs for less cost by utilizing a completely cast iron frame. Barbers, on the other hand, were reluctant to part with wooden upper-bodied chairs quickly. Therefore, manufacturers slowly introduced porcelain coated cast iron chairs into production. It took nearly twenty years before barbers fully accepted porcelain chairs, primarily because, after enduring terrible communicable disease breakouts including the plague from Europe, sanitation had become very important. The public wanted barbershops to be perfectly clean, white, washable, and germ free. Thereafter, completely porcelainized barber chairs were preferred. In terms of beauty porcelain chairs presented a step backward, but in terms of durability they went over the top. By 1920, barber chairs were being produced that could conceivably last forever. The castings were heavy, some Paidar chairs weighed nearly 250 pounds, and hy- draulic pistons and oil reservoirs were larger. Improved technology and machining capabilities made the mating of surfaces on the internal moving parts approach perfection, thereby reducing friction wear and adding to their longevity. Early 20th century barber chairs became the most durable ones ever produced. John Dloughy, the last head of the giant Paidar company and Emil J. Paidar's grandson, later admitted, "we made them too good. They just don't wear out. Nobody ever *had* to buy a new one!"

Between about 1920 and 1950, there were few major structural changes made to porcelain chairs; most innovations were cosmetic. In the late 1920s, the chromium metal plating process became more popular and by the mid-1930s it was used almost exclusively. Chrome was initially offered as an extra-cost option to standard nickel plating, but the shinier and more durable chrome was actually superior. At this time, too, leather was used less frequently as synthetic coverings were produced that wore and looked well, cleaned easily, and were less expensive than leather.

One mechanical change occurred in the 1930s when Paidar patented the Hy-Lo-Draulic chair which had two hydraulic cylinders that enabled the chair to be a little lower at rest and a little higher when pumped to full height. When the Kochs Barber Supply Company was sold to the Emil J. Paidar Company in 1940, Paidar, after steadily building a solid barber supply business since 1906, became the undisputed leader in barber chair manufacturing. Paidar did not eliminate the Kochs nameplate, but continued to market chairs under both names for many years, actually supplying 550 dealers worldwide.

By 1950, the long run of big porcelain and iron chairs had come to an end. American manufacturers, whose previous strategy had been to produce the longest lasting chair, were beginning to understand the theory of planned obsolescence. Also, the number of licensed barbers continued to decrease and less expensive chairs produced by Japanese makers became a factor. American manufacturers countered the competition by using different materials, such as aluminum, light gauge boxed steel and stainless steel. Post-1950 chairs were attractive and serviceable, but far lighter and less durable. They certainly do not possess the nostalgic lure of their early 20th century predecessors. Most of the chairs made since 1950 are not yet being considered collectible.

Chair Restoration Tips

Chair restoration projects can *really* become involved. My advice is to carefully think about the result you want in a finished chair. If you must have a chair in the $3000 + range of quality, be prepared to do a complete restoration: refinishing the body (both wood or porcelain models), re-plating all the metal parts, and adding new upholstery. If you do not need a showpiece, you may create a really nice example with little more than a thorough cleaning.

For information on identifying, appraising, and parts availability, you may want to contact a specialist in early barber chairs. Mark and Connie Stellinga have had as many as 77 fully restored wooden chairs in their collection at one time, they have discovered most of restoration tricks worth knowing, and they have graciously offered to share their vast research findings with fellow barbershop collectors. To contact them, mail a self-addressed and stamped envelope with your inquiry to 416 Sierra Trail, Coralville, IA 52241 or phone them at (319)354-7287 during daytime working hours only.

THE NO. 570-N.P.B. BARBER CHAIR
WITH ALL OF THE FAMOUS *Paidar* IMPROVEMENTS

Rugged and handsome is the No. 570-N.P.B. Barber Chair. Soft slanted upholstery for comfort for your customer. And it means working comfort for you as the customer sits up straight in the chair. Time-tested Duo-Hydraulic Mechanism. All exposed metal parts are brilliantly chrome plated. Sunburst design base with genuine "fired-on" Porcelain Enamel. Chrome plated metal band around back. Convenient hand hold is provided for reclining chair. Completely equipped with towel bar, strap ring, Comfo-Pad headrest, and manicure sockets.

MADE FOR YOU BY EMIL J. PAIDAR COMPANY
1120 North Wells Street
Chicago 10, Illinois
300 Meserole Street
Brooklyn 6, New York

The chair with the longer life!

KOCHS'
Hy-lo-draulic
HIGH ENOUGH–LOW ENOUGH
THE SUPERIOR BARBERS' CHAIR
PATENTED

No. 3380
PRICE:
$145
F. O. B.
CHICAGO

20th Century porcelain chairs showed little change for nearly 40 years. There were a number of cosmetic variations but few structural advancements. From about 1910 until the 30s, the average porcelain chair looked very much like the above Kochs model. From the late 1920s until 1950, more use was being made of chrome trim as seen on the above Paidar chair. Kochs Hy-Lo-Draulic in unrestored but excellent condition, $500.00 to $700.00. Paidar model 570 in unrestored but excellent condition, $400.00 to $600.00. Complete restorations on either chair would more than double the value.

Wooden Chairs.

If you have a Victorian model wooden chair in untouched condition, it's a good bet that you will need to consider a major restoration. At very least, the wood will need to be brightened up and there is no way that the upholstery will be presentable. Because it would have originally had thinly applied nickel plating, the old plating probably will be gone and you won't spend less than $500 to have the metal parts re-nickeled unless you have a friend in the business. If you *must* have chrome (not original in this period, but exquisite nonetheless), add about $150 more. A quality leather upholstery job won't cost less than $400 and could possibly approach $1000 if you desire pleating and button-tufting. While there are detractors of this type of upholstery who claim that it is not historically accurate, the accompanying original illustration from the August Kern Barber Supply Company of St. Louis, Missouri, shows that extremely ornate leather work was available. Fancy Victorian beauties were the best-of-the-best then, and remain so today. Based on the cost of the restoration alone (not taking into consideration your original acquisition price), one of these elegant chairs selling for below $3500 would be a bargain in today's market. Heavily carved wooden models could command even higher prices.

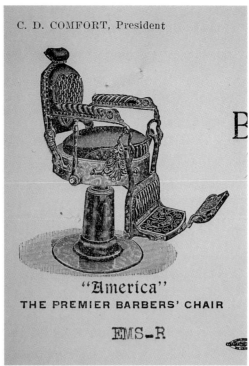

Example of button-tufted and pleated leather work seen on the "America" model by August Kern around 1900. This photo clearly shows that intricate upholstery was being done at that time. If completely restored, this chair would be $6,000.00+.

Louis Hanson manufactured barber chair is a good example of an unrestored find. Chair needs upholstery, wood refinishing, plating, and re-casting of one piece of trim. The chair is complete and works perfectly. Even in the condition that it is in, this scarce Hanson chair could bring up to $1,500.00. With full restoration, $3,000.00+. *Courtesy of Bill Wright.*

Koken round back, round bottom, porcelain chair with fluted base. This chair is among the most desirable of the porcelain chairs. Handsome just the way it appears as found and worth $1,200.00+. With plating and upholstery, the price could more than double.

Porcelain Chairs and Poles

If your project involves a porcelain chair or a porcelain pole, and you don't need complete restoration, you may find that elbow grease (your own hard work) will do the trick. Many porcelain chairs were built in the 1920s after manufacturers began using chrome. If yours is trimmed in chrome, most of the metal parts can be made to look like new with Number 0000 steel wool and automotive chrome cleaner. A notable exception is the footrest. Because of the usual wear on these surfaces, the original plating could be worn away and you may want to try buffing it with rouge on a polishing wheel. This will definitely put a bright shine on the bare metal. While it will look super at first, be prepared for some light residual rusting if the chair is placed in a humid-environment. The worst case scenario is that you may need to re-plate a few pieces.

Unless your porcelain is badly chipped or discolored, you can usually get it to appear surprisingly like new. The first thing to do is clean all of the porcelain surfaces with a grease cutting, household cleanser. Next, use a semi- abrasive tub and tile cleanser that has a bleaching agent. I use a product called Soft Scrub which I apply with a stiff-bristled scrub brush. Let it sit on the porcelain for a few minutes, but not so long that it begins to dry. Rinse thoroughly. Repeat these steps as needed. In most cases, you will get a satisfactory and pleasing result. If, as previously mentioned, your porcelain is badly chipped or deeply scratched, there are two preferred methods of restoration. The first would be to have the porcelain re-fired as new. This process is expensive. It could also necessitate high shipping costs of the cast-iron pieces since this service is not always available locally. A more affordable alternative would be to hire your local bathtub refinishing service. This process utilizes a synthetic type of porcelain that can be applied right in your garage. It has long been an accepted refinishing method for barber poles and chairs. When done properly, it is not only beautiful, but it shares the original porcelain's qualities. It will retain the color and is adequately chip resistant, even for commercial use.

If you need to replace the upholstery on a barber chair, it would be nice, but not necessary, to use genuine leather. After the 1920s, and particularly in the 30s and 40s, many of the original chairs were covered in synthetic materials. Therefore, a leather patterned synthetic would not only be historically correct, but it will look great and save money to boot. Based on a complete, professional restoration including genuine leather upholstery, (smooth, no pleats or tufting) chrome plating and porcelain refinishing, these chairs can cost about $2000.00 in today's market. It could cost even more for ornate leather work, or less if using synthetic upholstery fabric. Another element that will raise the price is a chair having ornamental or unusual iron castings. Conversely, a plain porcelain chair could be as low as $500.00 in excellent, but unrestored, condition.

Chair Handling Tips

MOVING: The first hurdle to clear in your new ownership of a barber chair, is how to safely move it. Attempting the task with muscle power alone is foolish. Ugly stories abound! If you can't borrow one, rent a commercial hand-truck of the type used to move household appliances. They can more than handle the weight. They have a large canvas webbed belt that, when cinched around the chair, will not drop your cargo. Always wrap a blanket around the chair *before* positioning it in the hand truck. This protects against scratches or nicks that can so easily happen during a move. When using a hand-truck, you must tilt the whole apparatus rearward to a fairly steep degree so that the wheels can roll. In order for the oil in the chair's hydraulic reservoir not to spill during the move, you must first pump the chair all the way to the top, and then lock the handle *before* loading it onto the hand truck. This tip would apply any time you need to move the chair if tilting it is necessary. Moving on stairs is not a problem since the commercial hand-trucks have rollers on the backside of the frame. These will allow the whole unit to virtually slide up or down steps. Using the method outlined here, you will be surprised to find that two people can complete this move quite easily and safely. Average hand-truck rental cost: $12.00 per day.

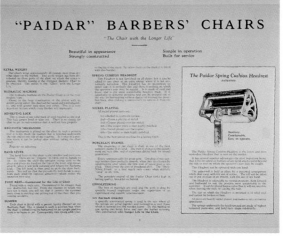

Catalog pages of the big three barber suppliers (Kochs, Paidar, and Koken) marketing their chairs selling points.

DISMANTLING CHAIRS: Taking apart a barber chair for cleaning or restoration is a fairly straightforward job that requires no special tools. You'll need two slotted screwdrivers. One should be very large, and one medium sized. A medium size adjustable wrench, a hammer, pliers, and a can of penetrating oil should be all you need. Begin by spraying penetrating oil on all accessible nuts and bolts. This does not apply to wood screws. Be sure to make a detailed drawing on a piece of corrugated cardboard as you take each piece apart. When putting the chair back together, you will be *real* glad that you did. If you use corrugated or other heavy cardboard for the drawing, each screw you remove from the chair as you're taking it apart, can immediately be screwed right into its corresponding place on the drawing. This way, the screws won't be lost and you can reinsert them in their original holes. I've found that the screws and bolts from 100+ year old furniture seem to prefer going back in the same hole they were removed from. This helps to eliminate undesirable forcing.

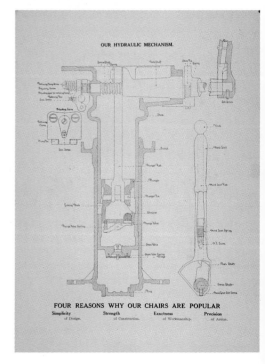

Once you dismantle the top half of the chair, you will see that the hydraulic unit needs to be removed from the base. There are no fasteners of any kind holding it there. It has a hidden-from-view piston shaft that extends downward into an oil cylinder in the base. Simply stand over it, take a firm grip on each side, and continuously lift upward. You may hear some gurgling or sucking sounds as the oil breaks the internal vacuum. This is expected. Keep lifting the unit upward until it comes completely out of the base. There will be some minimal oil dripping from the piston. Have a cardboard box or other receptacle ready to place it in. As the hydraulic piston separates from the oil reservoir base, a small, pie shaped piece of steel may fall out of its slot. This is the brake shoe and it could fall to the floor. If it does, wipe off any grit it may have picked up, and return it to the slot on the piston. To hold it in place until you are ready to reinsert the piston into the oil well at a later time, place a heavy rubber band around it. Now wrap the oily piston with paper towels or similar absorbent material. This will keep dust from building up on the oiled surface while the chair is apart. The next step is to empty the oil from the base. Simply turn the whole thing upside down and pour the oil into a waiting receptacle. When you turn the base right side up later, stuff a wad of paper towels into the opening so that the inside oiled lining doesn't get dust buildup. This is important because the piston and oil reservoir are mating surfaces and they have little tolerance for blockage. Even dust can sometimes be enough to clog up the works making it difficult to reassemble and operate. While the base is still upside down to drain the oil, you can access the screws that hold the base trim ring on. These large base screws (usually four or six) can be the most difficult of all to remove. This is primarily because they have had ground contact for many years. They've absorbed more moisture than any other part of the chair. Consequently, they could be rusted tight. If this is the case, saturate them with penetrating oil and take a long break. This will allow the oil enough time to soak in properly. Usually, it works well. If not, try giving the screw head a pretty good rap with a hammer. Many times this will encourage the rust crystals to break free deeper in the screw's threads. The worst case scenario would require drilling the old screw out and re-tapping the hole. Base screws are standard machine threaded.

REASSEMBLING CHAIRS: When all of your parts have been refinished or cleaned, reassemble them in a reverse order. The drawing you made when you took the chair apart will make the process easy. Place a few drops of liquid soap on all wood screws and lightly oil all machine screws or bolts. There are no other really "trick tips" for the re-assembly other than to proceed deliberately but, *do not* attempt the job by yourself. One person should hold each piece steady while the other uses the tools. Remember, you may have just spent as much as $2000.00 renewing these parts. Fresh new chips on the porcelain, scratches on the chrome, or a screwdriver hole in the upholstery can quickly neutralize any gains you may have been expecting. Be careful! When the chair is fully assembled you will need 2.5 pints of hydraulic oil. Pour about half of that amount into the reservoir and pump the handle several times. Pour the remaining oil in and pump the handle again. The chair should now be operational and ready to enjoy.

Original Materials Guide

The most valuable antique chairs are those that are restored with historical accuracy. The following information will help take the guesswork out of what types of fabrics, finishes, and trim to use. We have selected several of the more popular selling chairs through the Golden Years. These manufacturers also supplied chairs generically to various jobbers. For that reason, you can feel confident that the colors and materials listed would be authentic for most brands of chairs in the corresponding time frames. Many of the materials and processes that were utilized originally may still be found today.

BERNINGHAUS CHAIRS 1870s-1900

EUGENE BERNINGHAUS'
PATENT ADJUSTABLE BARBER CHAIR
"NOVELTY"

WOOD. These chairs were available in solid black walnut, French veneers, and oak. The finishes were varnished or oiled.

METAL TRIM. Enameled, bronzed, japanned, or nickeled.

UPHOLSTERY NAILS were available in nickel, gilded, or white porcelain heads.

FABRICS in order of desirability were, from least to most: Brussels tapestry carpet, terry cloth, morocco, figured plush, good and best grades of leather, moquette, best mohair plush, and silk plush.

COLORS for the upholstery were as follows: Brussels tapestry carpet was either red or green patterned; plush fabrics were green, crimson, and maroon; favorite leather colors were green, maroon, and tan.

OPTIONS during this period were cane or perforated wood seats for summertime or warm climates.

> *Unto thy secret thy false hair gives the lie; Upon thy skull I painted locks espy.*
> *Disgracefully bald! To shave hast thou no need;*
> *Use but a sponge, and from thy hair thou'rt freed.* -Unknown

Furnishings

ARCHER'S PATENT
ADJUSTABLE BARBER CHAIR, No. 9

WOOD. These chairs were available in walnut, cherry, ash, and ebony finished maple. Archer also had an accommodating policy of allowing a customer to choose any custom wood that was available. Finishes were either oiled or varnished. Archer also produced chairs with iron frames.

METAL TRIM. Enamel, nickel, or lacquered with gilt pin striping on iron based models.

UPHOLSTERY NAILS were plain brass, or nickeled brass.

FABRICS in order of desirability were, from least to most: Brussels tapestry carpet, figured plushes, best leathers, worsted plushes, clouded (heather) plushes, plain or embossed mohair, and moquette.

COLORS for the fabric upholstery were green, crimson, and maroon. Leather could be ordered in any custom color desired.

KOKEN AND KOCHS TRANSITIONAL PERIOD MODELS 1895-1910

WOOD. Walnut and mahogany were available on some models, but the majority of chairs turned out in this period were oak varieties. White oak, red oak, and finished in golden or antique shades. Transitional period chairs made heavy use of beautifully grained, quarter-sawn cuts. (tiger oak) Finishes were most often varnished.

METAL TRIM came in nickeled or plain brass on the upper portion of the chairs. One notable exception, is on the Koken chairs' footrests. For several years, these were never plated, but were polished and lacquered instead. If you have a Koken chair from the transitional period and it seems void of plating on the step plate or footrest, that is why. The round, pedestal, chair bases which defined the transitional period, had a variety of trim. They all shared a cast-iron base. Some were covered with wood veneers to match the upper wood on the chairs. Others were

painted with enamel or lacquer. These painted bases were usually trimmed in a process called japanning, (ornate symmetrical designs) or copper oxidized (strips of copper running over the metal which appear like Tiger stripes.) On Koken chairs, the metal ring at the bottom of the pedestal base, very often had a stamped ornamental design. These were nickeled steel, nickeled brass, or polished brass. On Kochs chairs, the base rings were usually smooth brass or nickel. One exception was their pullman and steamship model, chair number 105. The base ring on this Kochs chair had an ornamental stamped design. Kochs also produced a heavy rubber ring to replace the metal ones for a short time. A chair with one of these rubber base rings would date to around 1900.

Kochs' Columbia model 47 shows example of "japanned" base. Color schemes for japanned bases were usually a black or white field with gold symmetrical designs. Seen most often on transitional models. This chair unrestored, $900.00 to $1,200.00.

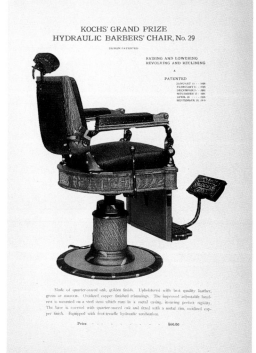

Kochs' Grand Prize model shows metal trim finished in oxidized copper. This "tiger stripe" appearance on metal trim was most popular in the 1890s and it rivaled nickel plating all through the transitional chair period. Even after the process was no longer used for barber chairs, it was still seen on some twisted-wire metal furnishings such as shoe shine or manicure items. This chair unrestored, $900.00 to $1,200.00.

UPHOLSTERY NAILS were plain brass, or nickel-plated.

FABRICS in this period had been narrowed down to the two most popular. They were plush mohair and best grade leather.

COLORS for Kochs mohair fabrics were green, crimson, maroon, or old gold. Kochs leather was offered in green or maroon with maroon being the most popular color. Koken chairs covered in mohair offered the standard green, crimson, and maroon. Koken offered green or maroon leather, but would supply it in any color requested.

OPTIONS were perforated wood or caned seat bottoms for the summer season. Some chairs were also sold with permanent cane backs and bottoms for hot climates.

PORCELAIN OVER CAST-IRON CHAIRS 1910-1950

CASTINGS. There were a great number of models through this period which lasted to about 1950. Their common bond was that they were all covered with porcelain. Most of the castings were fairly plain and had smooth surfaces. Some of the more interesting of them were the round bottom, round back design, the octagonal bottom, fluted bases, and other artistically cast designs. The unusually cast variants cost more to produce originally. They remain as the most desirable porcelain chairs and are priced accordingly.

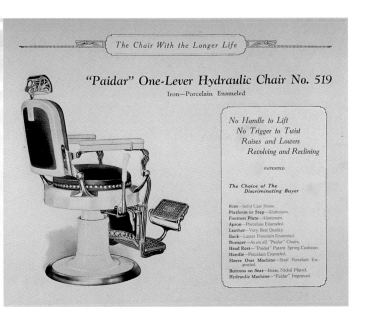

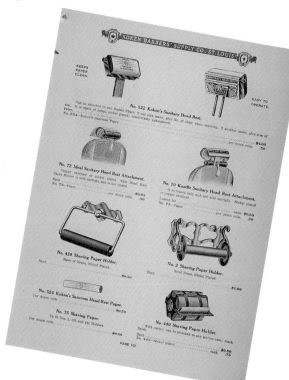

METAL TRIM was usually nickel or polished brass into the late 1920s. During the early years of this period, both Kochs and Koken used combinations of these metals on the same chair. This produced a beautiful effect. For example: the step, the footrest, and the outer base rim would be polished brass. All other metal parts were heavily nickeled. When restored that way today, it is stunning. You should be able to easily confirm any brass castings you may have on your particular model. By the late 1920s, these combo finishes weren't being seen as often. That was because of the practical benefits of chrome plating. By the mid-1930s, chrome was being used almost exclusively. It simply was shinier and lasted longer. Upholstery nail heads were brass or nickeled.

Accessories that were available for barber chairs included: dust covers, summer (cane) seats, various headrests with shaving paper rolls, hydraulic oil, and re-upholstery hardware. It is impractical to assign current prices to these items since they are not seen regularly enough to be gauge. Headrests are usually the first thing to become separated from a complete chair. As a result, they can be difficult to locate. When you do find one, the seller usually can tell that you *need* it. Expect the price to reflect that thought.

Furnishings

FABRIC saw a shift away from mohair which was popular during the beginning years of porcelain chairs. From the 1920s on, leather and synthetics became the fabric of choice. Mohair was still being used on some headrests until the late 1920s.

COLORS during this period applied not only to the upholstery, but to the color of the porcelain, as well. Upholstery colors were primarily green, red, brown, and black. Black and red were the runaway favorites. The porcelain colors were another story. During the teens and 1920s, the move to sanitize barbershops saw their decor become mostly white or neutral colored. White was a standard color for most porcelain chairs for years. By 1930, Kochs was attempting to infuse some color back into those boring, white, barbershops. At that time, a barber could order his porcelain furniture in the following colors: white, old ivory, pearl gray, Nile green, jade green, robins egg blue, orchid, black, desert tan, mottled green, and mottled buff. While some furniture in those shades does occasionally surface, most of the porcelain chairs you find will be white.

OPTIONS that were seen most often on porcelain chairs were manicure attachments and bowls. Another, was the side seat attachment which allowed the barber to remain seated while cutting hair.

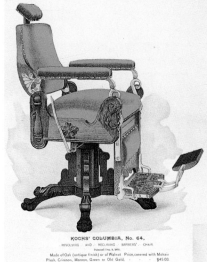

KOCHS' COLUMBIA, No. 64,
REVOLVING AND RECLINING BARBERS' CHAIR.
Patented Dec. 3, 1895.
Made of Oak (antique finish) or of Walnut. Price, covered with Mohair Plush, Crimson, Maroon, Green or Old Gold, - - - $45.00

KOCHS' HYDRAULIC, No. 97,
RAISING AND LOWERING REVOLVING AND RECLINING
BARBERS' CHAIR.
PRICE, - - - - $125.00

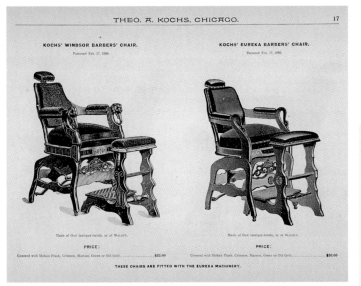

THEO. A. KOCHS, CHICAGO. 17

KOCHS' WINDSOR BARBERS' CHAIR.
Patented Feb. 17, 1880.

KOCHS' EUREKA BARBERS' CHAIR.
Patented Feb. 17, 1880.

Made of Oak (antique finish), or of WALNUT.
PRICE:
Covered with Mohair Plush, Crimson, Maroon, Green or Old Gold.........$55.00

Made of Oak (antique finish), or of WALNUT.
PRICE:
Covered with Mohair Plush, Crimson, Maroon, Green or Old Gold.........$30.00

THESE CHAIRS ARE FITTED WITH THE EUREKA MACHINERY.

These Kochs Two-piece chairs are representative of this style. Although sectional models were made by many different manufacturers for an approximately 40 year period, they were most popular from the 1850s until the 1870s. They were easily identified by separate, but matching, footrests. Many were nicely carved and upholstered. A variety of wood was used in their construction, but walnut was the favorite. Since two-piece chairs don't have anywhere near as many buyers as the late-Victorian models, sectional models can be a relative bargain in the $500.00 to $1,500.00 range depending on age and condition. Exceedingly ornate models would bring more.

KOCHS' HYDRAULIC, No. 94,
RAISING AND LOWERING REVOLVING AND RECLINING
BARBERS' CHAIR.
PRICE, - - - - $70.00

*Fair tresses man's imperial race ensnare,
And beauty draws us with a single hair. -Pope*

Right, top to bottom: Kochs late Victorian models show diversity of wood, fabric, colors, carvings, and embellishments. Each is more beautiful than the other. It is easy to see why the chairs produced in this period are the most sought after. Any one of the four with a complete restoration would be valued starting at $3,500.00 and could range much higher if at auction.

KOCHS' HYDRAULIC, No. 95,
RAISING AND LOWERING REVOLVING AND RECLINING
BARBERS' CHAIR.
PRICE, - - - - $75.00

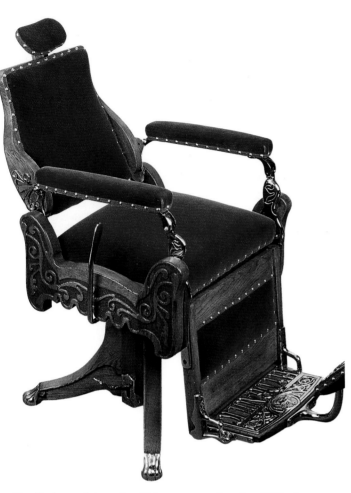

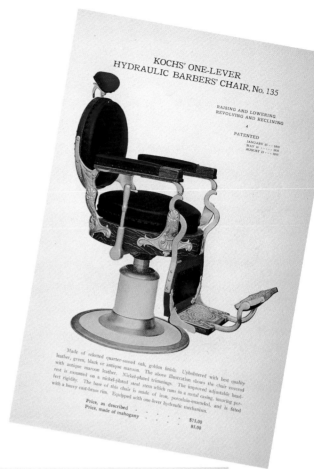

This Kochs model number 71 is representative of an 1890s, late-Victorian style chair. It has had a complete historical restoration including original mohair (then referred to as "plush") upholstery. Chair has nice embellishments but no carvings. Mint as seen, $3,500.00+.

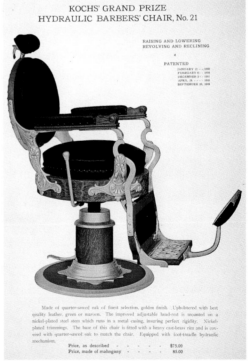

Three Kochs chairs that epitomize the "Transitional" years. These chairs overlapped the pre-1900, four-legged, Victorian models, and the 20th century, all cast-iron, porcelain chairs. Nearly all transitional chair bases are cast-iron pedestals with porcelain or wood veneer covering. Their upper bodies are solid wood. Most had leather or plush upholstery. Metal trim was polished brass, nickel, or oxidized copper. Some low-end models were non-hydraulic but most were fully mechanical. Round back, round bottom cushioned chairs seem more desirable to today's buyer and will be priced accordingly. The average range for a fully restored Transitional model chair will usually be from $3,000.00 to $5,000.00. Heavily carved examples or auction fever will boost the price.

Furnishings

Example of a fully restored Transitional era chair. This Koken "Congress" model was patented in 1895. It is often referred to as the "talc brush" model because of the oak carvings on the sides which represent a barber's powder dusting brush. It was also the chair model used for Norman Rockwell's famous *Saturday Evening Post* cover from April 29, 1950 entitled "Shuffleton's Barber Shop. Mint as seen with button-tufted upholstery, $3,500.00.

Example of an early 20th Century, cast-iron, porcelain coated chair. This Koken model, which was made prior to 1920, is typical of most barber chairs being manufactured by that time. Nickel plating. Heavy and durable, but short on eye appeal when compared to earlier wooden chairs. Their acceptance was due mainly to the public's demand for a white, sterile appearance since sanitation had become a societal concern. This particular chair also came with a scarce accessory in the "side-seat." It allowed a barber to actually sit down while cutting hair. Completely restored, early, porcelain chair as seen, $1,800.00+. Add $500.00 for the restored side-seat.

Example of an ornate cast-iron chair. Some were round. Others were octagonal. Occasionally, the base column was fluted. This Koken *fleur de leis* design actually had the signature design cast into the iron arms and base. The bulbous base (as opposed to column) also has symmetrical designs in the castings. The arm and seat bottom edges are gracefully shaped with a raised border. The time period for these Art-Deco inspired porcelain chairs was the late 1920s and early 1930s. Many women were patronizing barber shops for "bobbed" cuts in that time frame and perhaps the chairs designers were aiming to please that market. Completely restored and including genuine leather upholstery, chrome plating, (correct for the period) and porcelain refinishing, $2,200.00.

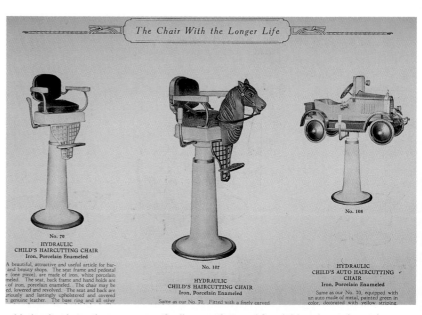

Hydraulic chairs that were specifically manufactured for children have always been sought after. A fairly large variety of seat treatments were available. The most popular were carved wooden horse heads and miniature vehicles appearing very much like pedal cars. Proportionately, there were many less children's chairs produced than their full sized counterparts. As you may expect, their prices (pound for pound) are proportionately higher. Prices vary wildly from a plain model in *as-found* condition at perhaps $1,000.00+, to a *fully restored* model featuring the pedal car style at $3,500.00+. Also desirable, were pre-1900 wooden child's chairs. They are scarce but can be found in the $500.00 to $700.00+ range. I consider them bargain priced only because they are currently less sought after than the newer porcelain models, not because they aren't more rare.

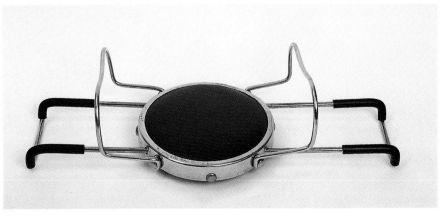

The most popular child's chair was the "twisted-wire", metal type. They were made from the 1890s until about 1930. Because they are affordable, they originally outsold porcelain, hydraulic, child's chairs. Outselling both of the above chairs combined, was the comparatively inexpensive "spanner" model which sat between the arms on a regular barber chair. Twisted-wire child's chair in condition as shown: $350.00+. Porcelain, hydraulic child's chair completely restored as shown: $1,800.00+. Add $500.00+ if carved horse head is present. Wire "spanner" type as seen from 1920s: $100.00.

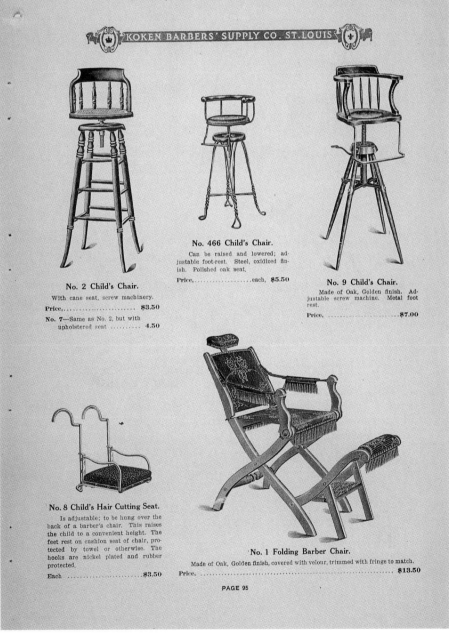

KOKEN BARBERS' SUPPLY CO. ST. LOUIS

No. 2 Child's Chair.
With cane seat, screw machinery.
Price,.......................... $3.50
No. 7—Same as No. 2, but with upholstered seat 4.50

No. 466 Child's Chair.
Can be raised and lowered; adjustable foot-rest. Steel, oxidized finish. Polished oak seat.
Price,....................each, $5.50

No. 9 Child's Chair.
Made of Oak, Golden finish. Adjustable screw machine. Metal foot rest.
Price, ...$7.00

No. 8 Child's Hair Cutting Seat.
Is adjustable; to be hung over the back of a barber's chair. This raises the child to a convenient height. The feet rest on cushion seat of chair, protected by towel or otherwise. The hooks are nickel plated and rubber protected.
Each $3.50

No. 1 Folding Barber Chair.
Made of Oak, Golden finish, covered with velour, trimmed with fringe to match.
Price, ...$13.50

PAGE 95

Furnishings

Theo. Kochs brand portable barber chair. Closes and opens like modern folding lawn chair. Originally sold in two presentations from the late 1890s until the 1920s. They came covered in plush (tapestry or velour) with gold trim for hotel room service. If restored as seen here: $750.00+. Another style was covered in khaki colored canvas (void of trim) for military field work. $350.00+ in good condition.

We have had a great many calls from barbers for a formula for a cure for Barber's Itch, so we submit the following, which is a good one.

BARBERS' ITCHINE

Tanic Acid	*90 grains*
Lac Sulphur	*180 grains*
Oxide Zinc	*1 ounce*
Starch	*1 ounce*
Petrolatum (white)	*2 ounces*

Shave every day and apply three times a day until cured, 1 to 3 days.— Professor Bridgeford, Barber's Instructor and Toilet Manual, 1899

"Bobbing" chairs became popular beginning in the 1920s as a result of the bobbed style of ladies haircuts. They were designed with, either a very low back height, or a portion of the chair-back would be scalloped at the top. A removable piece (not unlike a regular barber chair headrest) nestled down into the top of the back rest. When this piece was taken out of the chair back, a barber could better access a women's neckline which was the essence of the bobbed style. Many of them also doubled as facial chairs and reclined 45 degrees for providing that service to both men and women. Plenty of barber shops had large followings of women who preferred to have their "bobs" done by a barber. Of course, beauty parlors also used these chairs. To date, collector interest has been low and unrestored "bobbing" chairs are bargains in the $200.00 to $500.00 range depending on condition.

"Paidar" Bobbing Chairs

No. 77. BOBBING CHAIR
Hydraulic
Raising, Lowering, Revolving
Reclining

Can be used for bobbing and facials. Reclines to 45 degrees, and is 24½ inches from floor to top of seat when down, and 30 inches when raised as high as it will go. Made entirely of iron, porcelain enameled and covered with genuine gray leather.

No. 80. BOBBING CHAIR
Raises—Revolves—Lowers

This chair is fitted with hydraulic mechanism, so it can be pumped up or lowered, as desired, and will also revolve.

The base is of iron porcelain enameled. The top is of wood, white enameled and upholstered with genuine black leather. When at its lowest, it measures 22 inches from floor to top of seat and 28 inches when at its highest.

No. 74. EXTRA HIGH BOBBING CHAIR
Hydraulic, Raising and Lowering,
Revolving and Reclining
Bobbing and Massaging Chair for Operators Who Prefer to Stand
When Working

This is the chair to fill the requirements of one who wishes a chair to raise and lower. Made entirely of iron, porcelain enameled. Hydraulic mechanism. Revolving and reclining to 45 degrees. All metal parts heavily nickel plated. Raises about 5½ inches. Covered with genuine gray leather unless otherwise ordered. Height from floor to top of seat, 27½ inches when down.

81

Barbershop

Backbars

What we now commonly refer to as backbars, were originally known as wall sectionals or mirror cases. Their chronology through the Golden Years paints a clear picture of diminishing quality, both in aesthetics and materials. Next to the barber pole in front of a shop, backbars were the most important piece of barbershop furniture to own from a practical perspective. You can see very graphically by the following pictures just how these furnishings changed between 1880 and 1940.

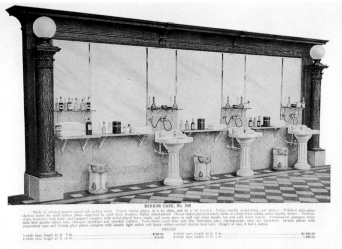

MIRROR CASE, No. 348

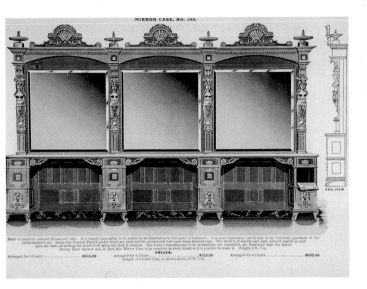

MIRROR CASE, NO. 195.

PRICES:
Arranged for 2 Chairs.................$358.00   Arranged for 3 Chairs.................$525.00   Arranged for 4 Chairs.................$692.00
Length of 3-Chair Case, as shown above, 13 ft. 5 in.

Pre-1900 Victorian backbar was typical of what was available and being utilized by 1880. This example is heavily carved mahogany but walnut was the most common during those years. Ornate hand carvings were the hallmark of late Victorian style barbershop furniture. If refinished, this, or a similar 3 station model could be valued at $12,000.00+.

This period of backbar innovation which began before 1910, shows that oak was still popular but there was very little, if any, carving still being done. Designs, in general, had become less ornate. Sinks had been added as an option by this time, but it was obvious that the quality of backbar materials was shifting downward. There was less woodwork and much more glass or marble. Glass was brighter, cheaper to produce, and easy to clean. If refinished, this, or a similar 3 station model could be valued at $8,000.00+.

This backbar was manufactured just after 1900 and reflects the changes from the previous period. Although hand carving was still being done, it was seen less often. The formerly favored walnut and mahogany materials had turned to golden or antique oak. Also in the post-1900 period, provisions were being made for more storage and display space along with a place for towel urns. If refinished, this, or a similar 3 station model could be valued at $10,000.00+.

MIRROR CASE, No. 214

Made of quarter-sawed oak, golden finish. Size of French beveled plates, 36 x 40 and 15 x 36. Italian marble shelf. The workstands are very neat and practical and have a shelf for clean towels; a drawer fitted with Yale lock and a shallow slide drawer which is very handy for such tools as razors, combs and shears. The feet of the workstands are metal, oxidized copper finish. The mirror case is provided with a compartment at each end for the display of toilet articles. These compartments are fitted with plate-glass doors, furnished with lock and key. Bohemian glass shaving-paper vases and glazed earthenware towel urns are furnished with this case. Height, 8 feet 7 inches.

PRICES
2-chair case, length 10 ft. 8 in.................$154.00   4-chair case, length 19 ft. 9 in.................$276.00
3-chair case, length 15 ft. 2½ in.................215.00   5-chair case, length 24 ft. 4 in.................337.00

Furnishings

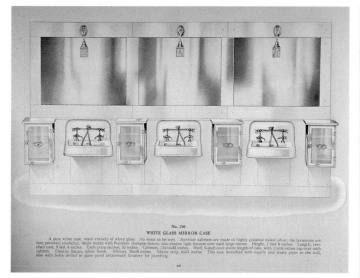

No. 700
WHITE GLASS MIRROR CASE
A pure white case, made entirely of white glass. No wood to be seen. Sterilizer cabinets are made of highly polished nickel silver; the lavatories are iron porcelain enameled, 18x24 inches with Rainbow shampoo fixture; also electric light fixtures over each large mirror. Height, 7 feet 6 inches. Length, two-chair case, 8 feet 4 inches. Each extra section, 53 inches. Cabinets, 12x14x22 inches. Shelf, 6-inch over entire length of case, with 11x16 inches top over each cabinet. Electric fixture, silver finish. Mirrors, 36x58 inches. Mirror strip, 6x35 inches. This case furnished with supply and waste pipes to the wall, also with holes drilled in glass panel underneath lavatory for plumbing.

43

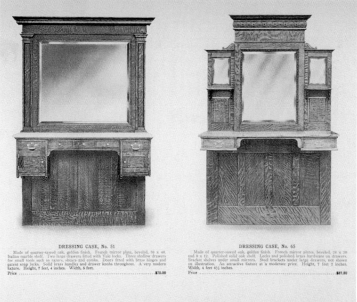

DRESSING CASE, No. 51
Made of quarter-sawed oak, golden finish. French mirror plate, beveled, 30 x 40. Italian marble shelf. Two large drawers fitted with Yale locks. Three shallow drawers for small tools such as razors, shears and combs. Doors fitted with brass hinges and patent soap locks. Solid brass handles and drawer knobs throughout. A very modern fixture. Height, 7 feet, 4 inches. Width, 5 feet.
Price $70.00

DRESSING CASE, No. 65
Made of quarter-sawed solid oak, golden finish. French mirror plates, beveled, 24 x 30 and 8 x 12. Polished solid oak shelf. Locks and polished brass hardware on drawers. Bracket shelves under small mirrors. Steel brackets under large drawers, not shown on illustration. An attractive feature at a moderate price. Height, 7 feet 2 inches. Width, 4 feet 6½ inches.
Price $37.50

As the 1920s were nearing, backbar construction had changed dramatically. The beauty of the earlier period's wooden units was gone. Everything was becoming white because of the sanitation movement. Notice the standard, built-in, sterilizer cases at each station. This period of innovation also made more use of lights on backbars since electricity had become readily accessible. While many backbars in this period were still being designed like sections of furniture or cabinetry, they were mostly white-painted wood, and mirrored or colored glass materials. Marble was still used but mainly for counter-top or mirror-borders on only the most expensive backbars. The diminished construction quality on the average backbar had become complete. If refinished, this, or a similar 3 station model could cost $2,000.00.

Single station backbars were also very popular for shops manned by a lone barber. The reason that the majority of remaining one-station wooden units seem to be early, is because they are. During the early and mid golden years, there were proportionately more one-man shops. As the years progressed, more and more shops employed multiple barbers which lessened production of single station type backbars. Most are walnut or oak and they have a special appeal to the modern collector who has a small display. Price range for refinished examples would be from $1,500.00 to $3,000.00 depending on ornate qualities.

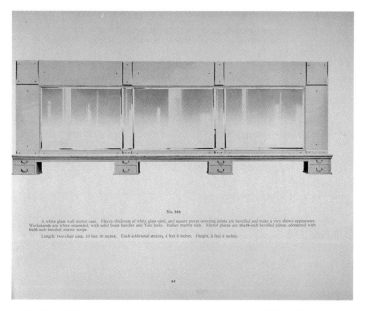

No. 355
A white glass wall mirror case. Heavy thickness of white glass used, and square pieces covering joints are bevelled and make a very showy appearance. Workstands are white enameled, with solid brass handles and Yale locks. Italian marble slab. Mirror plates are 36x48-inch bevelled plates, connected with 6x36-inch bevelled mirror strips.
Length, two-chair case, 10 feet 10 inches. Each additional station, 4 feet 5 inches. Height, 5 feet 3 inches.

60

By the 1930s, the average and low-end backbars had literally been reduced to a shell of their splendor just 20 to 30 years prior. The type seen here was not much more than a mirror and a glass or marble shelf. The border around the mirror was colored glass. With many units, there was nothing besides a drawer under the counter level. They were inexpensive, serviceable, easy to clean, and popular with lesser financed shops for years. This, or a similar, 3 station unit could be valued at $1,200.00 if found complete and undamaged. Note: Some fancier and more costly units *were* available during this time frame. Art-Deco was the aesthetic influence and they generally had multi-colored tile fronts. They would be valued at $2,000.00+ for 3 matching stations.

Mug Racks

Mug racks, as we call them today, were first sold as "cup cases" in the 1870s. By 1900, they were marketed as "mug cases." Of all barbershop furnishings, mug racks are perhaps the most sought after because of the large number of shaving mug specialty collectors who utilize the antique shelves to display their collections. Mug rack chronology parallels that of other barbershop wooden furniture. During the early Golden Years, racks were mostly made of walnut and very often had fancy embellishments or carvings. After 1900, oak became more popular and they were usually far less ornate. Racks were made in a wide variety of shapes and sizes. There were two main types of mug rack construction. The first were combination units which doubled as sinks, dressing cases, (with mirrors) and storage compartments. These were often very big units which sometimes reached nine feet in height and were six feet wide. Racks with compartments for 100 mugs were not uncommon. Hotels were where those large racks usually stood. The second, and far more common type, were wall mounted and only held mugs. They had no display or storage compartments. They were much smaller than combination racks and usually ranged from eighteen to sixty compartments. Early racks had compartments with solid dividers all the way from the front to the rear. Each compartment averaged five inches across although there is size variance between different manufacturers. The mug compartments were referred to as "pigeon holes" in early catalog descriptions. In later years, some manufacturers utilized only criss-crossed strips of wood across the front of a rack to designate each compartment. The manufacturers pulled a fast one here because they touted the advantage of strip-front racks as being "easier to dust." What they were..... was cheaper to build! These racks remain less desirable today since they allow the mugs to contact one another on the common shelf surface. That can lead to unnecessary chipping. With the price of collectible shaving mugs today, a fully compartmented rack is a good investment, especially if you are using it for high-end mug display.

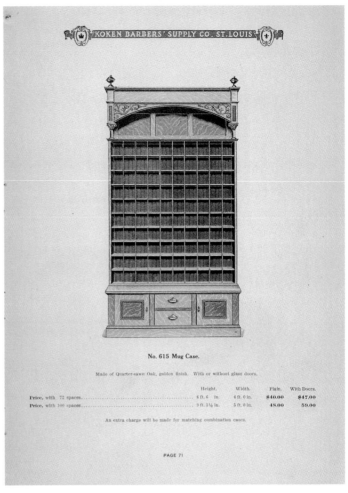

No. 615 Mug Case.

Made of Quarter-sawn Oak, golden finish. With or without glass doors.

	Height.	Width.	Plain.	With Doors.
Price, with 72 spaces	8 ft. 6 in.	4 ft. 0 in.	$40.00	$47.00
Price, with 100 spaces	9 ft. 3½ in.	5 ft. 0 in.	48.00	59.00

An extra charge will be made for matching combination cases.

PAGE 71

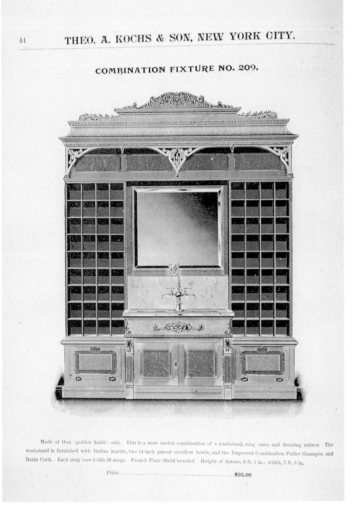

44 THEO. A. KOCHS & SON, NEW YORK CITY.

COMBINATION FIXTURE NO. 209.

Made of Oak (golden finish) only. This is a most useful combination of a washstand, mug cases and dressing mirror. The washstand is furnished with Italian marble, two 14-inch patent overflow bowls, and the Improved Combination Fuller Shampoo and Basin Cock. Each mug case holds 36 mugs. French Plate 30x34 beveled. Height of fixture, 9 ft. 1 in.; width, 7 ft. 5 in.

Price.............................$93.00

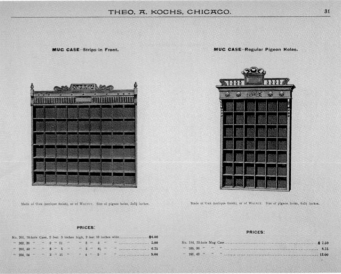

THEO. A. KOCHS, CHICAGO. 31

MUG CASE—Strips in Front.   MUG CASE—Regular Pigeon Holes.

Made of Oak (antique finish), or of Walnut. Size of pigeon holes, 3x3½ inches.   Made of Oak (antique finish), or of Walnut. Size of pigeon holes, 3x3½ inches.

PRICES: PRICES:

No. 201, 78-hole Case, 2 feet 5 inches high, 2 feet 10 inches wide.........$4.00   No. 184, 72-hole Mug Case.............$ 7.50
" 202, 36   " 2 " 11   " 3 " 2   " ....5.00   " 185, 90   " 8.75
" 203, 48   " 3 " 5   " 3 " 8½   " ....6.75   " 186, 42   " 12.00
" 204, 54   " 3 " 11   " 4 " 2   " 9.00

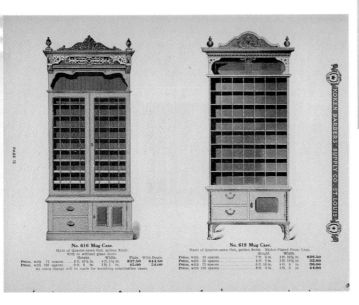

No. 616 Mug Case.
Made of Quarter-sawn Oak, golden finish.
With or without glass doors.

No. 619 Mug Case.
Made of Quarter-sawn Oak, golden finish. Nickel Plated Front Legs.

Furnishings

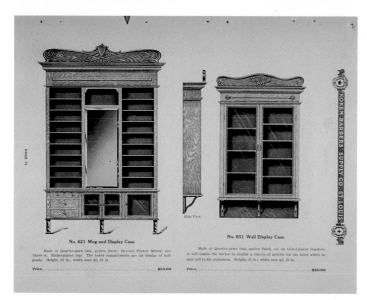

No. 621 Mug and Display Case.

Made of Quarter-sawn Oak, golden finish; Beveled French Mirror, size 15x40 in. Nickel-plated legs. The lower compartments are for display of bulk goods. Height, 92 in.; width over all, 43 in.

Price, ... $55.00

Side View.

No. 651 Wall Display Case.

Made of Quarter-sawn Oak, golden finish, set on nickel-plated brackets. It will enable the barber to display a variety of articles for the toilet which he may sell to his customers. Height, 40 in.; width over all, 40 in.

Price, ... $20.00

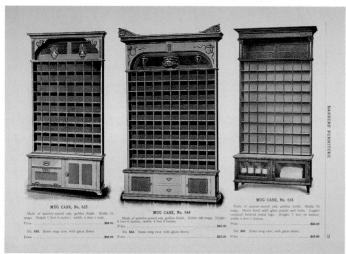

MUG CASE, No. 635

Made of quarter-sawed oak, golden finish. Holds 72 mugs. Height 7 feet 6 inches; width, 4 feet 1 inch.

Price $95.00

No. 636. Same mug case, with glass doors.

Price $99.00

MUG CASE, No. 644

Made of quarter-sawed oak, golden finish. Holds 100 mugs. Height; 8 feet 6 inches; width, 5 feet 8 inches.

Price $45.00

No. 645. Same mug case, with glass doors.

Price $52.00

MUG CASE, No. 638

Made of quarter-sawed oak, golden finish. Holds 72 mugs. Doors fitted with glass panels and locks. Copper oxidized finished metal legs. Height 7 feet 10 inches; width 4 feet 1 inch.

Price $38.00

No. 639. Same mug case, with glass doors.

Price $43.00

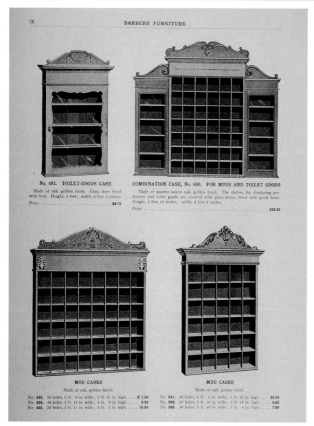

No. 681. TOILET-GOODS CASE.

Made of oak, golden finish. Glass door fitted with lock. Height, 4 feet; width, 2 feet 6 inches.

Price $8.75

COMBINATION CASE, No. 680. FOR MUGS AND TOILET GOODS

Made of quarter-sawed oak, golden finish. The shelves for displaying perfumery and toilet goods are covered with glass-doors, fitted with good locks. Height, 4 feet 10 inches; width, 5 feet 6 inches.

Price $22.25

MUG CASES

Made of oak, golden finish.

No. 423. 35 holes, 3 ft. 6 in. wide; 3 ft. 1 in. high	$ 7.50
No. 424. 48 holes, 3 ft. 11 in. wide; 4 ft. 6 in. high	9.25
No. 425. 56 holes, 3 ft. 11 in. wide; 5 ft. 2 in. high	10.65

MUG CASES

Made of oak, golden finish.

No. 241. 20 holes, 2 ft. 4 in. wide; 3 ft. 10 in. high	$5.50
No. 242. 25 holes, 2 ft. 10 in. wide; 3 ft. 10 in. high	6.25
No. 243. 30 holes, 2 ft. 10 in. wide; 4 ft. 4 in. high	7.00

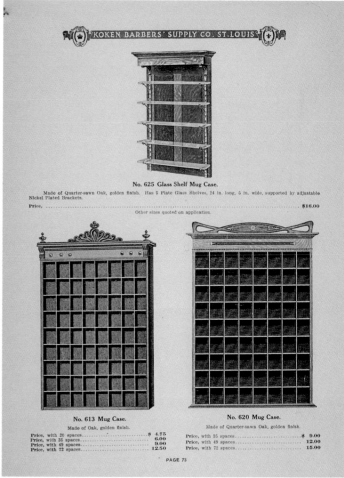

No. 625 Glass Shelf Mug Case.

Made of Quarter-sawn Oak, golden finish. Has 5 Plate Glass Shelves, 24 in. long, 5 in. wide, supported by adjustable Nickel Plated Brackets.

Price, ... $16.00

Other sizes quoted on application.

No. 613 Mug Case.

Made of Oak, golden finish.

Price, with 20 spaces	$ 4.75
Price, with 35 spaces	6.00
Price, with 49 spaces	9.00
Price, with 72 spaces	12.50

No. 620 Mug Case.

Made of Quarter-sawn Oak, golden finish.

Price, with 35 spaces	$ 9.00
Price, with 49 spaces	12.00
Price, with 72 spaces	15.00

PAGE 73

The chronology of mug racks is far less obvious than some other barbershop furniture such as chairs or backbars. Primarily, that is because mug racks had a shorter period of utilization. When shaving mugs began to fall from popularity in the 1920s, mug racks correspondingly became less necessary. During the years that they were in demand, racks were made of the popular wood at that time. Aside from a few variations like mahogany or cherry, the largest percentage of mug racks were walnut (Victorian) and oak (post-1900). Some racks, around 1910 and later, did get glass door coverings when sanitation awareness began growing. Yet others had their once-beautiful wood grains unceremoniously painted white for a more sanitary appearance. By the time that glass, Formica, wood laminates, and other modern materials became standard, mug racks were no longer being manufactured. For that reason, early and mid-Golden Years racks will always remain as a highly recognized and unique piece of hand-crafted wooden furniture. One with an exclusive use and an historically brief production span.

I would like to be able to price mug racks with an easily computed formula such as $25.00 to $35.00 per hole depending on condition and ornate quality. While that ballpark guideline isn't too far off the mark, it isn't always reliable since the actual selling prices with most good racks are based on supply and demand. Yes, more so than usual. Advanced mug collectors who seek out the already high-end racks have often bid them into the stars. If you find one at a flea market, you could get very lucky. If, on the other hand, you are bidding against somebody in an auction who is determined to own it, you'll need to be brave. There are lots of people buying antiques who *possess more money than brains!* Combination mug racks, when refinished, could be valued at $3,500.00+ depending on condition and ornate qualities. Wall racks range from about $350.00 for a small, plain, oak unit, to $1,500.00+ for a nice sized, early, walnut rack with some carving. The catalog pages show some average examples of presentation and size.

Display Cases

The height of popularity for freestanding showcases designed specifically for barbershops, was from about 1900 until the mid-1920s. There were showcases and retail display furniture items being made before and after that time, but the need for them was far greater during barbering's mid-Golden Years. It was in that period when sales of cigars, tobacco products, and retail, bottled tonics were at their peak. That time was also before building construction, in general, had provided enough closet or storage space. Take note that some freestanding display cases seen in antique barbershop catalogs have closed, bottom-level, storage space which was advertised for "surplus shop supplies." There simply wasn't enough storage space for everything, and multi-use display cabinet sales took off. Unfortunately, barbershops (and all businesses in general) occupied buildings where closet space reflected an earlier time when there had been less storage requirements.

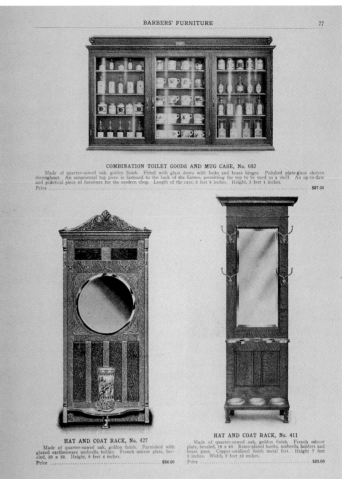

COMBINATION TOILET GOODS AND MUG CASE, No. 682
Made of quarter-sawed oak, golden finish. Fitted with glass doors with locks and brass hinges. Polished plate-glass shelves throughout. An ornamental top piece is fastened to the back of the fixture, permitting the top to be used as a shelf. An up-to-date and practical piece of furniture for the modern shop. Length of the case, 5 feet 6 inches. Height, 3 feet 4 inches.
Price $27.00

HAT AND COAT RACK, No. 427
Made of quarter-sawed oak, golden finish. Furnished with glazed earthenware umbrella holder. French mirror plate, beveled, 30 x 30. Height, 8 feet 4 inches.
Price $36.00

HAT AND COAT RACK, No. 411
Made of quarter-sawed oak, golden finish. French mirror plate, beveled, 18 x 40. Brass-plated hooks, umbrella holders and brass pans. Copper-oxidized finish metal feet. Height 7 feet 2 inches. Width, 2 feet 10 inches.
Price $23.00

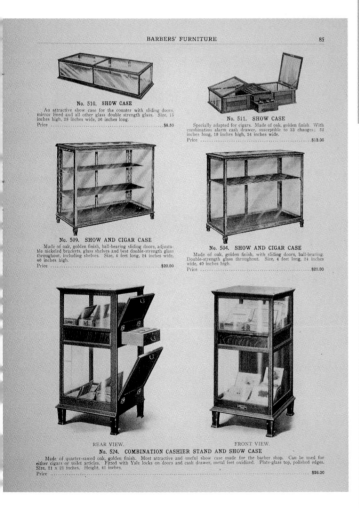

No. 510. SHOW CASE
An attractive show case for the counter with sliding doors, mirror lined and all other glass double strength glass. Size, 15 inches high, 28 inches wide, 36 inches long.
Price $8.50

No. 511. SHOW CASE
Specially adapted for cigars. Made of oak, golden finish. With combination alarm cash drawer, susceptible to 33 changes; 32 inches long, 19 inches high, 24 inches wide.
Price $13.00

No. 509. SHOW AND CIGAR CASE
Made of oak, golden finish, ball-bearing sliding doors, adjustable nickeled brackets, glass shelves and best double-strength glass throughout, including shelves. Size, 4 feet long, 24 inches wide, 40 inches high.
Price $20.00

No. 504. SHOW AND CIGAR CASE
Made of oak, golden finish, with sliding doors, ball-bearing. Double-strength glass throughout. Size, 4 feet long, 24 inches wide, 40 inches high.
Price $20.00

REAR VIEW.   FRONT VIEW.
No. 524. COMBINATION CASHIER STAND AND SHOW CASE
Made of quarter-sawed oak, golden finish. Most attractive and useful show case made for the barber shop. Can be used for either cigars or toilet articles. Fitted with Yale locks on doors and cash drawer, metal feet oxidized. Plate-glass top, polished edges. Size, 21 x 21 inches. Height, 41 inches.
Price $26.00

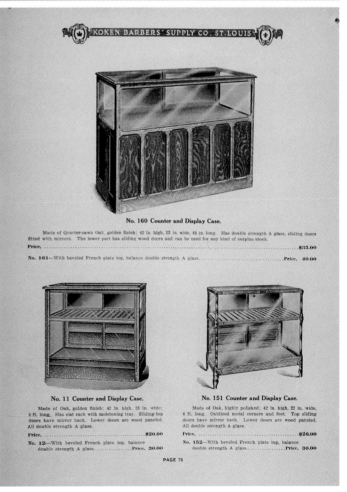

KOKEN BARBERS' SUPPLY CO. ST. LOUIS

No. 160 Counter and Display Case.
Made of Quarter-sawn Oak, golden finish; 42 in. high, 22 in. wide, 48 in. long. Has double strength A glass, sliding doors fitted with mirrors. The lower part has sliding wood doors and can be used for any kind of surplus stock.
Price, ... $35.00

No. 161—With beveled French plate top, balance double strength A glass .... Price, 40.00

No. 11 Counter and Display Case.
Made of Oak, golden finish; 42 in. high, 28 in. wide; 4 ft. long. Has slat rack with moistening tray. Sliding top doors have mirror back. Lower doors are wood paneled. All double strength A glass.
Price, ... $20.00

No. 12—With beveled French plate top, balance double strength A glass .... Price, 30.00

No. 151 Counter and Display Case.
Made of Oak, highly polished; 42 in. high, 22 in. wide, 4 ft. long. Oxidized metal corners and feet. Top sliding doors have mirror back. Lower doors are wood paneled. All double strength A glass.
Price, ... $26.00

No. 152—With beveled French plate top, balance double strength A glass .... Price, 30.00

PAGE 76

Furnishings

Within a decade's time after 1895, there was a proliferation of retail items and supplies to be displayed or stored. Most were tonic bottles that sat in rows upon the glass shelves. Perhaps the most popular retail items for sale in barbershops were cigars. As you can see by the following catalog page illustrations, cigar cases were available in counter-top, freestanding, combination-use, and a wide variety of sizes. Lesser grade models had no provision for humidifying which was important to the lasting quality and freshness of cigars and tobacco. Better grade (humidor) models had slotted shelves which held water in them and were quite effective in keeping tobacco products salable for a longer time.

It can be difficult to isolate some of this display furniture as having specific barbershop origins. Many items were generically produced and appeared to be identically presented in a variety of commercial furniture catalogs or outlets. However, most large barber supply houses placed their own small, brass, logo identification on generically acquired furnishings. These brass badges are how you can positively assign barbershop provenance to display furnishings or any other items seen on these pages. Unfortunately, many of those brass logo badges have been removed by antique dealers who hope that by making the piece generic once again, it will appeal to a broad-based buying audience. Display cases that are considered the most desirable by today's collector were produced in the mid-Golden Years. They were hand made and constructed mostly of walnut or oak. Display furniture designed after that time utilized newer materials such as laminates and Formica-type surfaces. While some of them are attractive when placed with Deco period displays, they don't yet have the same level of interest or value as solid wood models. Cigar, and showcases in general, have always been in short supply because of the obvious desire of current-day dealers and collectors to utilize them in showcasing their small treasures. For that reason, showcase prices have always seemed inflated when compared to other incidental furnishings. Recently, cigar display cases have seen an upward price-spike that sometimes happens when a particular antique category receives newly-found interest. The current cigar smoking renaissance around the globe, has, as you might expect, driven the price on cigar showcases higher than ever. Until recently, you could expect to find a nice, four foot wide, floor model example for less than $1,000.00. A counter top model for less than $600.00. Today, there isn't even a ballpark number because of the overwhelming current demand. If you really want one, your best bet is to haggle the best deal you can on the current asking price, or hope cigars fall out of favor again. Unrestored, general use cases (other than those specifically for cigars) usually range from $350.00 to $1,500.00 depending on size and condition.

Towel Steamers

Barbershop towel steamers, or sterilizers as they were also called, came predominately from the Golden Years period. They were used for several reasons. First and foremost, barbers needed hot towels to prep customers whiskers prior to shaving. As anybody who ever shaved can confirm, softened whiskers are more easily removed from the face. Nothing softens a beard better than the combination of rich, soap lather and steaming hot towels. Another use for steamers was to provide hot water for the barber to mix soap lather in his mug. Most steamers had a spigot to pour from, and only a few ounces were needed to complete the task. The water tank size varied but some held up to four gallons. It was this same tank of steaming water (usually regulated just below boiling at about 250 degrees) that sent the ster-

ilizing vapor upward into the towel compartment. One other use that sterilizers had was to warm hair and shaving tonics in the winter time, so that they would be more comfortable when applied to the patron's scalp or face. The tonic bottle was placed on top of the towels. Some specially designed steamers actually had external tonic warming racks.

Copper was the usual construction material for steamers because it conducted heat uniformly and was not subject to rusting. They were supplied with or without nickel plating. Interiors of better quality models had porcelain linings so the towels wouldn't become rust stained. The nickel plated models were the most desirable during the Golden Years. Today, most people feel that the polished copper type look better. Mainly because the steamers that had been nickled, have usually lost portions of their plating making areas of them appear dull. A polished copper steamer is uniformly shiny all over. There were three main styles of steamer construction. The most popular with today's collectors are floor models. They had the largest capacity and were used in the best shops. Most of them had large globe-like spheres that are very showy for an antique display. The two other types which were more economical to both purchase and operate, were table-top models and wall-hung models. They had about the same capacity and were chosen by the particular shop's space availability. The heat source for steamers or sterilizers was often an open-flame alcohol burner before 1900. Two other popular fuel burners were coal oil and gasoline vapor. As natural gas became more popular and available, steamers were produced with a regulator and Bunsen-burner that accepted a direct gas line from the outside.

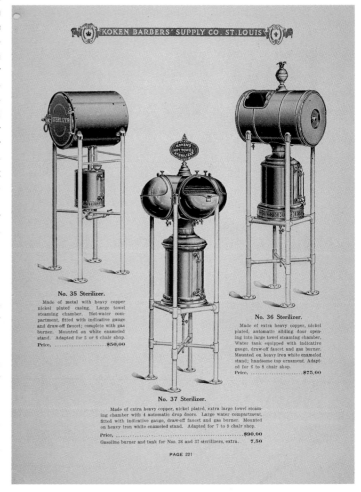

No. 35 Sterilizer.
Made of metal with heavy copper nickel plated casing. Large towel steaming chamber. Hot-water compartment, fitted with indicative gauge and draw-off faucet; complete with gas burner. Mounted on white enameled stand. Adapted for 5 or 6 chair shop.
Price, ... $50.00

No. 36 Sterilizer.
Made of extra heavy copper, nickel plated, automatic sliding door opening into large towel steaming chamber. Water tank equipped with indicative gauge, draw-off faucet and gas burner. Mounted on heavy iron white enameled stand; handsome top ornament. Adapted for 6 to 8 chair shop.
Price, ... $75.00

No. 37 Sterilizer.
Made of extra heavy copper, nickel plated, extra large towel steaming chamber with 4 automatic drop doors. Large water compartment, fitted with indicative gauge, draw-off faucet. Mounted on heavy iron white enameled stand. Adapted for 7 to 9 chair shop.
Price, ... $90.00
Gasoline burner and tank for Nos. 36 and 37 sterilizers, extra. 7.50

PAGE 221

Example of "The Sun" floor model, polished copper, towel steamer. Fully restored and operational. 5' tall.

"The Globe" nickel plated, hot towel sterilizer. Mint condition restoration. *Courtesy of Tony Gugliotti.*

Large capacity "Simplex" copper steamer featuring a ruby-glass top piece. Unrestored. *Courtesy of Bill Wright.*

Furnishings

"The globe" hot towel sterilizer. As-found condition. Originally nickel plated but fading. *Courtesy of Bill Wright.*

Floor model steamer and sterilizer believed to be manufactured in Mexico. Copper and brass construction with isinglass doors. Unrestored but excellent condition. *Courtesy of Bill Wright.*

Examples of steamers including a rare crescent shaped model that fit around a stovepipe for heat. Also seen are a few different types of heat sources for steamers.

Nickel plated "Acme" floor model steamer by The Labate Company. In unrestored but excellent, useable condition. *Courtesy of Tony Gugliotti.*

Scarce, pre-1900, alcohol burner made by the Kingorv Company in Buffalo, New York. Features side pods for sterilizing tools or heating tonics. *Courtesy of Tony Gugliotti.*

Nickel plated example of a pre-1900 table-model steamer. In unrestored, but excellent, useable condition. *Courtesy of Bill and Marlene Levin.*

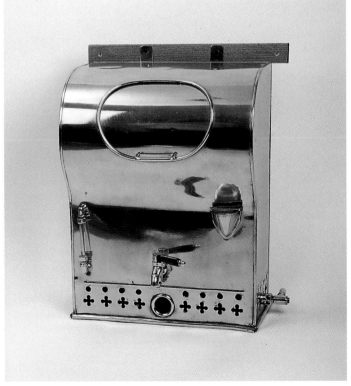

Restored wall-hung model. These scarce models used little space at 16" wide by 21" tall.

A beautifully restored steamer is a *really* stout addition to any barbershop collection. To a shaving mug collection, a steamer is the ultimate enhancement. **Alcohol fueled table models** are the oldest and range from $300.00 "as found" to $700.00+ in refinished or polished and lacquered condition. **Natural gas fired wall hung models** are the least common. They require no floor space and are worth $500.00 in good "as found" condition, to $1,000.00+ when polished and lacquered. **Floor standing pedestal models** are currently the collector's favorite. If found in excellent but unrestored condition, they will bring $1,000.00+. With a complete (usable condition) restoration including the porcelain base, re-soldering the water tank, and plating or polishing, $2,000.00+. **Note:** During WORLD WAR II, President Roosevelt appealed to the nation to turn in any unneeded copper items to be recycled into ammunition. Many barbers (who were by that time using hot tap water for shaving towels) complied with a huge number of previously favored, but no longer needed, copper steamers. This fact eliminated many steamers. As more barbershop collectors seek to acquire them, the supply is quickly diminishing for worthwhile (many are hopelessly dented) examples. Correspondingly, the price has been rising on towel steamers.

Barbershop Sinks

Throughout the Golden Years, sinks were a standard fixture in nearly every barbershop. Their first function was obvious in enabling the barbers to wash their hands frequently for good hygiene. Of course, plenty of customers chose to wash up too. Shampoos were another reason for sinks. Although not every shop offered shampoo service, many barbershop sinks had a hose and sprinkler as standard equipment. In the later Golden Years, barbershop shaving was in serious decline (as discussed in chapter one) and barbers couldn't justify keeping a steamer going all day. As a result, they began using the sink's hot water tap for individual hot towels.

The chronology of barbershop sinks was quite obvious over the years. In the late Victorian era, they were wonderfully elaborate with multiple marble bowls, back-splashes, and counter tops. They had solid wood cabinets in walnut, mahogany, and oak. Some had carvings. Others had French veneers or inlays. Less expensive models had beautiful lathe-turned wooden legs. Hardware was brass or nickel. By 1900, sinks were going the way of barber chairs and poles: they were being made with cast-iron and porcelain coatings. In truth, this construction produced a more practical and lasting sink. One that cleaned easily and appeared more sanitary. In the beginning, most porcelain over cast-iron sinks were designed with fluted pedestal bases. As the Victorian era three and four basin "cluster" sinks became less available, some porcelain models were being made with two bowls. After the Deco look came into style in the 1920s, the sink bases were less ornate and became smoothly geometric. As the Deco period passed, pure space-saving function took over and the popular sink style became wall mounted. These had no cabinetry or pedestal bases of any kind.

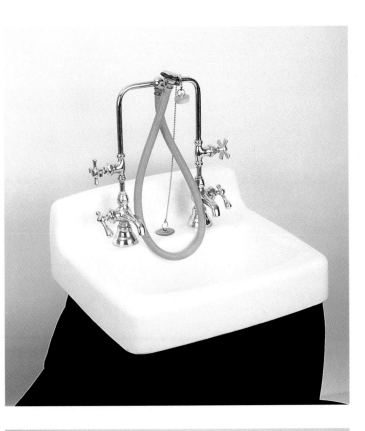

Victorian era marble sinks with cabinetry are fairly scarce. Because they have not been in big demand, they remain a bargain in the $400.00 to $700.00+ range unrestored. **Fluted column, porcelain sinks** are far more plentiful but also are the most popular. Unrestored, single bowl examples range from $300.00 to $500.00 depending on condition. A porcelain restoration can easily add $500.00 to their value. The usual buyers of pedestal iron sinks are antique home renovators who change the hardware and make them functional. **Wall-mounted barbershop sinks** from the 1930s are just now beginning to see demand from modern shop owners who are retro-fitting their shops with motifs from that period up to the 1950s. They are available in the $200.00+ range as found. If porcelain reconditioning has been done and the sink is useable, $350.00+.

Barbershop Coat Racks

Most coat racks (originally called "hall trees" in Victorian times) advertised in barbershop catalogs were generically produced. They could have been found in any commercial outlet throughout the Golden Years. In the 1800s, coat racks were typically turned-walnut or oak spindles with bronzed iron hooks and bases. After the turn of the 20th century, they were made of a combination of tubular sheet steel, cast iron bases, and brass hooks. They were also being referred to as "costumers" by 1910. There was a variety of sizes and metal finishes including oxidized copper, and nickel plating which were very ornate when compared to today's counterparts. The best of them had rotating tops for easier garment retrieval in close quarters. Some had small, round, face mirrors. Others had cane or umbrella holders with copper drip pans. As with generically manufactured showcases, some barber supply houses affixed their logo to the coat racks. Aside from that, there would be no way to assign true barbershop status to these functional accessories.

Another hall tree presentation was the furniture type. Without a barber supply, brass, logo badge, these too were generic items. Most were produced during the mid-Golden Years when both hall trees and oak wood furniture were very popular. They required more space but they also offered more utility to the barbershop. Most had large mirrors (so a gentleman could prop-

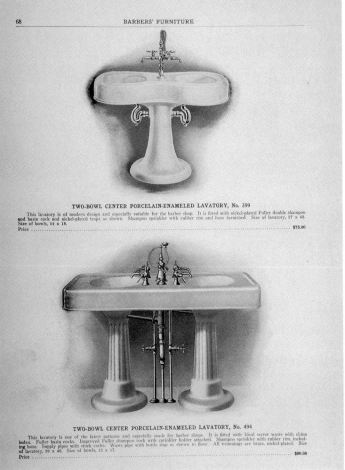

TWO-BOWL CENTER PORCELAIN-ENAMELED LAVATORY, No. 399

This lavatory is of modern design and especially suitable for the barber shop. It is fitted with nickel-plated Fuller double shampoo and basin cock and nickel-plated traps as shown. Shampoo sprinkler with rubber rim and hose furnished. Size of lavatory, 37 x 42. Size of bowls, 14 x 18.
Price $75.00

TWO-BOWL CENTER PORCELAIN-ENAMELED LAVATORY, No. 494

This lavatory is one of the latest patterns and especially made for barber shops. It is fitted with Ideal secret waste with china index. Fuller basin cocks. Improved Fuller shampoo cock with sprinkler holder attached. Shampoo sprinkler with rubber rim, including hose. Supply pipes with stock cocks. Waste pipe with bottle trap as shown to floor. All trimmings are brass, nickel-plated. Size of lavatory, 26 x 46. Size of bowls, 13 x 17.
Price $90.00

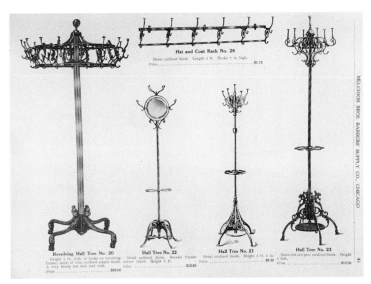

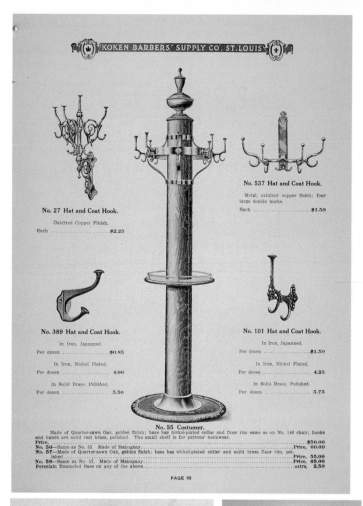

erly re-tie his neckwear) attached to the natural grained woodwork. Cast-iron or brass hooks were strategically placed to accept both hats and coats. Some hall trees also had a bench seat that was hinged to reveal extra storage space which was always welcome in most barber shops. Wooden hall trees are currently a popular target for antique furniture buyers in general.

Barbershop coat racks that were made specifically for the trade were always called "costumers." They were recognizable by their appearance which was not unlike that of a barber pole without stripes. Of course, there was a ring of hat and coat hooks that circled the pole near the top. Early models were wooden top to bottom, with a cast-iron circular base that was porcelain coated, and similar (though smaller in diameter) to a barber chair. Later models saw a fluted, cast-iron and porcelain treatment extend halfway up the costumer where a neckwear tray was placed. At first glance, these models appeared as though a coat rack had been mounted on a child's barber chair base. However, measurements reinforce that both bases are different and were custom made for each application. Wood used on the costumers was mahogany or quarter-sawn oak. Some were painted white. The tops of these seven foot tall racks were seen in a variety of presentations. There were lathe-turned wooden tops in the shape of a ball or spindle designs. Others had white, glass globes that were wired for electricity. My research suggests that barbershop costumers were only produced during a small window of time shortly before, and after, 1910. They may have fallen from favor because of their comparatively expensive cost. For example, in 1910 a good wall mount hat and coat rack could be had for $2.00. A top quality metal rack was $6.00. Mahogany, barbershop costumers by contrast were a whopping $65.00. These scarce, *and still functional* costumers make a bold addition to a barbershop display.

Victorian, wood-spindled coat racks can be found in the $150.00 range. A barber supply logo could add more value. **Post-1900 metal coat racks** range from $100.00 to $250.00+ depending on size, condition, and ornate quality. A barber supply logo could add more value. **Wooden hall racks** vary in price from region to region as with most antique furniture. Average pricing is difficult but a representative model in oak (with some embellishments) and refinished could be in the $600.00 to $900.00 range depending on size and quality. **Genuine Barbershop Costumers** are the most sought after by current collectors and recent demand has seen their value rise accordingly. These scarce, purpose-built racks will currently bring $1,200.00 unrestored. With a professional restoration, $2,200.00+.

Miscellaneous Furnishings

The remaining items in this chapter are an assortment of incidental barbershop furnishings. Some, like clocks and cash registers have groups of collectors who specialize in only those items. Because of that, the prices are sometimes inflated. Another item seen here is a barbershop hollow-wire gasoline lighting system that (except for the lamps) no longer exists at any price. I show it because of the historical significance that it brings to our hobby.

Opposite page, all four: Grouping of catalog pages showing an assortment of **stationary and portable work-stands.** Unrestored, $250.00 to $500.00. **Cash drawers.** Unrestored, $75.00 to $150.00. **Early "Monitor" type cash registers.** Unrestored, $300.00+. **Brass cash registers** are the most desirable and have a broad range that is kept high by specialty collectors.(see caption on page 56) **Cash register stands** as seen, $300.00 to $600.00.

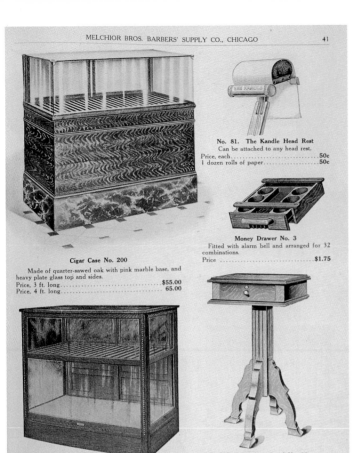

No. 81. The Kandle Head Rest

Can be attached to any head rest.

Price, each.....................................50c
1 dozen rolls of paper.........................50c

Money Drawer No. 3

Fitted with alarm bell and arranged for 32 combinations.

Price $1.75

Cigar Case No. 200

Made of quarter-sawed oak with pink marble base, and heavy plate glass top and sides.

Price, 3 ft. long..............................$55.00
Price, 4 ft. long..............................65.00

Cigar Case No. 95

Made of oak, golden finish; glass, double thick; heavy beveled plate glass top; moistening pan furnished.

Price, 3 ft. long..............................$21.00
Price, 4 ft. long..............................26.00

Cash Register Stand No. 32

Made of quarter-sawed oak, golden finish, with drawer and slots in top to insert checks. Yale lock on drawer. Size of top, 20 x 20; height 38 in.

Price $19.00

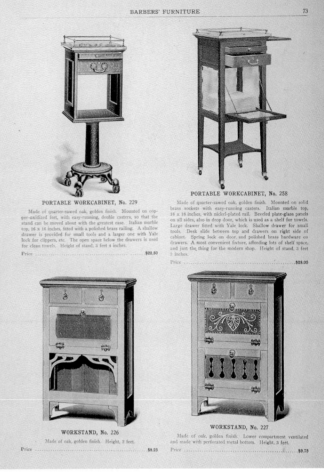

PORTABLE WORKCABINET, No. 229

Made of quarter-sawed oak, golden finish. Mounted on copper-oxidized feet, with easy-running, double casters, so that the stand can be moved about with the greatest ease. Italian marble top, 16 x 16 inches, fitted with a polished brass railing. A shallow drawer is provided for small tools and a larger one with Yale lock for clippers, etc. The open space below the drawers is used for clean towels.

Price $22.50

PORTABLE WORKCABINET, No. 258

Made of quarter-sawed oak, golden finish. Mounted on solid brass sockets with easy-running casters. Italian marble top, 16 x 16 inches, with nickel-plated rail. Beveled plate-glass panels on all sides, also in drop door, which is used as a shelf for towels. Large drawer fitted with Yale lock. Shallow drawer for small tools. Desk slide between top and drawers on right side of cabinet. Spring lock on door, and polished brass hardware on drawers. A most convenient fixture, affording lots of shelf space, and just the thing for the modern shop. Height of stand, 3 feet 3 inches.

Price $28.00

WORKSTAND, No. 226

Made of oak, golden finish. Height, 3 feet.

Price $8.25

WORKSTAND, No. 227

Made of oak, golden finish. Lower compartment ventilated and made with perforated metal bottom. Height, 3 feet.

Price $9.75

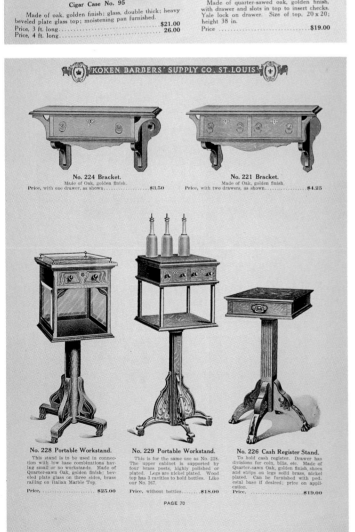

No. 224 Bracket.

Made of Oak, golden finish.

Price, with one drawer, as shown.............$3.50

No. 221 Bracket.

Made of Oak, golden finish.

Price, with two drawers, as shown.............$4.25

No. 228 Portable Workstand.

This stand is to be used in connection with low base combinations having small or no workstands. Made of Quarter-sawn Oak, golden finish; beveled plate glass on three sides, brass railing on Italian Marble Top.

Price.................................$25.00

No. 229 Portable Workstand.

This is for the same use as No. 228. The upper cabinet is supported by four brass posts, highly polished or plated. Legs are nickel plated. Wood top has 3 cavities to hold bottles. Like our No. 267.

Price, without bottles........$18.00

No. 226 Cash Register Stand.

To hold cash register. Drawer has divisions for coin, bills, etc. Made of Quarter-sawn Oak, golden finish, shoes and strips on legs solid brass, nickel plated. Can be furnished with pedestal base if desired; price on application.

Price.................................$19.00

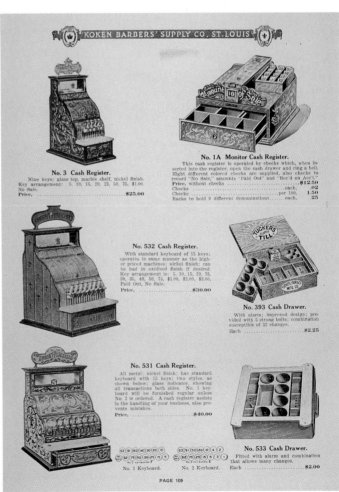

No. 3 Cash Register.

Nine keys; glass top, marble shelf, nickel finish. Key arrangement: 5, 10, 15, 20, 25, 50, 75, $1.00. No Sale.

Price, ...$25.00

No. 1A Monitor Cash Register.

This cash register is operated by checks which, when inserted into the register, open the cash drawer and ring a bell. Eight different colored checks are supplied, also checks to record "No Sale," amounts "Paid Out" and "Rec'd on Acc't."

Price, without checks $12.50
Checks ....each .02
Checks ....per 100, 1.50
Racks to hold 9 different denominations......each, .25

No. 532 Cash Register.

With standard keyboard of 15 keys; operates in same manner as the higher priced machines; nickel finish; can be had in oxidized finish if desired. Key arrangement is: 5, 10, 15, 20, 25, 30, 35, 40, 50, 75, $1.00, $2.00, $2.50, Paid Out, No Sale.

Price, ...$30.00

No. 393 Cash Drawer.

With alarm; improved design; provided with 5 strong bolts; combination susceptible of 32 changes.

Each $2.25

No. 531 Cash Register.

All metal; nickel finish; has standard keyboard with 15 keys; two styles, as shown below; glass indicator, showing all transactions both sides. No. 1 keyboard will be furnished regular unless No. 2 is ordered. A cash register assists in the handling of your business, also prevents mistakes.

Price, ...$40.00

No. 533 Cash Drawer.

Fitted with alarm and combination that allows many changes.

Each $2.00

No. 1 Keyboard   No. 2 Keyboard

Barbershop towel cabinet in cherry. Provided to barbershops by the Peerless towel laundry ca, 1915. Has interior warning for barbers not to place wet towels inside. 18" x 30" and held approximately four dozen folded towels. Complete with brass logo badge and paper provenance. Restored as new, $375.00+.

Cast-iron, porcelain based, cash register stand ca. 1910. Mahogany cabinetry. Marble counter. Slots for barbers checks. Opens to writing desk with compartments. Unrestored. $600.00. *Courtesy of Bill and Marlene Levin.*

National cash register model 313 ca. 1900. Often referred to as the barbershop model. Keys rang up to $1.95 as opposed to $.49 with the number 312 candy store model. Patented in 1890s. Brass finish and operating mechanics professionally restored to "as new" condition. $1,500.00+. Brass and glass National check-stub receiver. Refinished, $150.00+.

Waterbury Clock Company, 10 inch drop octagon advertising clock with reversed dial and hands moving counterclockwise. For barbershop mirrors. Winds at 6; eight-day spring movement. Restored, $600.00+.

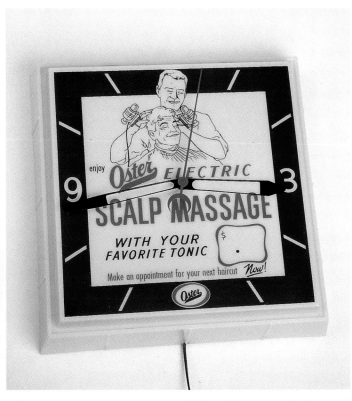

Oster electric barbershop clock ca. 1950s. 16" square molded plastic frame. Mint condition. Motor replaced and runs perfectly. $275.00+.

Barbershop merchants desk with Koken nameplate. If refinished, $750.00+. Large cashier's stand, $600.00+. Large wall-hung display case with glass doors, $600.00.

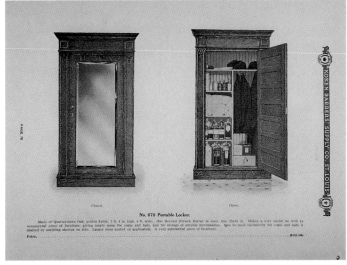

Rarely seen portable locker for barbershops. Heavy oak construction. If refinished and bearing Koken identification, $1,200.00+.

Catalog page offering of the hollow tube system that was required to light a barbershop with gasoline in 1910. Interesting to note the bicycle style pump that was used to pressurize the system.

Furnishings

Chapter 3

Backbar Essentials

The backbar, as it is commonly referred to today, was originally called a mirror case. There are examples of them to be seen in this book in the furniture chapter. If there was any one thing that a good barbershop could not do without, it was the backbar. These shallow cabinets and counter tops were cram-packed with nearly everything that a barber would use within the course of his work. In this chapter, we're going to look at the many items placed over, under, on, or about the backbar. Some articles, such as shaving mugs, straight razors, and tonic bottles, have been established antique categories for many years. Other items that you will see may not have previously been considered as collectibles. All, however, are interesting and certainly applicable under the barbershop collector's umbrella.

Single Mirror Case

No. 48.   Single Mirror Case.

Made of select quarter-sawed oak, golden finish. Beveled French plate mirror 36 x 48 in. Italian marble shelf. Yale locks on drawers. Polished brass trimmings. Heavy copper oxidized metal legs under cabinets. Height 8 ft. 6 in., width 5 ft. 8 in.

Price $75.00

Shaving Mugs

Of all of the different categories in barbershop antiques or collectibles, shaving mugs are surely one of the best known. They have a legion of *very* enthusiastic collectors. Some continue to build upon inherited collections that were begun sixty years ago and contain hundreds of advanced grade mugs. Others are just beginning with entry grade mugs. As more mugs become dedicated to privately held collections, the dwindling availability of newly found mugs comes more into focus. Competition to acquire these small works of art has never been more keen. It would not be unusual to spot an "occupational mugs wanted" advertisement appearing in a local newspaper in rural Pennsylvania which was placed there by a collector from California. In national antique publications, mug buyers' advertisements make statements like "I pay more," and "call me first." Auction prices are setting records for more desirable types of mugs. The obvious passion that some collectors have for their mugs is well warranted and goes beyond dollars and cents. Decorated shaving mugs are fine examples of hand painted art and they stand as lasting mementos of a time gone by. These artists' renderings were intended to personalize a man's shaving mug which made each one unique to it's owner.

It was within the Golden Years that hand decorated shaving mugs had their popularity rise and fall. Personalized, china mug decorating began in the 1870s when, because of emerging awareness of sanitation, the barber's "one for all" mug fell out of favor. Men were encouraged to have their own mug and brush that remained in the barbershop solely for their personal use. That was the most sanitary option in a time rife with infectious disease which was sometimes suspected of being spread by the barbers' communal mugs. The era of shaving mugs widest popularity was effectively ended in the 1920s. There are some who will tell you that the decline in shaving mugs was because men began using safety razors to shave at home instead of going to the barbers. That fact *did* mean that there were less personalized mugs on the racks in barbershops. However, those same men were *still* shaving, and even if it was at home, they *still* needed a lather source to do it. If anything, they needed more lather than ever with the style trend leaning toward clean shaving and less beard styles around WWI. Men simply weren't using the mug and brush method as much. Not only decorated mugs, but mugs in general. Why? The real culprit in the decline of mugs wasn't *who* was doing the shaving or *what type of razor* was being used, it was the advent of manufactured shaving cream. It became available in the 1890s and immediately posed a threat to the previously popular mug-soap cakes. Anything that threatened soap cakes also signaled bad times ahead for shaving mugs since they depended on

58

each other's success. Heavy, national advertising pushed the obvious benefits of manufactured creams and sticks. Benefits which were nearly identical to those of safety razors: sanitation and convenience! With manufactured cream, (which was perfect every time and came packaged in a tube, stick, or jar) a man had instant, rich, and convenient lather. No mandatory mug or brush, no muss, no fuss. Just as men had embraced safety razors, they also embraced manufactured shaving cream during the same time period. Barbers even began using shaving cream dispensed from glass jars on their backbars. There were also pump style cream dispensers invented by the Fitch Company. Even though soap cakes for shaving mugs had previously been a huge source of revenue for F.W. Fitch, he publicly held the shaving mugs' "funeral service" complete with obituary in November of 1927. He gambled, correctly, that manufactured shaving cream would soon become the favorite of barbers and the public as well. The writing had been on the wall for some time: shaving mugs in general had seen their best day. Yes, some men who used cream and stick soaps still preferred the relative luxury of a hot brush to lather up with. However, all they had to do was soak the brush under hot tap water. *They didn't need a mug!* Manufactured creams for home shavers and heated soap dispensers at the barbershop became the overwhelming favorites. *Nothing* was more sanitary or convenient!

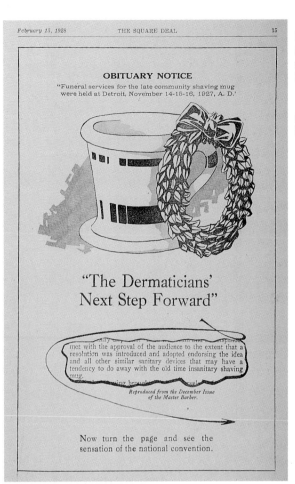

F.W. Fitch's shaving mug obituary of February 15, 1928. 6" x 10" in black and white. $25.00+.

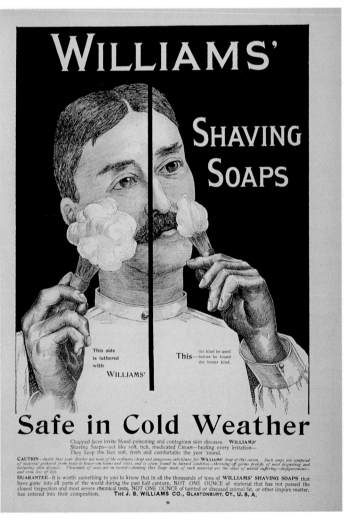

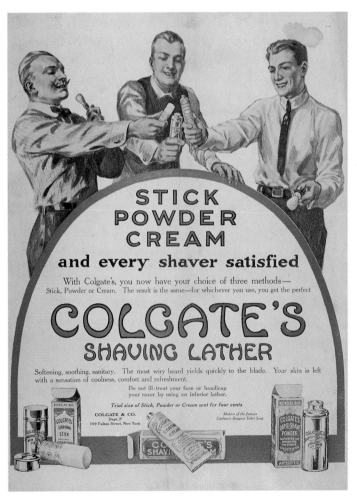

Typical advertisement (Williams) from 1893 extols the virtue of mug soap cakes. Typical advertisement (Colgate) after 1900 pitches manufactured creams and sticks. Each advertisement 11" x 14' in excellent condition. Williams ad, $20.00. Colgate ad, $15.00.

Backbar Essentials

The Koken barber supply company is estimated to have personalized one million mugs in their fifty years of providing that service. Those years were from 1874 until 1924. Koken was only one of many china decorating companies back then which means that millions of mugs were produced. Obviously, they are still available to be found because they continue to reach the antique marketplace regularly. This is good news for those of you who are interested in beginning an entry grade collection. The most popular mugs falling into that category are floral, decorative, and the name or monogram only type. While these can be quite beautiful, they are currently the most plentiful and affordable on the secondary market. Very often, you can still find these mugs in the $25.00 to $35.00 price range. So you see, a nice mug collection can still be had quite reasonably.

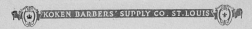

Price List of Shaving Mugs (Cost to Barbers).

Numbered Mugs.

	MEDIUM	LARGE
Gold Striped, per dozen	$3.50	$4.50
Gold Banded, per dozen	4.00	5.00
Gold Banded, with gold wreath, per dozen	5.00	6.00

Plain Mugs.

	MEDIUM	LARGE
Plain Imported China Mugs, per dozen	$1.75	$2.50
Plain Gold Band Mugs, per dozen	.75	3.50

Extra Charges.

For Script Letters	$0.10
For Autographs or Fac-Simile of Handwriting	.25
For Gold Shading on Black or Blue Letters	.10
For Roman Letters	.10

Cups and Saucers.

Cups and Saucers, with same design as on Shaving Mugs, will cost from 25c to 75c more than the latter.

Various Styles of Letters Used in Decorating Mugs:

ROMAN. — JOHN N. BLEECK.
OLD ENGLISH TEXT. — Andrew Johnson.
BLOCK LETTER. — GEO. F. ROGERS.
SCRIPT. — R. Wendell.
Roman and Script, 10c more per Mug than Old English.

We can make any Mug shown in other catalogues or mug sheets at prices quoted therein

Price List of Decorated Shaving Mugs.

Trade Designs, Lodge, Society and all other Emblems.

The prices here quoted are for barbers only and are for Mugs complete, including name and design for each Mug.

For Lather Brushes, see Pages 194–196.

PAGE 136

IN this department we keep to the front with new and advanced ideas in design and finish.

The guarantee of a good shaving mug depends upon: The artist, the material used and class of finish. In each of these we employ only the best.

Our artists are men of long experience, who have learned their art from the ground work of the apprentice to the delicate and intricate work of the finished artist. They can elaborate on any given design and carry out any idea desired by our customers.

The materials used are the most reliable money will purchase, enabling us to produce mugs which wear and are permanent in color. The finish is done with especial care. It does not crack or craze and is developed under a degree of heat which makes the finish both hard and durable.

As this department is organized expressly to execute shaving mug decorations, you will find by trial our work is not surpassed by any art productions on china.

No. 502.

PAGE 123

DECORATED SHAVING MUGS

Prices quoted below are the prices to barbers only, are net cash, and are not subject to any discount, except the usual discount of 5 per cent on orders of $10.00 or over. Please be careful always to state whether medium or large mugs are wanted. If no size is given, medium-sized mugs will be sent.

LIST OF MUGS WITH FANCY DECORATION

Please note that prices quoted above are for complete Mugs, with name and decoration.

EXTRA CHARGES

For monograms of two letters there will be an additional charge of	20c.
For monograms of three letters there will be an additional charge of	30c.
For facsimiles there will be an additional charge of	20c.

For black and gold letters on mugs not so specified, there will be an extra charge of 10 cents.
Prices for mugs quoted are for the mugs as they are described, and extra charges will be made for any additional decoration that is wanted.

NUMBERED MUGS

	Medium	Large
Gold striped, per dozen	$3.50	$4.50
Gold banded, per dozen	4.00	5.00

PLAIN MUGS

	Medium	Large
Plain Mugs, per dozen	$1.75	$2.50
With gold band at top, per dozen	2.75	3.50

Barbershop

Most of the advanced collectors of occupational, fraternal, and figural mugs don't have it so easy. These are the categories of long standing elite mug collectors. They are currently the most competitively sought mugs and can sell from hundreds to thousands of dollars each. They don't turn up at the local flea market too often since most of the dealers are aware of their value. Usually, these high-end mugs get channeled directly to steady customers or specialty auctions. When a rare mug *is* spotted on the table of an unknowing seller, it can cause a normally calm mug buyer to become spastic. Mugs are fun and interesting at any level and it is easy to see why they remain so popular.

It would take a separate book to include all of the interesting research known about shaving mugs. Our purpose instead, is to provide an introduction and to promote understanding of the main areas of interest. For some excellent, in-depth research on shaving mugs, please refer to the books listed in the bibliography. An especially comprehensive book is by author Keith E. Estep and is entitled, *Shaving Mug And Barber Bottle Book*. The prices shown on the following mugs are intended to be current median prices and could certainly fluctuate based on condition. This is one barbershop collector's category where good, definitive information is available. Do your homework and make an informed purchase. The following catalog pages show how mugs were marketed during the Golden Years. Can you find a mug that you own or would like to acquire?

THE ALBRECHT BARBER SUPPLY & DRUG CO., AKRON, OHIO   103

TRADE DESIGNS AND SOCIETY EMBLEMS

AN APPROPRIATE CHARGE WILL BE MADE FOR SPECIAL DESIGNS. WRITE FOR PRICES.

Please note that prices quoted above are for complete Mugs, with name and design.

---

60   MELCHIOR BROS. BARBERS' SUPPLY CO., CHICAGO

Barbers' Prices of Designs, Including Mugs

---

66   THEO. A. KOCHS & SON, NEW YORK CITY.

DECORATED SHAVING MUGS.

PRICES TO BARBERS ONLY.

Prices are *Net Cash*, and not subject to any discount except on orders of $10.00 or over.

Gold lettering on all mugs, unless otherwise mentioned below.

Please be careful to state in each order whether medium or large size mugs are wanted. If no size is given, medium mugs must be sent.

EXTRA CHARGES.

For monograms of two letters there will be an additional charge of $0.20
For monograms of three letters there will be an additional charge of .... .30
For fac similes there will be an additional charge of .... .20
For cups and saucers we charge from 35c. to 60c. more than for mugs, according to design.
For black and gold letters on mugs not specified there will be an extra charge of 10 cents.
Prices for mugs quoted above are for the mugs as they are described, and extra charges will be made for any additional decoration is wanted.

NUMBERED MUGS.

	Medium.	Large.
Gold striped, per doz.	$3.50	$4.50
Gold banded, per doz.	4.00	5.00
Gold banded, per doz., with gold wreath	5.00	6.00

PLAIN MUGS.

	Medium.	Large.
Plain French China mugs, per doz.	$1.75	$2.50
With gold band at top, per doz.	3.00	3.50

We can make any mug shown in other catalogues or mug sheets at the prices quoted herein.

Backbar Essentials

Shaving Mugs

Shaving Mugs.

Barbershop

62

DECORATED SHAVING MUGS

653 — Chas F. Wright
322 — Paul Krüger
592 — Peter Knights
336 — Herbert Kinze
310 — Sam McGrath
780 — S.B. Keener
220 — T.L. Fischer
205 — E.A. Girl
253 — Thos W. Spencer

TRADE DESIGNS AND SOCIETY EMBLEMS

301 — U Workmen
321 — J. Darriberr
327 — Ben Ballinger
342 — R.B. Layer
343 — Henry Walls
355 — C.L. Wooker
364 — Paul Fallet
372 — Ky.D. May
431 — A.C. Ward

KOKEN BARBERS' SUPPLY CO. ST. LOUIS

Shaving Mugs.

526 — Wayne
529 — F.C. Kuntze
530 — C.R. Wesner
531 — Bros
532 — J. Cassens
535 — B.F. Steer
536 — Brown
537 — A.H. Pironce
538 — W.M. Fuller

PAGE 125

TRADE DESIGNS AND SOCIETY EMBLEMS

453 — E.A. Flager
457 — Albert Michu
459 — Chas Thyrel
471 — H.E. Farmer
493 — Val H. Monk
526 — Geo.D. Lake
571 — S.H. Joubert
591 — A.O. Roby
599 — Alf. Miles

DECORATED SHAVING MUGS

258 — D.H. Gibson
217 —
251 — William Tell
255 — J. Dave Gray
214 — Harry Maymon
223 — A.D. Bertram
256 — T.P. Battis
929 — R. McDonald
219 — Jos Geronimo

Backbar Essentials

Floral, Name-Only, And Decorative Mugs

Of all of the early mugs to be found, these are the most plentiful and they provide an excellent source for beginning collectors. Since they are not always sought out by advanced collectors of occupational mugs, these entry grade mugs are also more affordable. While they don't illustrate what the mug's original owner did for a living, some of the floral or decorative art work is still very beautiful. They *are* hand painted, and when originally offered, they often cost just as much as the currently more expensive occupationals and fraternals. The most basic of personalized mugs are those which only had the owners name on them. The names were usually presented in Old English, Block, or Script styles. It is interesting to note that the mugs with Script were available as artists facsimiles of the owner's actual signature. Some mugs only had the owner's monogram. One other presentation that is seen less often, are mugs with the owners names which have been printed on a paper under glass label. With each new collection that is begun using entry grade mugs, mug values overall will increase accordingly. When purchasing name mugs, florals, and decoratives, try to buy the best ones available. Remember, there is a fairly good supply of them and the best mugs will not only look better in your collection now, but they will appreciate in value as time goes on. *The following entry level mugs appear courtesy of Keith Estep.*

Gold name decorated mug.
"Goldfladen" $35.00+.

Floral decorated with name. "Lutz" $40.00+.

Floral decorated with
name. "Tubbs"
$60.00+.

Example of floral decorated name mug with brush. $45.00.

Irish-American decorative. $175.00+.

Early gold name with straight-blank sides. "Dornwelder" $25.00.

"Horses in a storm" decorative. $125.00+.

Figural Or Character Mugs

While these mugs were *not* marketed through barber suppliers, they are nonetheless appreciated and sought after by many collectors. They are known for their portrayals or amusing caricatures of animals, people, or objects. Often, they show exaggerated features such as mouths, lips, or eyes. Sometimes, there is a side opening on the mug similar to plain scuttle mugs. (on scuttle mugs, the shaving brush went into a hole on the side instead of the top) Some character and figural mugs were originally sold as one part of a matching set of household china items. For that reason, the most valuable of these mugs today, are those which are mated to a matching shaving brush. The heavy relief of the china castings, bisque finish, and accompanying art work make the best of these mugs exquisite to view. Most of them originated in Germany or England and were exported prior to 1930. *The following character mugs appear courtesy of Dave Giese.*

Exaggerated mouth opening scuttle-style mugs. Made by Schafer and Vater, Germany. Valued at $300.00+ each.

65   **Backbar Essentials**

Elephant figural with matching brush. Schafer and Vater, Germany. $1200.00+.

Glass-eyed monkey figural. Made by E-Bonne and Son. $800.00+ without matching brush.

Glass-eyed owl with matching brush. Made by E-Bonne and Son. $1600.00+.

Fraternal Mugs

This is a category that would appeal to collectors who appreciate not only the beauty of a mug's presentation, but who also enjoy researching its provenance. Fraternal mugs are characterized as those which depict the organization to which the mug's original owner belonged. There was a good variety, not the least of which were religious groups, academic fraternities, secret societies, and a host of trade unions. Fraternal mugs definitely appeal to the academic mug collector. Because, in order to fully appreciate this category, it helps to explore and understand the origins of the organization that the mug represents. This can often times lead to some interesting research which makes own-

ing these mugs even more rewarding. The National Shaving Mug Collectors Association, whose address appears at the end of chapter one, has a bibliography available to all members that would be invaluable to anyone interested in fraternals. Most of that information comes directly from Mr. Bernie Lucko who is a leading authority on this subject. Quite possibly, fraternal mugs may serve up the most information on society in general during barbering's Golden Years; more so than other mugs in many cases. This is especially true of a mug that may include the owner's name, his occupation, *and* his fraternal or social affiliation! Fraternal mugs have many different levels of desirability and rarity. Expect a fairly wide price range. *The following fraternal mugs appear courtesy of Bernie Lucko.*

Laundry Workers International Union featuring the union label. $1000.00+.

Double fraternal features the Junior Order of American Mechanics and the Daughters of Liberty. This rare double features related male and female social organizations. $450.00+.

Ancient Order of United Workmen. Name is worn but this is a rare presentation for this organization. $250.00+.

Double fraternal symbols on one mug indicated that owner belonged to two social groups. In this case, the Improved Order of Redmen and (probably for this groups good burial benefits) the Odd Fellows. $250.00+.

Rare example mug of the United Mine Workers of America. $750.00+.

Backbar Essentials

Example of the Alpha Tau Omega-College fraternity still in existence today. $300.00+.

Fraternal Order of Moose was a common fraternal organization still in existence today. Their large membership during the early 1900s was bolstered by the fact that you could get alcoholic drinks there on Sunday. $250.00+ in this presentation.

Occupational Mugs

Of the previously discussed categories in shaving mug collectibles, it is generally accepted that occupational mugs stand alone at the top. Closely viewing one of these charmers will quickly show you why their competitive owners can't get enough. They are artists' representations which are painted on china soap mugs and they feature the occupation, or favorite pastime of the mugs original owner. These graphic vignettes of brilliant color document Americana in an intoxicating way: *buy one, and you will want another.....and another.* There are *many* factors to consider in making a purchase. Some collectors specialize in one area of occupational interest such as bartenders or butchers. Others may prefer just recreational scenes such as baseball or hunting. Most occupational mug collectors try to find as many different representations as possible. No matter what the area of interest, there are different levels of presentation and fairly concise guidelines to help determine a mug's worth. One of the most obvious factors, as with all antiques, is rarity. For example, there was a huge number of carpenters employed in 1900. Correspondingly, there were a huge number of mugs personalized for carpenters at that time. As the ripple theory would suggest, a proportionate number of them still exist. On the other hand, if you were able to purchase a mug that vividly portrayed such an unusual occupation as a taffy candy maker at work, hire a guard to help you get it home: *It is rare!*

Beautiful rendition of the Order of Independent Americans. The owner's name appears on the rear in facsimile script. $250.00+.

This occupational mug epitomizes what constitutes a "rare" designation. "Taffy" candy makers were few and far between. This beautifully detailed mug names the business which is "Shanty Of Sweet." It shows the men in the process of "pulling" (mixing) taffy over a wood-burning heater. The completeness of detail even shows wispy curls of smoke rising from the burning wood. The mug is one of a kind and perfect. A realistic value could not be placed on a such a mug because it would be viewed as a slice of the Holy Grail for many an occupational mug collector. Most of whom would bid it out of sight at an auction.

It is also quite possible for two mugs which portray the same occupation to have a fairly significant price difference. For example, you may have a carpenter mug which is "symbolic." This means that the art work only illustrates the tools of the trade such as a hammer and saw. Conversely, there may be a "working" carpenter mug that actually shows the carpenter engaged in his labors. Of course, the detailed mug will always be worth more. The same would be true for a mug which portrays a fisherman enjoying the local trout stream. It would not be worth anywhere near as much as a mug with detailed art work showing a steam trawler and a commercial fisherman on deck hauling in nets. The first mug may simply be the man's favorite pastime. The second leaves no doubt as to the owner's occupation. Another very significant consideration is the artist's capabilities and his attention to detail. Very often, you will see two "working" mugs side by side, both of which will be portraying the same activity or occupation. One mug will be exquisitely rendered and the other will appear amateurish by comparison. One may include intricate details relating to, and greatly enhancing, the overall scene. Another mug may depict only the bare essentials. It is always a plus when the artist includes provenance in his work such as the location, the year, or perhaps a company name. As you can see, collecting occupational shaving mugs is something you may want to thoroughly read up on before you jump in. It is a branch of barbershop collectibles that is not for the feint of heart. Yes, you may be able to find some for less then $200.00, but don't forget that at least one of these little rascals has gone for $10,000.00! Many have changed owners for between $3,000.00 and $6,000.00! Hey, look at it this way, it's a neat way to fund your retirement.

Carpenter mug is "working" occupational which *shows the worker engaged in his labors.* Although carpenter mugs are not uncommon, this particular mug has excellent artistic interpretation and is valued at $550.00+.

Butcher occupational is a top-grade artistic example. The mug is loaded with details including customers, rows of hanging meats, etc. Valued at $600.00+.

Carpenter mug is "symbolic" meaning it shows *only the tools* of the trade. This one has very good detail and is valued at $300.00+.

Backbar Essentials

Machinist's mugs are normally routine but this well detailed example tells us the city, state, country, and the year. The machine room scene is also well done. Valued at $700.00+.

Baker occupational shows two men at work, loaves of bread rising on the table, open oven door, barrel of flour, etc. Valued at $550.00+.

Bartender mug scenes were relatively common, however, this mug has a very colorful artists representation which includes plenty of detail including a cigar case on the bar. Valued at $375.00+.

Interior renditions of iron foundries are rare. This exceptionally detailed example shows no less than six men engaged in different jobs to prepare molten metal. Valued at $1,500.00+.

Although nicely done, this common Grocery Wagon mug is void of much detail and as a result would be valued at $350.00+.

town for an interim period of time, and who desired their "own" mug during barbershop visits. Other numbered mugs were provided to steady barbershop customers who did not own a personalized mug. Even back then, being a "number" was less desirable than being a "name." For that reason, the mere presence of number mugs provided good leverage for the barbers who were always trying to sell personalized mugs to their steady customers. The need for large sets of number mugs was greatest in cities, and more specifically, in hotels. Few photographs of small town barbershops show numbered mugs. They are rarely found in complete sets. When they are, they make a spectacular addition to real barbershop displays. Even if they are not all there, numbered mugs are neat and have an interesting occupational history.

The last type of barbershop mugs bore advertisers names and they were often provided to the barbers for free. Manufacturers of various products, such as hair tonics or razors, had their company name printed boldly on the side of the mug. The company gave the mugs to barbers with hopes that the barbers' customers would read that advertising over and over. It was effective advertising and plenty of barbers took the offer.

Commercial Barbershop Mugs

Barbershop mugs are those that were specifically marketed and sold to barbers for commercial use in their shops. These mugs don't always have the eye-appeal of previous categories that we have looked at in this book. Mostly, because barbershop mugs were made of plain material and usually void of decoration. Many were plain metal, others were clear or milk-glass, but *all* were *heavy and sturdy.* Some had the red cross or other sanitary designation. Advertisements for these mugs would directly make reference to them being "for the barber's bench or counter." When found today, many barbers' mugs will exhibit lots of "character" with heavy use being obvious.

One type of commercial barbershop mug that *has* seen some interest from collectors, are those which are numbered. Numbered mugs were white china and were hand decorated with gold or black trim. The trim was limited to the number, handle, and pin-striped bands around the lip and base. Some also had a flourish under the number. They could be ordered in sets from one dozen to one hundred. These mugs were intended for men who were in-

Complete set of 18 consecutively numbered barbershop mugs in unused condition. They date to the early 1900s and are the only known unused set in existence. They are Limoges china and are hand decorated with 22 kt gold. Rare. $2,500.00+.

Backbar Essentials

Variety of mugs intended specifically for barbershop commercial use. Although void of decoration, they were heavy, serviceable, and easily sterilized. Most were produced in heavy glass and metal. Still plentiful in both materials, they range from $15.00 to $35.00+ depending on presentation and condition. Advertising mugs are much more scarce and have a range from $50.00 to $200.00 depending on rarity of the product being advertised and the condition of the mug.

Barber Bottles

You may have wondered just what was in those tonic bottles that often lined a barber's backbar from end to end. For that reason, we have included the above recipes for hair-care products that were taken directly from an 1890s barber instruction manual. They show, very definitively, just how creative barbers were. But even before barbers became active in mixing their own concoctions in the 1870s, it was druggists and chemists who sold a wide variety of "prescription" hair remedies. Their products came in small clear bottles with the maker's name in raised lettering, and they pitched tonics like "Hope For The Bald," Dandruff Remedy," or "Hair Renewer." We will be taking a closer look at some early Golden Years bottled products in the retail products chapter. In hindsight, we now understand that many of the scalp related complaints of those days were simply a matter of oily scalps and infrequent bathing. Curiously enough, it turns out that many of the above potions were actually making some people worse, since they contained wood alcohol. Some preparations contained up to 96% of the poisonous liquid! Many years passed before F.W. Fitch would present the U.S. government with

his hypothesis that wood alcohol was responsible for much of the population's "scald head" or scalp problems. It was a direct result of Fitch's research that the American Pure Food and Drug Act of 1906 included a provision which stated "wood alcohol is condemned as a dangerous poison unfit for use in preparations intended for man or beast." Any product bottled after the enactment of the FDA required that agency's approval before it could be sold to the public. Thirty years earlier however, the success of druggist's potentially endangering hair tonics, *and resulting profits,* was not lost on the barbers. There were no particular regulations in effect at that time on who mixed up these products. Before long, barbers were stirring up their own tonics and cures. They began selling squirts of their "house" tonics as an adjunct sale to the price of a haircut or shave. Tonics were put up in what have come to be known as art-glass barber bottles. These beautiful bottles helped promote the sale of barber's tonics in a way now referred to as "graphic marketing." They were gorgeous to look at on the barber's backbar and they helped encouraged a patron to agree to pay extra for a portion of their "beneficial" contents. As the style of barber bottle containers and their contents changed throughout the Golden Years, liquid hair-care products proliferated and became more popular then ever commercially.

The two photographs show open book pages with barbershop formulas. The left-hand pages read:

THE BARBERS' MANUAL.

—FORMULAS.
HAIR TONIC (BALDNESS.)
HAIR TONIC.
IMPROVED SEA-FOAM.
HAIR BLEACH.
BAY RUM.
BARBER COLLEGE BRILLIANTINE.
BARBERS' POWDER.

REMEDY FOR DANDRUFF.
HAIR DYE.
SHAMPOO PASTE.
HAIR POMADE.
OINTMENT FOR BARBER'S ITCH.
GLYCERINE FACE LOTION.
VIOLET WATER.

Barbershop recipes for hair and scalp potions before the FDA restrictions were imposed in 1906. Prior to that, barbers had been mixing and selling hair remedies for 30+ years.

After the Pure Food and Drug Act became law, refillable art-glass bottles were still being produced and sold. The difference in their use after 1906, was that they were (supposedly) being refilled with FDA approved, bulk quantity, tonics that were manufactured by suppliers. The barbers could no longer *legally* make their own tonics without FDA approval however, there was some boot-legging that went on into the teens and early 1920s. Tonic manufacturers and suppliers were thrilled when the FDA was formed. They knew that the public had become totally accustomed to using tonics and that barbers couldn't *legally* provide their own mixes any longer. The suppliers immediately began bottling their products in "proprietary" backbar sized, clear glass (or label under glass) containers. In the chronology of barber bottles, the proprietary type was destined to become an interim style followed by paper-labeled disposable bottles which remain popular today.

At one time, most barber bottle enthusiasts tended to be interested mainly in the art-glass type. While they remain as the cornerstone of barbershop bottle collecting, all of the other varieties that come under the barbershop umbrella have seen increased interest. This is good because it provides the beginning collector with affordable items. As their new collections grow, they may choose to move into advanced grade bottles. Also to be considered, is that there are buyers who are only looking for bottles that accurately reflect the period of their personal barbershop display. For instance, if you had a "Gay Nineties" display, art glass bottles would be historically correct. If you were doing from 1900 into the "Roaring Twenties," you could mix in clear glass, or label under glass, proprietary bottles. If your display was more recent, such as the thirties or forties, opaline and early paper-labeled disposable bottles would be the perfect compliment. While some of the bottle style changes overlapped throughout the Golden Years, you should now understand the main periods of innovation.

If you find bottles that are not otherwise damaged, but do have some inside discoloration, don't let that stop you from buying. It is understood that these bottles are aged and have been well used in some cases. Unless the staining is extreme, careful cleaning will usually render them quite presentable. If it is a refillable type bottle, it may add a dimension of value if an accompanying cork and squirt tube applicator is present. This is especially true if you are viewing these bottles from a barbershop's historical perspective since they were only used with bottle tubes. On the subject of bottle tubes, there seems to be some confusion of their chronology throughout the Golden Years and also of their current worth. We have included illustrations of the most popular types that were taken from a variety of barber supply catalogs. You can see for yourself when certain model tubes were popular and how they were offered. I believe that it is time for bottle tubes to be recognized as an important compliment to refillable barber bottles. Since many bottles are found without tubes, I feel that they should have a designated accessory value of their own. The prices that I have given them fairly reflect their

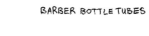

BARBER BOTTLE TUBES

Long-neck Brittania tube. most popular pre-1900.

Sold new in 1891 for 15¢ current value: $20. in good condition.

Barbers best self-closing bottle tube. Popular from 1890s through 1930s.

Sold new in 1912 for 40¢ current value: $20. in good condition.

Low-rise China tube. Sold as "opal" in late 1800s. Fell out of favor by 1900.

Sold new in 1891 for 10¢ current value: $20.

Crown stopper. Screw type. Usually seen in pewter or white metal. Variations known from late 1800s until 1940s.

Sold new in 1911 for 50¢ current value: $20. in pewter or $12. in white metal (in working (not frozen) condition.

Brittania tube with design on collar. Offered in catalogs from 1891 until about 1930s.

Sold new in 1891 for 10¢ current value: $15. in good condition.

Small size Brittania tube. Sold for use in Brilliantine bottles.

Sold new in 1910 for 30¢ current value: $20. in good condition.

China tube appears more like metal tubes by 1920. China became popular again because of move by industry to white and sterile look.

Sold new in 1920s for 60¢ current value: $15.

Short-neck, white metal bottle tube. Nickle-plated. Most popular metal style by mid-1930s.

Sold new in 1935 for 50¢ current value: $12. in good condition.

NOTE: "Bubbled" plating on metal tubes and chips or cracks on China tubes will reduce the value of those items. Replacing disintegrated corks does not affect values.

Backbar Essentials

worth to a barber bottle's historically accurate presentation. Most collectors agree that the currently available lead reproductions may be fine for display purposes, but they have no value beyond their purchase price. They should not be represented as having originally come with the bottle. Lets look more closely at the main bottle categories throughout the Golden Years.

Art Glass Bottles

This rainbow-like array of colorful barber bottles is made up of common examples. Although beautiful, their average price would be in the $75.00 to $150.00+ range.

This is one more area of barbershop memorabilia that has had a dedicated group of collectors for many years. When art-glass barber bottles are displayed in a color spectrum, there are few other barbershop collectibles with as much eye appeal. They form a glittering rainbow that invites your attention. The history of these barber bottles began in the 1870s when large supplies of hand blown bottles were being inexpensively imported from Europe. The glass blowing craftsmen, especially in Bohemia, were turning out thin-walled blown bottles that were often hand decorated with geometric or floral designs. All of them had wide mouth openings to make refilling more easy. They rarely carried any bottom marks that identified their origin, however, they do have small, circular shaped, pontil scar marks on the bottom which indicate that the bottle was hand blown. Pontils were iron rods that stuck into the molten glass and provided a way for the glass blowers to steady their work. After the molten glass was formed

and began to cool, the pontil rod was snapped from the finished product. Some of these pontil indentions were rough to the touch, others have been polished smooth. Later on, bottles were blown in molds and they show no evidence of pontil rod separations. Some mold blown bottles may have an obvious circular pattern on the base. This symmetrical casting mark should not be confused with the more crudely appearing pontil scar. As the Golden Years of barbering progressed, American made art glass bottles ultimately became more popular than the imports. It was because they were usually mold blown and the glass was much heavier. These bottles were less prone to breakage and were often formed into shapes that allowed them to be easily decorated. This was especially true of the milk glass type. There was a wide variety of glass styles such as opalescent, cut, overlay, milk and carnival. Currently, the most sought after bottles are hand painted or personalized varieties. Some, such as Mary Gregory and Whitall, Tatum & Co. bottles are bringing record prices. Jim Hagenbuch of Glass-Works Auctions in Pennsylvania, reports that a recent absentee sale saw barber bottles bring prices up to $2,585.00. For you new collectors reading this, take heart. There are plenty of interesting entry grade tonic bottles to be had from $20.00 on up. Once you have become familiar with all of the varieties, barber bottles can become a good flea market target. I have, on occasion, purchased art glass barber bottles without tubes that were described to me by the seller as "nice old bud vases" for less than $10.00. It does happen! For more frequent and varied purchases, you would do well to join the N.S.M.C.A. barbershop collectibles organization listed at the end of chapter one. In that group, you will find nearly 600 members who regularly buy, sell, and trade bottles along with all other barbershop items. Another excellent source for bottles and memorabilia is the above mentioned Glass-Works Auction. You can order picture and description catalogs from them by calling (215) 679-5849, EST. *The following art- glass bottle photos are courtesy of Glass-Works Auction.* Prices placed on bottles seen here were estimated bid ranges for a recent auction sale. Actual winning bids averaged 25% above the high estimates and in some cases were doubled!

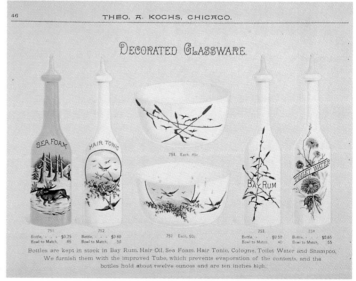

Early examples of American produced, white, glass bottles which lent themselves to hand decorating and personalizing.

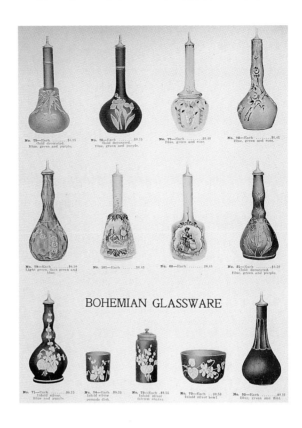

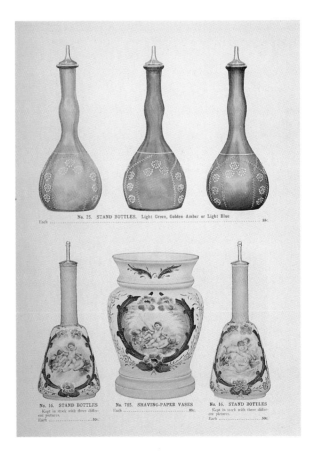

Backbar Essentials

From left to right: Carnival glass, $275.00 to $375.00+. Green bell-formed, enamel decorated, $175.00 to $250.00+. Cobalt blue Art Nouveau style, $200.00 to $300.00+. Cobalt blue cut-to-clear, $250.00 to $350.00+. Deep purple Art Nouveau style, $250.00 to $350.00+. Frosted turquoise Art Nouveau style, $200.00 to $300.00+. Cranberry with white coin spot design, $100.00 to 150+.

From left to right: Rare presentation of a china bottle, $350.00 to $475.00+. Frosted topaz with laid-on enamel, $225.00 to $350.00+. Amethyst colored Mary Gregory decorated, $175.00 to $250.00+. Cobalt blue paper vase, $400.00 to $700.00+. Personalized Whitall, Tatum and Company, $350.00 to $550.00+. Bohemian ruby cut-to-clear, $200.00 to $300.00+. Amethyst Mary Gregory style with rare "fountain" scene, $300.00 to $500.00+.

From left to right: Frosted mint green, Art Nouveau style, $300.00 to $400.00+. Deep cobalt blue, bell-form, $200.00 to $300.00+. Emerald Mary Gregory decorated, $250.00 to $350.00+. Bohemian style paper vase, ruby cut-to-clear, $700.00 to $1,000.00+. Teal colored Art Nouveau style, $300.00 to $400.00+. Emerald and gold Art Nouveau style, $375.00 to $475.00+. Satin mint green with laid-on enamel decoration, $275.00 to $375.00+.

From left to right: Tiffany style art-glass, $400.00 to $600.00+. Personalized Whitall, Tatum and Company, $350.00 to $550.00+. Blue milk glass, $80.00 to $120.00. Personalized Whitall, Tatum and Company bottle missing screw-cap, $275.00 to $375.00+. Cherub decorated, $250.00 to $400.00+. Label-under-glass, amber tonic bottle, $175.00.

From left to right: Ceramic "whisk broom" figural bottle, $175.00+. Rib-pattern, purple amethyst Bay Rum decorated, $150.00 to $225.00. Rib pattern green "Cybeline" tonic bottle, $375.00 to $550.00+. Opalescent swirl "Bay Rum" (letters not complete) $80.00 to $120.00. Green and gold Art Nouveau style, $300.00 to $400.00+. Purple and gold Art Nouveau style, $300.00 to $400.00+. Clear glass thumbprint, floral decorations, $275.00 to $400.00+.

Backbar Essentials

Proprietary Bottles

Proprietary bottles were basically intended to put barbers on notice that these bottles were not to be refilled with anything other than the suppliers products. After the FDA enactment in 1906, manufacturers and suppliers alike wanted to make it clear that *their* tonic was the *only* tonic these bottles should hold and dispense. They hoped that warnings embossed directly into the clear glass (or printed on labels sealed under glass) would insure that barbers would order more of their brand of tonic for refilling. Lettering on proprietary bottles stated words to the following effect: "This bottle the property of the manufacturer. Professional use only. Must not be refilled or you risk prosecution or penalty." Proprietary bottles also coincided with the interim period when art-glass bottles were on the decline and paper labeled disposable bottles hadn't fully arrived. Proprietary bottles are scarce today because of their short window of manufacturing time. Also, because most of them have been discarded since they previously didn't fit any particular collectible category. The problem with the earliest proprietary bottles, was that the neck opening was cork-width and they were very tempting and easy for a barber to refill with his own boot-leg tonic. It didn't take too long for the suppliers to reduce the wide opening on the proprietary bottles to a tiny squirt hole with a screw cap. That change allowed the bottles to still dispense tonic nicely, but it made them impractical to refill. Although there were many more of the squirt top variety produced, they too got discarded just like the earlier wide mouth type. Because of that, both types of raised letter, or label under glass, proprietary bottles aren't often seen. While they don't share the art-glass bottle eye appeal, they are, nonetheless, a scarce category. Interest in these bottles to date has been minimal so prices have been correspondingly low. Expect this to change soon as more collectors seek to acquire proprietary tonic bottles. While it is true that they can appear similar from lack of coloring, that is easily remedied. General bottle collectors have shown their clear glass bottles with colored water for years. It can add a whole new dimension of beauty to clear glass displays, including proprietary bottles. All you need is water and some readily available food coloring from you local supermarket.

Examples of proprietary bottles with raised-glass lettering and small molded-glass squirt holes. These were difficult to refill (as the manufacturers intended) and helped eliminate product bootlegging by barbers. $15.00 to $35.00+ with original metal caps intact. Add value for accompanying paper labels. Left: Newbro's Herpicide Right: Weyers Tonic.

Examples of wide-mouthed proprietary bottles attractively displayed with colored water. All have raised-glass labels. Average price range in good condition. $15.00 to $35.00+. Increase value if original bottle tubes are present. Brands from left to right: Pinol, Noonan's, Wildroot, Odell, Jeris.

Barbershop

Wide-mouth proprietary bottles in clear glass. *Without* paper labels,
$15.00 to $35.00+. *With* paper labels and original bottle tubes.
$50.00 to $150.00+. Brands from left to right: LaFoma, Noonan's,
Jeris, F.W. Fitch's.

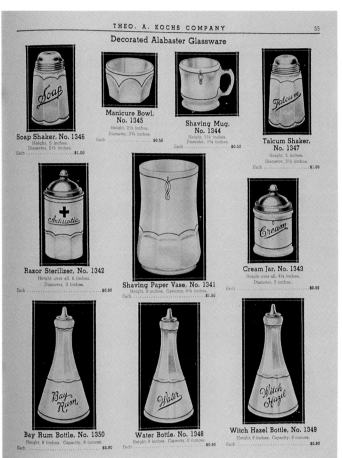

Decorated Alabaster Glassware

Soap Shaker, No. 1346
Height, 5 inches.
Diameter, 2½ inches.
Each _____$1.00

Manicure Bowl,
No. 1345
Height, 2½ inches.
Diameter, 3¾ inches.
Each _____$0.50

Shaving Mug,
No. 1344
Height, 3½ inches.
Diameter, 3¾ inches.
Each _____$0.50

Talcum Shaker,
No. 1347
Height, 5 inches.
Diameter, 2½ inches.
Each _____$1.00

Razor Sterilizer, No. 1342
Height over all, 6 inches.
Diameter, 3 inches.
Each _____$0.90

Shaving Paper Vase, No. 1341
Height, 8 inches. Opening, 4¼ inches.
Each _____$1.50

Cream Jar, No. 1343
Height over all, 4¾ inches.
Diameter, 3 inches.
Each _____$0.50

Bay Rum Bottle, No. 1350
Height, 8 inches. Capacity, 8 ounces.
Each _____$0.90

Water Bottle, No. 1348
Height, 8 inches. Capacity, 8 ounces.
Each _____$0.90

Witch Hazel Bottle, No. 1349
Height, 8 inches. Capacity, 8 ounces.
Each _____$0.90

Opaline Bottles

As the use of proprietary bottles was winding down and paper-labeled, disposable bottles were becoming standard, one popular style of refillable bottles was still being produced. Marketed in barbershop catalogs as "Opaline" bottles, they are easily recognized as having wide, open-mouth necks with cork and tube tops. They were also bell shaped and quite heavy. Their coloring was off-white and is sometimes referred to as "clam broth" appearing. Their popularity was initially due to the public's concern about sanitation. Opaline bottles *did* appear sanitary, but like proprietary bottles, they lack the appeal of earlier produced art-glass bottles. These pre-labeled bottles could be purchased individually or in complete groupings as seen below. The contents of opaline bottles were sometimes identified with letters that were stenciled on. Yet others, (usually from earlier years) had hand decorated descriptions similar to the way shaving mugs and bottles once did. Another variety had silver-metal overlays. The most popular labels were Bay Rum, Witch Hazel, Antiseptic, and Water. Several others were Lilac, Shampoo, and Astringent. As you can see by the descriptions of their contents, opaline refillable bottles primarily held preparations for after shaving and shampooing, *not* hair tonics. Because by the late 1920s, barbers were no longer refilling bottles with bulk hair tonic. By then, nearly all hair tonics were sold in paper-labeled throwaway bottles. Except for some unusual variants, such as custom hair tonic designations, silver overlays, and cream or pomade jars, opaline bottles are still reasonably priced. They are another great target for entry level collectors. Opaline bottles are also one of the historically correct items for period barbershop displays from the 1920s through the 1950s.

Opaline barber bottles with *stenciled labels* and original bottle tubes.
Each, $25.00 to $40.00+.

Opaline barber bottles with *hand decorated labels* and original bottles tubes. Each, $35.00 to $50.00+. Opaline, hand painted, cream jar with original metal lid. $75.00+.

Early examples of paper-labeled disposable tonic bottles from Wiley's Barber Supply. Dated 1925. $45.00 each with contents and original metal screw caps.

These bottles are often misrepresented by unknowing dealers as Opaline glass. They are simply frosted glass bottles that were manufactured in sets in the 1940s and 50s. However, they are not found in plentiful numbers, especially if in sets (from two to five, *all different*.) With lettering and squirt-caps intact as shown, $60.00+ for the set of three.

Modern Era Bottles

This is one more barbershop bottle that should not be overlooked. These were disposable bottles that were manufactured following the clear, raised-glass, proprietary type. While modern era bottles are also clear glass, they do *not* have proprietary markings in raised glass which claim ownership and exclusive usage of the manufacturers products. Instead, they have paper labels, metal or plastic screw caps, and were intended to be thrown away when empty. Many of them indicate barbershop provenance with embossed glass or printing on the label that states "For Professional

Disposable Fitch's tonic bottles with vine-embossed glass, paper labels, contents and original screw-caps. $40.00 each.

Barbershop

80

Use." Colorful, and sometimes very graphic paper or painted labels are the lure here. When they are filled with the original contents, modern era bottles make a very attractive advertising display. Although they currently turn up more often then art-glass bottles, they are still not your everyday flea-market item. Especially those from the 1920s and 30s. They had become popular by the 1920s and were the standard of the industry by 1940. Hair tonic barber bottles that are new enough to have bar scanning codes (small series of parallel black lines) aren't usually old enough to be thought of as collectible. On the flip side of that, it should be pointed out that some bar-coded bottles may be nearly 25 years old and perhaps shouldn't be passed up for the "right" price. Pre-1950s modern era bottles make a nice addition to any late Golden Years barbershop display. They are most valuable when containing the bottle's original contents and when bright undamaged labels are intact. These could be the sleepers in the barbershop bottle category as more collectors begin to seek them out. Remember, *they are ephemera*. This means that they were never intended to be collected, but instead, to be thrown away when emptied. *Most of them were!* The currently desirable modern era bottles were manufactured roughly from 1920 to 1950. Determining their exact age is difficult. The graphics on 1920s bottles are obviously older appearing, even to the untrained eye however, from the 1930s on, most label graphics had a more modern appearance to them. Their real value factor is influenced by odd shapes, true barbershop provenance, (designated "for professional use only") how obscure the brand is, and condition. Time will prove the earliest of these bottles to be scarce. Get them while they seem available. Best place to find them: country store and advertising shows.

Assorted barbershop skin and hair tonic bottles. **From left to right:** Pinol Skintone with cap and contents, $35.00. SKYNTONAC with cap and contents from the 1920s, $45.00. Pennsylvania Excelsior Tonic with cap and contents, $40.00.

Matching set of disposable West Point Tonics with labels, contents, and metal screw caps. $40.00 each.

Wildroot selection from 1930s to 1950s. Bright labels, original contents and caps. Each, $30.00+.

81   **Backbar Essentials**

Three backbar styles of Kreml's tonics. **From left to right:** Anti-Dandruff, $35.00. Kreml's Tonic, $45.00. Kreml's Corrective, $40.00.

Pair of Jeris tonics from the 1930s. (although taken from the same packaging box, the Antiseptic tonic has a Bakelite cap, the Hair Oil as a metal cap) With contents, $20.00 each.

Assorted paper-labeled disposable barber bottles ranging from the 1930s to 1950s. **From left to right:** Odell's Tonic, $25.00. Lilac Water, (gem-cut bottle) $40.00. Healox Lavender Lotion, $25.00. 3 Roses Tonic, (gem-cut bottle) $40.00. Lucky Tiger Tonic, $25.00. Westphals Auxiliator Tonic, $35.00. Pinaud's Eau De Quinine, $20.00.

Lan-Lay Incorporated produced these bottles as advertising gifts to barbers. They were one of the last known sets of backbar ("stand") bottles produced. As seen, $50.00+.

Straight Razors

This subject is undoubtedly the oldest area of still obtainable barbershop collectibles. Cutlery enthusiasts were swapping razors before personalized mugs were ever thought of. While some really fine straight razor examples like those seen above still exist from the 1700s, most, as you might imagine, are in the hands of advanced private collectors or museums. The desirable razors that *are* still available today, originate mostly from the Golden Years. If you find a razor that is worth collecting in today's marketplace, it was probably produced between the mid-to late 1800s, and 1940. Razors that were made earlier then that aren't frequently spotted at the flea market, and anything newer doesn't generally have collector appeal.

If you are just now becoming interested in straight razors, you'll be glad to know that there seems to be no shortage of them. Yes, a lot of the most beautiful and desirable "straights" are already privately held. However, the original production of these razors was prolific and many millions were produced. They are still available in plentiful numbers with different blade and handle designs. New collectors first goals are usually to acquire as many different handle types as possible. There are many gorgeous varieties and their value is determined by their presentation, age and condition. Expect to sometimes tire of finding plain, black, composition handled razors with rusted, broken blades. It seems as though *every* dealer in the world has three of these duds and is "willing to let them go" for *only* twenty bucks apiece. Be patient. You *will* find plenty of nice razors. Advanced collectors get right down to the most minute details and nuances of straight razors. They have been students of the game for a long time, and just like advanced mug collectors, they own the best. Their interests are almost always focused on acquiring the most unusual, high end razors. When they go hunting for that type of razor, it is more then likely to visit another advanced collector for a trading session. They also find good razors through specialty catalog auctions. These auctions, like that of Phil Krumholz (Box 4050, Bartonville, Illinois 61607), offer razors from entry level right up to advanced grade. High bidder wins and you would be surprised to learn that very often, the winning bid is lower then some dealer prices. The problem with being a new collector who may want to participate in an auction, is sometimes simply not understanding the catalog descriptions. While it doesn't take long to understand all of the terms once you've been at it for a while, getting started can be confusing. For that reason, we're showing some basic nomenclature here on these pages. It would take a whole book to learn all there is to know about "straights", but this should point you in the right direction. The accompanying illustrations were gleaned from A.B. Moler's barber school instructional manual and it is the same information that was taught to aspiring barbers for decades.

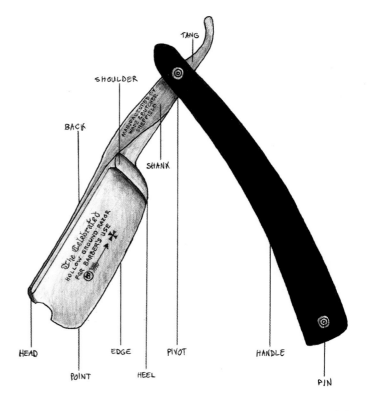

59. Ornamented razors. (England, 17th Century.) From collection at the Schloss Museum, Berlin. Handles are of silver, gilded. Marks of manufacturer indicated.

223

83

Backbar Essentials

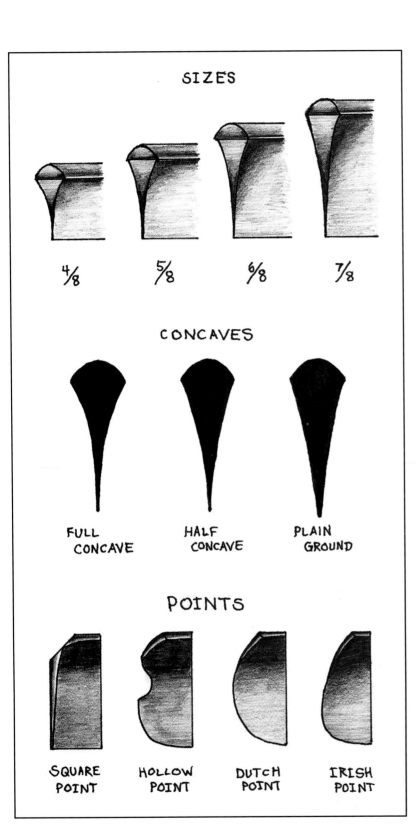

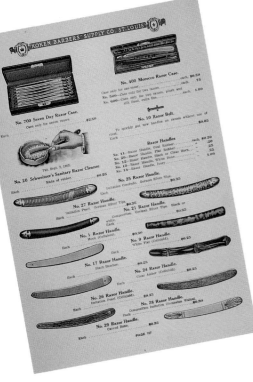

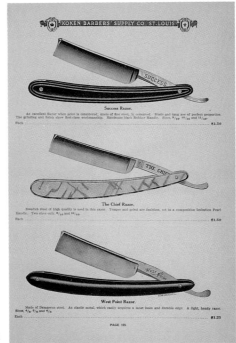

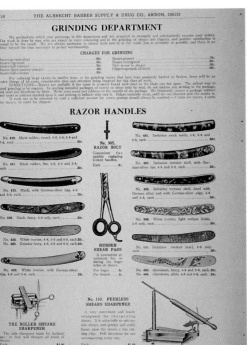

Since this book is written from the Golden Years barbershop perspective, I would like to point out that today's most desired examples of straight razors were not specifically intended for barbers' use. The razors that I am referring to are the beautiful models with handle presentations in pearl, ivory, sterling, or those which are exotically carved. No doubt there were barbers who owned a few of these good-lookers, but probably more for their personal use, and then, because they had received them as a gift. Throughout the early part of the Golden Years, there were many cutlers and generic suppliers of straight razors. Millions of them were sold as one of the most popular men's gift of the times. The presentations were endless but one of the most popular was sets of razors for each day of the week. It was believed by some that if you used a different blade to shave with each day, that would allow the other blades to somehow replenish themselves which made them last longer. Barbers didn't always subscribe to that thinking because they knew that "resting" a razor had nothing to do with its service. Proper stropping and honing was all that was needed. Beautiful handles didn't matter much to barbers either. Razors sold in barbershop catalogs were utilitarian appearing by comparison. It stands to reason that barbers were not concerned as much with looks as they were with performance and durability. Some barbers preferred a very heavy razor with a wide blade while others liked a short narrow blade. Most of them kept both. The larger and heavier blade was for wide sweeps of beard removal. The short and light blade is better for making the shaped hollows and cutouts in some beard styles. It seems that one thing barbers all had in common was their preference for good grinding. Their razors saw truly *heavy* use. They were expected to be beautifully concave and to contain high quality steel to withstand repeated honing and stropping. Razors that were sold through early barber catalogs usually had basic handles of composition or possibly horn, but most had terrific blades, balance, and longevity.

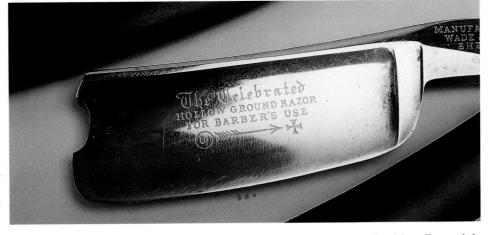

Outstanding example of horn-handled massive barber's razor. The blades on these Wade & Butcher manufactured razors measured nearly 1.25" wide. In condition as seen, $125.00+.

85

Backbar Essentials

In case you have ever wanted to put an edge on a razor and weren't quite sure how to go about it, we have included textbook instructions for you to follow. They are taken directly from a page out of A.B. Moler's barber school manual and are still totally applicable. If you decide to follow these directions to "put your razor in shape" just like the barbers did, *proceed carefully and with patience*. You will be surprised and pleased with the results. However, regardless of what you have been told about straight razors, *nothing,* (including a *good* barber) will shave you as well as a modern, stainless steel, Teflon coated, disposable blade.

NOTE: the accompanying instructions seemed more quaint when left verbatim. As a result, they reflect the original spelling and grammatical errors.

PREPARING A RAZOR FOR USE

First, see that your hone is clean and free from embedments of steel from the razor, (as the hone will not cut properly if the grains are full of steel accumulated from the razor.) If you hone your razor over three or four strokes use thin lather. Not water. Slowly and carefully hone your razor, keeping the hone completely covered with lather, and every few second gently pull the razor across the thumb or finger nail, having nail covered with lather, allowing the razor its own weight. Should the razor incline to stick to nail from the point to the heel, and at the same time feel smooth, its ready for stropping.

In event the razor feels rough or slips on the nail in places, continue to hone the razor until it does stick to the nail from heel to point, before carrying it to strop.

2. Dry the razor, hone also. Then with towel or palm of your hand rub over the strop, both sides, to remove any accumulations, if you have a canvass, strop the razor a few seconds first, if your strop is made of leather on each side, strop razor on the heavy grain piece of leather first. (The object of this is, to remove any fringes of steel from edge of razor and the canvass, or heavy grain leather will remove same quicker than a fine grain piece of leather will.) Then strop your razor briskly upon the fine grain piece of leather for a few seconds, and occasionally pull the razor across the nail of your finger, have nail dry, allowing razor its own weight. In event the razor inclines to feel slightly rough or wirery place the razor on the thumb nail, (as a rule the thumb nail is thicker than the finger nail), press down on the razor slightly (and if you cannot make the razor feel smooth by pressing down on thumb nail, it is necessary to hone the razor more) (As you have either honed the razor too much or not enough at the time taken off the hone.) In event you can make the razor feel smooth, then return the razor to the smooth or fine grain side of the strop, and strop same until the razor will feel smooth on the finger nail, allowing the razor its own weight. When this is accomplished the razor should stick to the ball of the finger or thumb, having same damp, sliding the razor from the heel to the point. Should the razor feel slick to the ball of the finger, it is in need of more stropping, until it does feel smooth and stick to the flesh.

3. A razor should not be honed on a wet hone more than once or twice a week.

4. In honing razor on dry hone, the razor should be tested the same as using a wet hone.

5. In stropping a razor, remember the friction created from stropping causes the edge of the razor to heat, and therefore, causes same to expand. The more the edge expands the thinner it becomes, and the thinner it becomes the sharper it is until the edge becomes so thin, until it crumbles, and therefore, same has been stropped to an extreme, so be careful and do not strop a razor too much at a time.

PREPARING HONE FOR USE

Hones become slick from use and when such is the case, one can detect same by the shiny appearance of the Hone, then you should with a pummey stone clean your hone. You can either use water or lather in cleaning hone. The hone must be wet while using the pummey stone. After rubbing the hone to where it will hold water, then stop. Do not hone your razor very much on your hone after using pummey stone, as the grains of the honest are larger and cuts faster.

In event that you do not have a pummey stone, you can clean the hone to some extent by rubbing it with paper.

PREPARING AND KEEPING PREPARED STROPS

For an unbroken strop (meaning leather only), lay the strop upon a smooth surface board or marble slab. Apply very thick lather completely covering the strop, and with the smooth part of a bottle rub the strop briskly for thirty minutes, (keeping plenty of thick lather on the strop all the time). After this dry strop off with dry cloth. Then apply a piece of tallow about the size of a pea, and briskly rub leather with same bottle for fifteen minutes. Again apply lather and for ten minutes rub briskly with bottle. Dry the strop with cloth free of all lather or tallow. Apply a good grade of powder completely covering strop, and with hand rub powder on strop for few seconds. (The lather first used is to flush the strop, the tallow is applied while the leather is flushed, as it will penetrate the leather. The second application of lather is applied to remove remains of tallor from strop not penetrated. The powder is used to harden the strop.)

(This performance should be carried out for three times every other day.) After the completion of these performances, every evening when day's work is finished, cover the leather part of your strop with very thick lather, and allow some to remain until morning. Then with your hand remove remains of lather. (In event you are using a canvass be careful not to allow any water or lather to come in contact with same.)

The following straight razors (*courtesy of Don Perkins*) are representative of the most popular presentations. They include handles of multi-colored and embossed celluloid, pearl, ivory, silver, inlays, bone, and stag. Also seen, are "sets" of razors and huge manufacturers models. Prices are intended to be median and would fluctuate widely for condition, presentation, and rarity. You may refer to the bibliography in this book for sources of additional straight razor information.

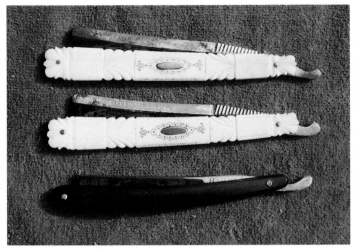

These razors underscore how wide the value spread is with straight razors. The razor on the bottom is a plain, black, composition handled straight of common manufacture. Its value: $5.00. The two razors appearing above it are a matched set in hand-carved ivory featuring intricate "pin work" designs. Their value: $800.00+.

Examples of different handle materials. Values listed are for razors in the condition as seen and would fluctuate accordingly. **From top to bottom:** Sterling silver, $250.00+. Tinted celluloid embossed with feathers and bird's foot, $150.00. Tinted celluloid embossed with stag scene, $80.00. Celluloid with rope pattern, $20.00. Deeply embossed snake scene on celluloid, $300.00. Nude on tinted celluloid, $80.00. Sterling silver, $250.00+.

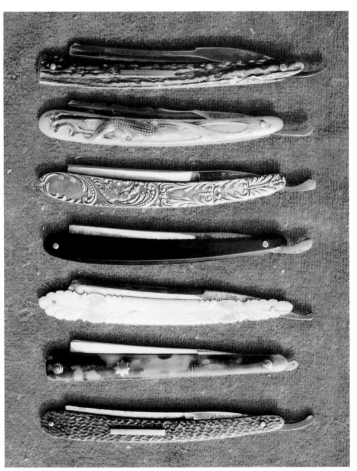

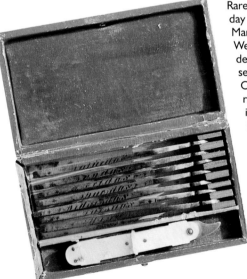

Rare example of a seven-day razor set ca. 1825. Manufacturer unknown. Wedge blades are detachable from the separate pearl handle. Close examination reveals weekdays inscribed in script form on the razor backs. Presented in a red velvet-lined, leather covered, wooden box. Value, $600.00+.

Examples of different handle materials. Values listed are for razors in the condition as seen and would fluctuate accordingly. **From top to bottom:** Stag-horn, $250.00. Deeply embossed and tinted celluloid with Alligator scene, $300.00. Solid sterling silver, $250.00+. Black composition, $5.00+. Carved ivory, $200.00+. Tortoise shell, $75.00. "Picked" bone, $200.00+.

Backbar Essentials

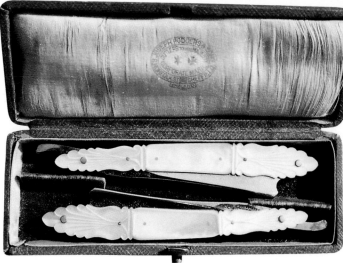

Set of two mustache razors from the mid-1800s. Manufactured by Joseph Rodgers & Sons. They feature pearl handles and are presented in a black-velvet and golden, silk-lined, wooden clasp-box. Value, 450.00+.

Representative seven-day razor sets. **Top:** Early 1900s, J.A. Henckels manufactured, black celluloid handles. Each of the seven blades are inscribed with the corresponding day of the week. Presented in red satin, fabric covered, wooden clasp-box. Value, $300.00+. **Bottom:** Late 1800s, manufacturer unknown. Ivory handles. Each of the seven blades are inscribed with the corresponding day of the week. Presented in a black, velvet-lined, leather over wood box with a key lock. Value, $400.00+.

Additional Backbar Items

Hones

The purpose of honing a razor was to remove a minute amount of steel from the edge of a rounded, dull blade to prepare it for a fresh, sharp edge. Hones came in two main varieties: natural quarry stone, and manufactured synthetics. The most popular natural stone hones prior to 1900 were known as water or oil hones. Although those were slow to put an edge on a razor (because they were minimally abrasive) it was a consistently good edge. They were named for the liquids used to lubricate them during honing and the best of them were mined and exported from natural stone quarries in Europe, particularly Germany and Belgium. Some barber suppliers, such as Theo. A. Kochs, personally traveled abroad to select the finest stone material. After 1900, synthetics such as Alumine, oil residue (dry hones) composition, and carborundum hones became very popular. The Franz Swaty brand was one of the most successful. Synthetics were just as durable, but relatively inexpensive when compared to stone hones. They were also convenient, as they could be used with oil, water, or shaving lather to lubricate the honing process. If there was a gripe with man-made hones, it was that they were often too abrasive. That fact made it easy to accidentally

Two examples of oversized "model" razors. Notice the normal sized straight razor at the bottom of the picture to see the size difference. They were produced for special displays and gift presentations. **Top:** Manufactured by J.A. Henkels in the late 1800s. This razor named "The Nymph" measures over 40" long when opened and weighs 12 lbs. The intricately detailed handles are made of nickel plated steel and

the blade is heavily etched. It is believed to be one-of-a-kind. **Bottom:** This model razor was made in 1876 by the Wade & Butcher to commemorate the centennial of the signing of the Declaration Of Independence. It is nearly 40" long when opened. The scene on the solid ivory handles recreates the original signing. The back of the blade is intricately "worked" and the manufacturers name is etched on the blade. **Value:** There is no accurate way to assign value to these razors because of their extreme rarity and exquisite presentations. If either were placed for sale in a current auction they would set new high-bid records.

over-hone which caused a crumbling of the edge and required a second attempt. That rarely happened with natural stone hones which meant your razor would last longer. Most barbers kept both: the smoother, natural stone for unhurried quality when time permitted; the more-abrasive synthetics for a faster job if needed. Both types of hones clogged rather quickly from the tiny steel particles that were ground from the razor's edge. However, they were easily cleaned with emery paper, wet pumice stones, or plain paper with water and lather.

Prices for hones are reasonable at between $5.00 to $15.00 for average cardboard-sleeved models. If marked with a barber supply logo, $15.00 to $25.00. Those having elaborate presentation boxes in metal or custom wood cases sometimes range up to $50.00+.

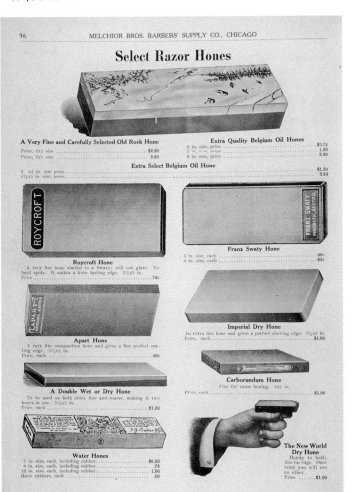

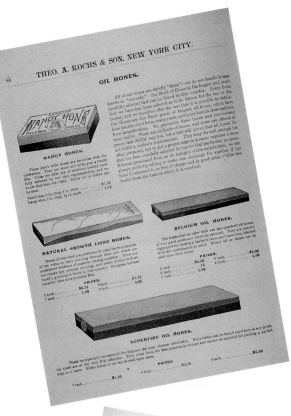

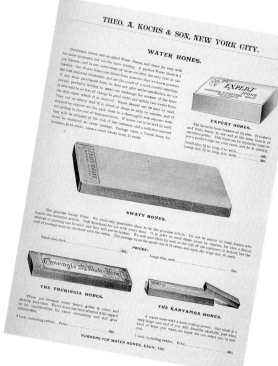

Strops

A quality leather strop is used to complete the sharpening process for a straight razor. Honing stones provide a virgin-steel fairly sharp edge. The subsequent leather stropping draws and smoothens the blade to a refined, hairsplitting edge. A "proper" strop should *actually be a pair of strops*. One canvas and one leather. That is because the razor should always be drawn over the canvas strop first in order to clear the blade of any grit that it may have accumulated. When sure that the blade is perfectly clean and the edge is "drawn," (minutely roughened by the canvas) you switch to the leather strop and "finish" the edge. Both the canvas

Backbar Essentials

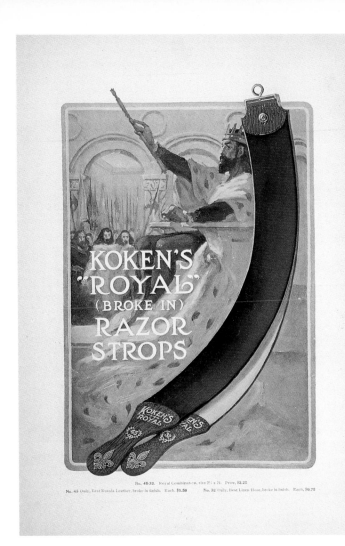

No. 45-32. Royal Combination, size 2½ x 21. Price, $2.25.
No. 45 Only, Best Russia Leather, broke in finish. Each, $1.50   No. 32 Only, Best Linen Hone, broke in finish. Each, $0.75.

for a while) began to roughen from use, no amount of strop dressing or attention could salvage them leaving them undesirable to barbers.

Prices on strops are still reasonable and range from $5.00 to $50.00 depending on condition. Most of them are *well worn*. New/old stock examples will bring the highest prices.

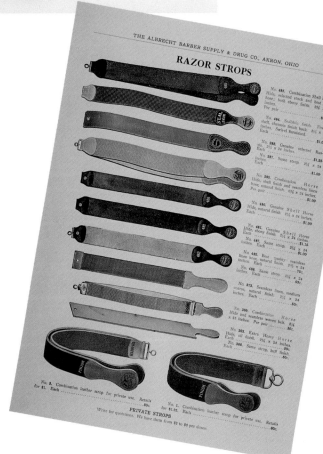

and leather strops were available in grades. The fabric side had three main grades and materials: high-grade linen, canvas, and cotton. The leather side also came in three main grades and materials: Russia leather, (thick cowhide) Shell leather, (thick horsehide) and regular (less-thick) horsehide. There were occasional variants such as pigskin, (fairly popular) porpoise, and sharkskin. Barbers rarely dipped below the top two grades for their strops. The runaway favorite was Russia leather which, although it could take many weeks to laboriously break in, was the heaviest, smoothest, longest lasting strop you could own. Many barbers utilized the same Russia leather strop throughout an entire career. Many people have asked "what constitutes a Russia leather strop." In the 1800s, we imported many cowhide strops from Russia that were very heavy and exceptionally well made. They were identifiable not only by their "heft" and pungent cowhide odor, but also by the corrugated appearance that was stamped onto their reddish colored reverse side. As the Russian imports cooled, American producers simply continued calling their highest grade *cowhide* strops "Russia leather." The second most popular strops were called "shell" leather which came from the horses rump area and was more of a sinuous fiber that helped controlled the animals tail movement. Although not cowhide, the best of those strops received the "Russian Shell" label and many even had the red embossed backside. Supplies were obviously limited which kept the price high on these very serviceable strops. Many barbers favored them because, like pigskin, they were naturally smooth and required no break in time. Less expensive grade (thinner and more pliable) horsehide strops were sold to the "private" trade for home shaving. Because, as the softer leather (nice

Prices on lather dispensers such as the F.W. Fitch pump style range from $125.00 to $175.00 depending on completeness and condition. The small, bulb-squeeze models were for individual applications (home shaving) and are often found for $25.00 or less. Electric models range from $25.00 for not working, poor condition examples, to $100.00+ for excellent condition working examples.

Soap Lather Dispensers

As the demise of shaving mugs was unfolding, alternate means of providing shaving soap lather were being developed. Of course, manufactured creams had steadily been gaining popularity from their inception in the 1890s. Barbers often had a jar of shaving cream on the backbar. F.W. Fitch developed a practical pump-style dispenser that delivered the exact amount of sanitary shaving cream every time. Rivals companies soon made competing pump dispensers as well. The problem with these sanitary doses of shaving lather from jars and pumps, was that *they were cold on the skin*. Patrons complained that they missed the relative comfort of hot lather which shaving mugs used to provide. Hence, the invention of electrically heated lather dispensers. First prototyped around 1920, electric "latherizers" are still utilized today.

91

Shaving Brushes

The primary accessory to shaving mugs was the lather brush. Prior to 1900, and before the sanitation movement, many lather brushes were made with beautiful natural materials such as wood, bone, stag, horn, and ivory. Many of them used twine to bind the bristles. Shortly after 1900, those brushes (although still available) were sold mostly to home shavers as the barbers could no longer use them in a practical sense. The reason was because sanitation awareness called for a new criteria for barbershop shaving brushes. Barber's brushes by that time, were expected to be able to stand in boiling water for "effective" sanitizing. Of course, the natural materials were not capable of that kind of punishment so most barber's brushes after 1900 had handles of hard rubber or metal. The bristles were set in molten rubber with aluminum ferrule wrappers. The preferred bristle for shaving brushes was badger hair which came in two grades. Mixed, which was a *combination* of the softest (pure) strands and also coarser strands, or pure which had *only* the softest Badger hair. There were brushes that contained other very durable animal hair, but none were as comfortable as Badger. For the ultimate hair-bristle to lather-up with, Camel was highly thought of, however you could only accomplish one shave before the bristles would become totally flaccid. They needed to totally dry out before the next shave. For that reason, expensive Camel hair brushes were out of the question for barbershop commercial usage.

Prices for shaving brushes are reasonable and range from $5.00 to $10.00 for synthetic handled styles, and $25.00+ for pre-1900 natural handled models. Carved ivory, silver, pearl, or stag could be higher. In all cases, the brush would be devalued if not containing most of the original bristles.

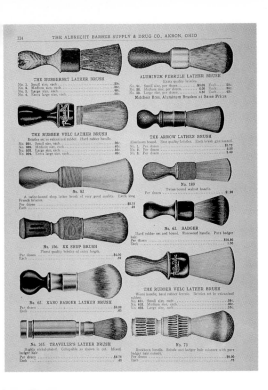

Scissors

Early in barbering's Golden Years, some scissors were produced as a combination of cast metal and laid-on steel edges. These were less desirable with barbers because of their weight, lack of good balance, and shorter life span. All-steel scissors (preferably forged) were the best for barbershop use. While there was not a lot of variance from one good shear to another, the most noticeable was the finger and thumb ferrule (ring) styles. There were two main types: German, which had a flatter, broader finger ferrule, and French which was smaller and round. Most barbers preferred the French style because they offered better control which produced a finer and more precise cut. They were also lighter in weight. All good haircutting shears are produced as two blades of a precision matched set. When both blades are fully closed, they should be touching each other *only* at the very tip. If one didn't know why, it wouldn't be unusual to believe something was wrong with them. They require this slight bow in each blade so that, as they are being closed, the built-in tension will cause them to "bite" and cut the hair cleanly instead of the hair sliding along the edges. Most Golden Years barber shears were finished in one of three ways: plain steel, crokus, and polished nickel. Sizes in length ranged from 6.5" to 8" and was measured in half-inch increments. The barbers' favorite size has always been the 7" model. Professional barber shears that were offered to the trade prior to 1925 are *not* easy to find.

Prices for barber shears, when found, remain bargain priced at between $15.00 and $25.00 for good examples of 1800s barber supply house brands. $10.00 to $15.00 for post-1900 generic models.

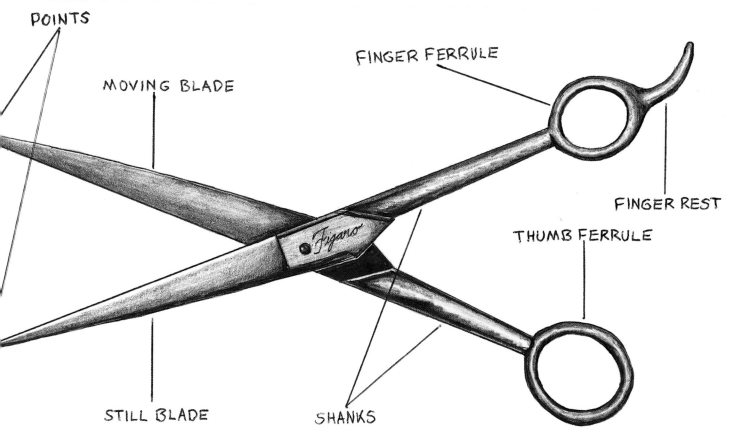

POINTS

FINGER FERRULE

MOVING BLADE

FINGER REST

THUMB FERRULE

Figaro

STILL BLADE

SHANKS

Backbar Essentials

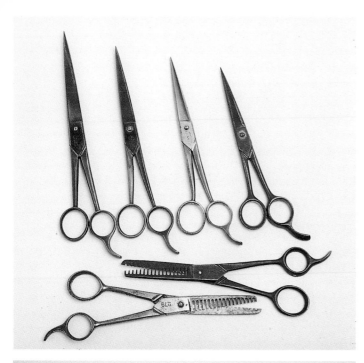

person to person. (not to mention to the barber himself) This spawned the invention of individual applications of styptic as seen below. There was styptic powder, styptic fiber applicators, alum matches, styptic (cauterizing) pencils, powdered alum, and finger cots for sanitary application of those products. Many were generically marketed since home-shavers also need to buy them. It is sometimes difficult to determine the age of these applicators when found because some of their presentations were similar for decades. Being able to identify early printing styles and packaging could help.

Prices on styptic and alum. My experience in buying various styptic or alum applicators is that they rarely exceed $5.00 no matter what their age. I have, for example, purchased a beautifully preserved pack of styptic matches as seen in an 1890s cata-

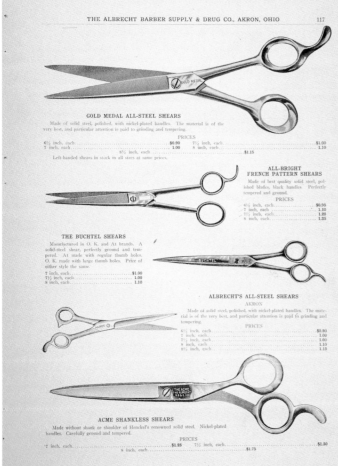

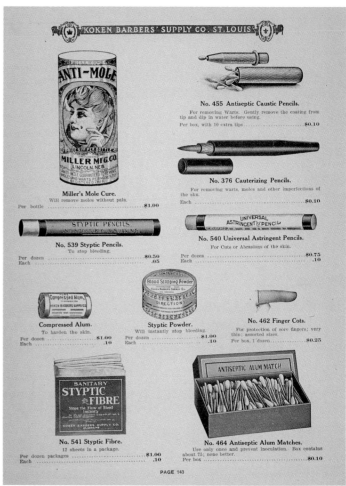

Styptic

Putting surgically sharp instruments in the same space with customers ears and necks, sometimes ended quite predictably. Barbers *do* cut people. Only rarely of course, but with the same result each time.....*bleeding!* Before Lister's revelations on sterilization in the mid-1800s, barbers used the same communal block of alum to stop bleeding on everybody. While that one block of alum stopped everybody's bleeding, it also spread disease from

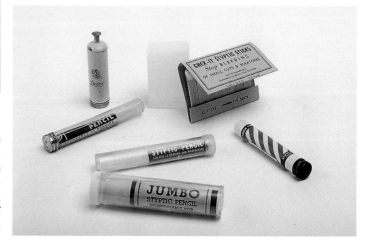

log for .50 cents. Most serious barbershop collectors would be glad to pay $10.00+ for styptic products that are labeled as being from barber supply companies such as Koken or Kochs. They are not often seen.

Hand Clippers

Hand clippers were an interim method of cutting hair that spanned the time between scissors only hair cutting, and the invention of electric clippers. It was a relatively short window of manufacturing time (as can be understood by reading the origin of hand clippers). It lasted only long enough to see two main styles of innovation. Most original hand clippers (pre-1900) had spring-steel strips or barrel springs that rode between the handles. The improved models had coil springs nestled inside of the cutting head. Another way to determine hand clipper age, is to observe the bottom of the blade. If it is flat steel, that would indicate a very early model, since it was discovered this type stuck to a patron's neck if he was perspiring. It was learned that by corrugating the bottom blade, it allowed the clipper to glide smoothly upward on the neck. Before (and sometimes even after) the advancement to corrugated bottom blades, barbers had to heavily powder the neck to keep the blade from sticking. Both styles were capable, albeit sometimes uncomfortable, for the patron: anything less than a *perfect* closing of the handles meant pulled hair! Anybody could operate hand clippers successfully for a short time, but barbers had to do it *all day*. It required a strong-wristed, steady-handed barber to continuously squeeze the handles together in a way so as not to "pull" more hair then they cut.

Hand clipper prices for early (exposed spring) models, $20.00 to $30.00+ in good working condition. Later models with springs concealed in the head, $5.00 to $12.00 in good working condition. Rust is the problem with pre-1900 hand clippers since they weren't always nickel plated as with later year models.

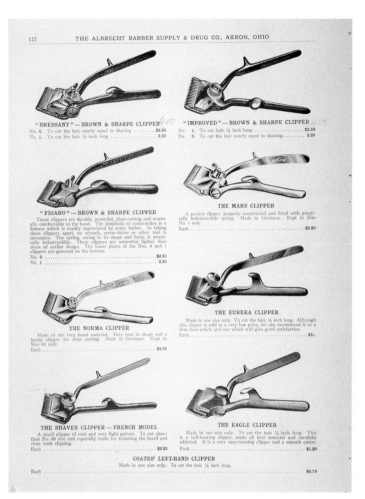

How the Use of Hair Clippers Came About

One hot summer, nearly 50 years ago, some boys in Providence, R. I., created a sensation by appearing with the first "Pineapple Haircuts." These "Pineapple" cuts attracted attention — they were new — and everyone wondered how they were accomplished with scissors. It was learned, however, that the boys had been cutting each other's hair with horse clippers. These horse clippers had been made for the trade by the Brown & Sharpe Mfg. Co., for several years, but their use for cutting human hair was new and resulted in the hair clipper in use today.

The horse clippers were unwieldy articles whose use required two hands. The clumsiness of the long wooden handles and wide plates made them unsuited for the barber shop.

The Brown & Sharpe Mfg. Co., quickly realized how needful a clipper, made for barbers' use, would be and in 1879 secured the first patent for a clipper especially intended for cutting human hair. This early clipper was designed with vision and foresight and was of great value to barbers. It accomplished a wide range of work that previously had been difficult to do with scissors. It was an important advent for barbers.

Brown & Sharpe Hair Clippers can be bought everywhere in all good hardware, cutlery, and barbers' supply stores.

Write us, if you do not find them, and we shall see that you are supplied.

2

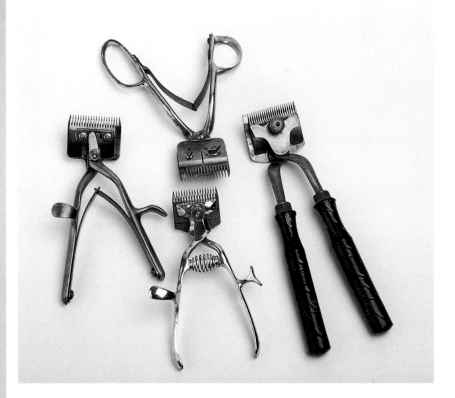

95   **Backbar Essentials**

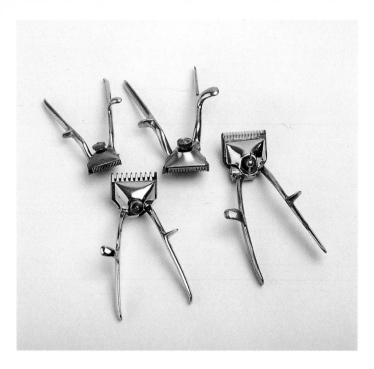

comb. Undoubtedly, the all-time barbers favorite comb would be a hard rubber comb that tapers from end to end and has half-coarse, and half-fine teeth. It is the most versatile comb ever made for haircutting because a barber could use it for delicate neck tapering or bulk hair removal simply by reversing the working end.

Combs, Brushes, and Cleaners

The above illustration show the favorite types of combs by barbers at about 1900. At that time, nearly all good combs were horn. (either hand-cut or machined) Others that were somewhat less popular were made of aluminum or hard rubber. As the years progressed, hard rubber combs became the overwhelming favorite for barbers. That was because they didn't warp like horn combs often did, and aluminum combs would quickly dull scissors and clipper blades if accidentally contacted with the metal

BARBERS' FAVORITE COMBS

Center Taper

Aluminum Curved

End Taper

Narrow Neck

Dressing

Mustache

Although hair brushes were obviously a necessary implement in the barbershop, the middle portion of the Golden Years made it tough for them. Brushes are much more difficult than combs to keep clean. When sanitation and sterilization became barbershop buzzwords after 1900, hairbrushes were seen as dirty carriers of disease. It was a dilemma even for barbers who *wanted* to sterilize their brushes. The problem was that the backs of early brushes were wooden or horn and they simply couldn't be submerged in soapy solutions for too long, let alone boiled as was recommended. Some states actually passed legislation banning hair brushes in barbershops for a period of years. Fortunately, ingenuity rose to the occasion and they began to produce brushes with bodies made of vulcanized rubber which could be submerged in soap indefinitely. They were also producing metal (mostly aluminum) bodied brushes which could actually be boiled. Brushes were also being made that, even though they still had a wooden handle, the bristles were removable for boiling separately. Methods for sanitizing combs and brushes in the Golden Years ran from the above mentioned boilings, to sprinkling Sea Foam (alcohol based skin and scalp lotion) on them. Most barbers realized that before you could sanitize a comb, you had to clean it. There was a good variety of comb and brush cleaners manufactured. Most had metal or rubber tines that were intended to be dragged through the comb or brush which loosened accumulated dandruff and other residues. Another popular comb cleaner was a series of parallel strings stretched between a wire frame. Running the comb back and forth over the wires removed all built-up residue. Once this cleaning was done, the sanitizing could better be accomplished with soap, alcohol, or boiling water.

Comb prices are rarely more than a few dollars. In truth, few combs stamped with barber supply logos exist, and those that can be found are bargains at $2.00+. Mustache combs in aluminum or celluloid seem to be more of a novelty in today's market and therefore range up to $20.00. Ivory examples would be higher. **Brush prices** for early, screw-back, wooden models routinely sell for $10.00+. Newer, rubber or metal models are even less. **Comb and brush cleaner prices** have a fairly disparate range. The earliest of them appearing here is silver plated and is dated 1879. It is very ornate and bears the Victorian design influence. I have only seen a few, and none for less than $65.00. Conversely, the plastic, pre-WORLD WAR II, Fuller brush models can be spotted at flea markets for $2.00. Not everybody knows what comb and brush cleaners actually are and most can be bargains.

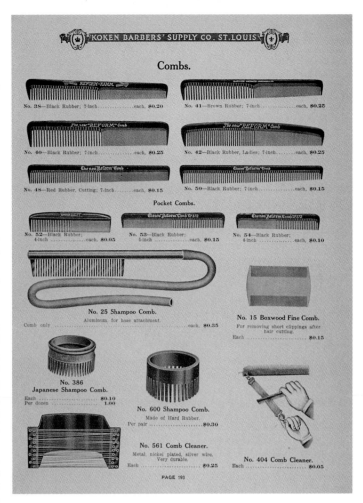

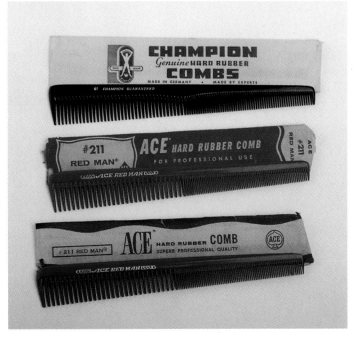

Backbar Essentials

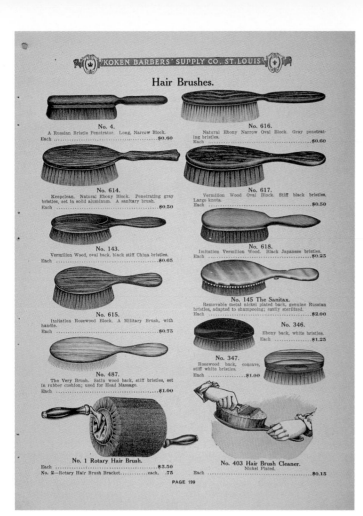

Hair Brushes.

No. 4.
A Russian Bristle Penetrator. Long, Narrow Block.
Each $0.60

No. 616.
Natural Ebony Narrow Oval Block. Gray penetrating bristles.
Each $0.60

No. 614.
Keepclean. Natural Ebony Block. Penetrating gray bristles, set in solid aluminum. A sanitary brush.
Each $0.50

No. 617.
Vermilion Wood Oval Block. Stiff black bristles. Large knots.
Each $0.50

No. 143.
Vermilion Wood, oval back, black stiff China bristles.
Each $0.65

No. 618.
Imitation Vermilion Wood. Black Japanese bristles.
Each $0.25

No. 615.
Imitation Rosewood Block. A Military Brush, with handle.
Each $0.75

No. 145 The Sanitax.
Removable metal nickel plated back, genuine Russian bristles, adapted to shampooing; easily sterilized.
Each $2.00

No. 346.
Ebony back, white bristles.
Each $1.25

No. 487.
The Very Brush. Satin wood back, stiff bristles, set in rubber cushion; used for Head Massage.
Each $1.00

No. 347.
Rosewood back, concave, stiff white bristles.
Each $1.00

No. 1 Rotary Hair Brush.
Each $3.50
No. 2—Rotary Hair Brush Bracket............each, .75

No. 403 Hair Brush Cleaner.
Nickel Plated.
Each $0.15

PAGE 199

Imported Hair Brushes.
Exclusive Patterns.

No. 603.
Solid Rosewood Sextant shaped Block. 11 rows penetrable set long gray Russian bristles.
Each $2.00

No. 602.
Solid Cocobolo Block. 11 rows penetrable set black bristles.
Each $1.50

No. 601.
Solid Rosewood Oval Block. 11 rows extra long Russian bristles.
Each $1.75

No. 604.
Solid Satin Wood Block. 8 rows unbleached Russian bristles. Heavy knots.
Each $1.50

No. 605.
Satin Wood Square shaped Block. 8 rows extra long penetrable set Russian bristles. Large knots.
Each $1.50

No. 606.
Long Narrow Rosewood Block, with open back. 5 rows penetrable Russian bristles. The best sanitary and sterilizing brush.
Each $1.00

No. 607.
Narrow Oval Convex Satin Wood Block. 10 rows black bristles set penetrable.
Each $0.75

Imported Mustache Brushes.

No. 608.
Rosewood Block. 9 rows white bristles.
Each $0.35

No. 609.
Narrow Oval Satin Wood Block. 7 rows black bristles.
Each $0.35

PAGE 197

Barbershop

98

Electric Clippers

The invention of electric clippers was responsible for reducing the length of time that it took to complete a haircut. In an oblique way, it effectively provided the barbers with more income without raising their prices. The first electric clippers (around 1920) were gear and cable-driven by a remote location motor which hung from the ceiling. Multiple chair shops sometimes had a trolley cable across the ceiling so that a lone electric clipper could be slid back and forth to be used by all of the barbers. Later, rolling floor stands were provided for even more convenience. While the cable-driven clippers were quick, they had three glaring faults. The first, was that they were attached by cable to the motor. This greatly limited mobility as the barber worked around the patron's head. Secondly, because of how unwieldy the units were, the motors were constantly being pulled from their hanging position causing them to fall to the floor. Since the motor housings were cast metal, they broke easily and often. So often, that many barbers couldn't afford the replacement expense, and they returned to using their manually operated hand clippers. When those scarce early electric machines are found today, most will have cracked motor housings. Motor cracks are *so* common that it does not count as a fault against their current antique value. The third problem that the original electric machines presented, was that they were not readily adjustable in blade cutting length. It was too expensive to buy three or four sizes of them as barbers had done with the original, inexpensive, hand clippers. Even as barbers were discovering that cable-driven electric clippers had an impractical side, self-contained, hand-held, electric clippers were being developed. When perfected, they would offer far greater mobility, lighter weight, and ultimately, changeable or adjustable blades. By the late 1920s, these small wonders had become standard equipment in barbershops across the country. Most self-contained electric hand clippers (like Wahl machines) were too small to utilize standard electric motors, and instead, had oscillating motors not unlike those that activate door bells. The Oster corporation was an exception as they developed a tiny electrical motor capable of powering a gear-driven blade. They were the most powerful electric clipper at the time, and they remain so today. If you find an early one that seems to *want* to run but doesn't, soak the blade in kerosene for an hour and then try. Very often they are simply "gummed" up. Flea markets seem to offer up old hand-held electric clippers quite regularly. Cable driven models are difficult to locate *anywhere*.

Cable-driven electric clipper prices reflect the scarcity of these items and they average about $50.00+ for a "bare" clipper, meaning it is minus the cable and motor. Popular brands to be on the lookout for include Moore, Coffman, Race, Van Osdel, and Universal. If complete, but not running, $100.00+. If operable for demonstration, $150.00+. If complete with original hanging stand or ceiling trolley and operable, $200.00+. **Self-contained, hand-held, electric clipper prices** range from $50.00 for operable models from the 1920s, down to $20.00+ for operable models from the 1940s. Popular brands were Oster, Wahl, Racine, and Andis. Models that date after WORLD WAR II are not yet viewed as collectible.

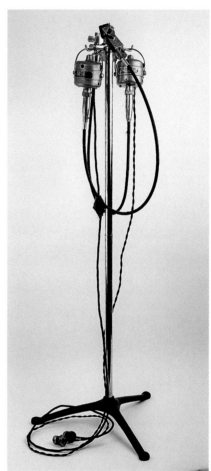

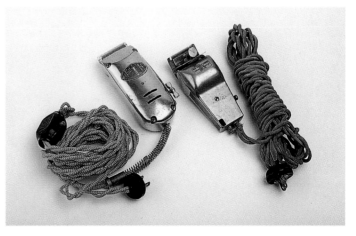

99

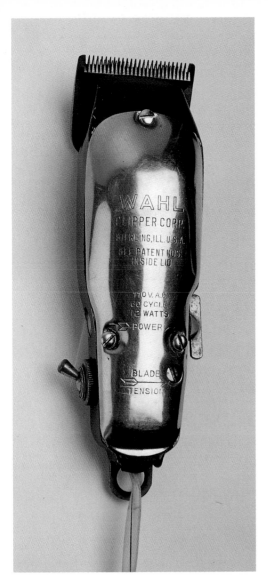

Neck Duster Brushes and Fans

To spare a patron the annoyance of leaving a barbershop with freshly cut hair on his neck, duster brushes were a must. As evidenced by the above photo of 17th century neck dusters (*courtesy of the Schloss Museum, Berlin*) which were made of pigs' bristles and silver bindings, itchy neck hair has been a problem for a *long* time. Throughout the Golden Years, a broad variety of neck dusters were seen. Some had to be hung on a hook, others had flat bases that allowed them to stand upright on the backbar. The least sanitary, were those that laid flat with no provision to keep the bristles from contacting the counter surface. Most early models had nicely turned wooden handles in walnut or oak. The best dusters had flared bristle-ends to better spread the powder on a patron's neck. Some models, particularly in the mid-to-late Golden Years were known as "fountain" models. They carried a supply of talc in their hollow bodies, and when a button was pushed, a bit of talc was released directly into the bristles. Horsehair was the most common bristle used until the 1930s when synthetics (mostly nylon) became popular. Although usually considered more abrasive on the skin, synthetics held up better to repeated washing. Both, natural fiber, and synthetic brushes may still be purchased today. The rarest example of all dusters is pictured below and is a circular bristle brush. It has off-set crank handles so that when turned, the brush rotates 360 degrees in a continuous "sweeping" action, not unlike a modern street sweeper. They were used to brush clippings out of extremely short haircuts in the 1890s like the "Society" style. (now called crew-cuts) It also was very effective as a neck duster and shirt collar brush. Circular brushes were much more costly to the barbers than regular dusters and apparently, because of that, were sold in small quantities and only for about 10 to 12 years. Good examples remain rare. Especially if found with the original walnut hanging rack.

Fans were as much a part of early barbershops as straight razors or scissors. Nearly every picture of a properly appointed barbershop in the Golden Years showed evidence of a fan or two. Their usual resting place was on the backbar tucked between the tonic bottles and the mirror. Lack of air conditioning was the main reason for fans which were usually made of thatched palm fronds or cardboard. Many of them were provided "gratis" from area businesses in hopes that the customers would see the advertisements printed on them. It was important to provide this cooling comfort to a patron who was getting freshly cut hair on his skin. On a hot summer day, that annoying, sticky, problem was magnified. Another use for fans was to soothe and dry the skin after a shave or facial treatment. Fans were much appreciated barbershop equipment until the widespread use of air conditioners. Fans with *barbershop advertising printed on them* remain scarce today. The hand-held squeeze fan pictured below was purpose-built just for drying men's faces after applying skin lotions in barbershops. By slowly squeezing the handles, this fan blows a forceful stream of air. It is offered for sale in the 1910 Koken barber supply catalog. Few of these rare fans are known to still exist.

Prices for neck dusters. Victorian era hair whisks in ebony, $35.00. In ivory, $60.00. 360 degree rotary whisk in perfect condition, $200.00+. If mated with original walnut hanging rack, $300.00+. Early, formed-metal (sometimes silver plated) or turned-wooden brushes in good condition average $25.00+. Flat walnut and celluloid brushes $15.00+. Standing brushes in good condition, $15.00+. Fountain handle with push-button talc dispenser, $35.00+.

Prices for barbershop fans. Thatched palm or other natural fiber with *barbershop* advertising, $40.00+. Cardboard with barbershop advertising, $30.00+. Koken hand squeeze fan in perfect working order, $500.00+. Generic advertising fans, $10.00+.

Backbar Essentials

Talcum and Powder Containers

Neck duster brushes wouldn't have been nearly as effective if they hadn't been used in conjunction with talcum powder. Before air conditioning was available, it was simply taken for granted that talcum powder would be spread on your neck, sometimes before and *always* after, a haircut. It absorbed perspiration or moisture that was leftover from the shaving process and it was responsible for less hair sticking to the skin. Mennen, Williams, Pinaud, and Fitch were early manufacturing leaders of bulk talcum powders which, in the beginning, were white in color. Later, tins of Jeris brand talc became the favorite of barbers everywhere. It seemed to have the perfect consistency, was priced right, and came in white or *flesh colored* which most barbers and their customers preferred. Early, Golden Years, talcum dispensers were glassware, bowl-like containers that were shallow in depth, but which had a wide mouth opening. In barbershop catalogs, they were variously advertised as being utilized for powder, water, or as sponge bowls. The later two uses were to rinse the barbers fingers and wipe excess soap from his straight razor after shaving. When bowls were used for powder application, "puffs" made of animal fur were dipped into the powder and then dabbed on the patron's skin. Some bowls were designed as sets to match artglass or decorated barber bottles. They were made with or without lids. One other type of talc dispenser seen in late 1800s barber catalogs was a 6" pewter bottle with a domed and perforated lid. During the mid-Golden Years, purpose-made containers began showing up in barbers catalogs that were for talc application. They were decorated art-glass with an upright cylindrical shape and also had perforated brass caps. These talk sifters were intended to be refilled. Decorated art-glass sifters were only made for a relatively short period of time because of the advent of powder tins which came with a closeable shaker-top and were to be thrown away when empty. There were also some opaline glass, talcum sifters produced which matched the popular, sterile appearing, opaline barber bottles of those years. By the end of the Golden Years, tins were used exclusively and the pre-1920 glass bowls and decorated art-glass sifter models have become scarce to rare. For that matter, even the tins are difficult to locate since they were designed to be thrown away when emptied.

Prices for powder or sponge bowls. Late 1800s hand painted talcum powder bowls, $150.00+ if perfect. If they match a corresponding barber bottle, the price range is wide depending on rarity and presentation. Most will be $200.00+. **Art-glass talc sifter bottles** (*those seen here courtesy of Tony Gugliotti*) are truly scarce and have been a bargain in the $150.00+ range. **Pewter metal talc sifters** are not often seen but previously low buyer interest also makes them bargains at $15.00+. **Opaline glass talc sifters** have been trading at the $35.00+ range for stenciled letters, $45.00+ for hand lettered. **Disposable tins** average $65+ for pre-WWII lithograph examples. More recent painted tins average $20+.

Backbar Essentials

Cologne Atomizers

During barbering's Golden Years, small atomizers were used by barbers to put a light misting of cologne on a patron. It was offered at the completion of services and was favored as a "finishing" touch. Cologne was too expensive for barbers to pour from stand bottles, so vaporizing it was the only cost-effective dispensing method. Another practical reason for vaporizing cologne, was because it was important for the barber to see that cologne only got on the patron and not himself. If barbers poured cologne from a bottle into their hands in order to apply it to patrons, the scent of cologne on themselves would become overbearing as the day wore on. Colognes were much more powerful and lasting than lightly scented Bay Rum or Witch Hazel astringents. Those two could be (and were) slathered on generously by hand with only a mild residual scent. The atomizers seen in barber catalogs, and also those seen in Golden Years barbershop photographs, are *not* to be confused with ladies perfume atomizers (currently hot collectibles) for home dresser use. Ladies perfume atomizers were highly ornate, imaginative, and *decidedly feminine* appearing. Those were items you could not have *given* any self-respecting barber. Barbershop atomizers were plain and functional tools. There were a few that were whimsical or figural in nature, but most were only one step up from medicinal atomizers. In fact, I've spotted a number of generic DeVilbiss medicinal atomizers on backbars in old barbershop photos. (they were probably less expensive for the barber to buy and were just as effective and durable.) The most desirable barbershop atomizers are those that had internal pump mechanisms instead of the usual rubber squeeze-bulb to propel the spray. The reason for their popularity was simply because the barber needed only one hand to activate pump-style atomizers. That convenience left his other hand free to reach for a towel, duster brush, or whatever else may have been needed. Pump mechanism atomizers cost considerably more when new, and because of that, there were far fewer of them made. They remain scarce, especially if hand decorated to compliment barber bottles. Compressed air, atomizing systems for barbershops are the most elusive of all to find. Only the best shops could afford them and these systems provided each barber with his own atomizer connected to a built-in air compressor line. (see catalog below) Prices below are for functional atomizers with undamaged bulbs or mechanisms.

Prices for barbershop atomizers made with smooth glass bottles, $15.00+. With designs in clear or colored glass, $25.00+. Nickel plated over brass atomizers $35.00+. Hand painted, artglass, pump mechanism style, $175.00. Various, generic, medicinal styles, $10.00+. Air compressor outfits if complete, $350.00+.

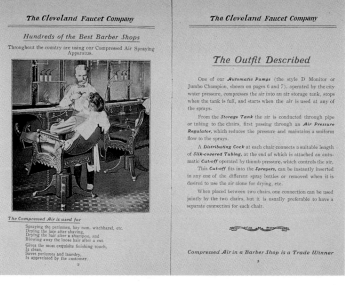

Sanitary Neck Strips

One of the industry's first concessions to the public's request for better barbershop sanitation came in the late 1800s in the form of individual "neck" strips. They were small cotton strips that served as a buffer between the patron's neck skin and the barbers' communal hair cloths. In their earliest form, neck strips were about 2" wide by 18" long pieces of fabric. There was no container for them and they hung loosely on a piece of hooked, bent-wire resembling a string of fur pelts. Of course, they could be washed after being used, but not too often because the edges weren't bound and they would quickly unravel. There was an obvious need for improvement. In the 1890s the Koken Barber Supply was the first to supply flip-top cans of a product they labeled as "Koken's Toilette Requisites." These hinged-lid containers were seen as a more sanitary way to store and dispense cotton sanitary strips. In short time (just after 1910) disposable paper strips came about and quickly took over in popularity. They weren't perfect, as the flat paper would stick to a perspiring neck. However, the sanitation wary public didn't have to *wonder* if the paper strips had been laundered as they did with the earlier cotton neck strips. Just after 1920, a company was started called Sanek. They developed a wrinkle-textured, paper (patented as Cellucotton) neck strip that wicked moisture away from the skin and came in pre-folded dispensers. These strips were bundled in a way so that when the barber pulled one out of the metal dispensing case, another strip automatically popped up. They provided sanitation, quality, and convenience that to this day remains unequaled for hair-care professionals.

Prices for sanitary neck strip dispensers. Koken Toilette Requisites, hinged dispenser. Tin-lithograph, 6" tall, as seen, $125.00+. Original 1920s, white, Sanek dispenser as seen, $45.00+. Deco style, rust colored, wrinkle finish model, $35.00+. Post-WORLD WAR II Sanek dispensers, $15.00. All Sanek dispensers could be valued higher if containing original neck strip contents.

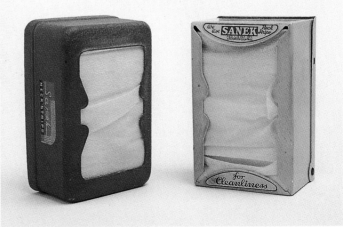

Electric Hair Dryers

While hair dryers were sold in nearly all barber supply catalogs after the widespread availability of electricity, they did not appear in all barbershops. Because then, as is still the case, traditional barbers did not "style" hair. They cut hair (proudly) in a precision manner to make it look good. Traditional barbers left the styling to ladies beauty parlors. Of those barbershops that did have electric hair dryers, they utilized them for more practical use, and often as a courtesy to enhance the overall service. Of course, drying a man's hair after a shampoo was the main purpose of keeping one in a barbershop. However, plenty of barbers would vigorously shake the hair with their free-hand while di-

Backbar Essentials

recting the dryer at the hair and hopefully blowing away all of the loose, freshly cut hair. Another alternate use for a dryer was to direct the air-flow at a gentleman's freshly shaved face in order to be sure all off the moisture was gone before sending him outside into possibly freezing temperatures. In the summer, the dryer was switched to the cool air setting in order to help dry the neck of a perspiring patron before getting wrapped with the neck strip and hair cloth. These extra touches with electric hair dryers only took the barber a few seconds, but they encouraged many a patron to be generous with a gratuity, thereby making dryers a handy barbershop tool item. Most barbershop hair dryers were hand held although floor models were also available. Floor models were often heated with gas but had electric blower motors. These units were large, bulky, and they were most often seen in beauty parlors.

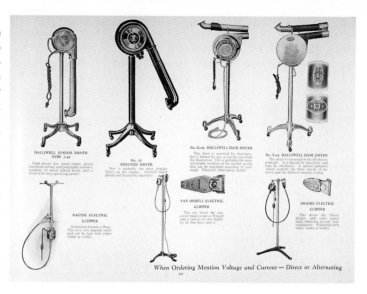

When Ordering Mention Voltage and Current — Direct or Alternating

Eye Protectors and Shields

Eye protectors were sold for many years in barber supply catalogs. Their purpose was straightforward in that they were intended to prevent fresh-clipped flying hairs from entering the patron's eyes during a beard trim. Unlike a shave, where the whiskers being removed were absorbed into the creamy soap mixture, a beard trim utilized scissors which caused the wiry, dry, beard hairs to fly about when snipped. While getting a hair splinter in the eye could be a seriously irritating concern, I have never been able to understand why the barber and his patron couldn't simply agree that the patron should keep his eyes closed during the trimming process. In my 34 years of trimming beards, each time before I begin, I say "close your eyes now please." No problem! Maybe with all of the straight razors being twirled around in those days, men felt a *real need to keep their eyes open*. At any rate, barbershop eye protectors were sold from the 1890s until sometime after 1910. They were available in a number of styles including, celluloid, wire mesh, clear glass, and darkened glass (handy when lying on your back and looking up into the lights) I suspect that many eye protectors were generically produced and also served the stagecoach, and later, the motorcar trade. One common characteristic of barbershop eye protectors seemed to be soft frames. That is to mean that the part of them that contacted the face was often made from very soft glove-appearing leather or felt material.

Eye shields were made expressly for the barbers themselves to wear. The shields purpose was to help reduce the glare from the bare incandescent electric light bulbs. It was an interesting time for barbers who went from gas, kerosene, and oil lamp light, (none of which were truly sufficient) to brilliant, un-filtered, in-

Prices for electric hairdryers. Both dryers shown below date to before 1910 and are typical of hand held dryers from that era. They have wooden handles, tin or aluminum bodies, and both are in running condition as most (surprisingly) are. Better models will have hot or cold air capabilities. Working models as seen here are sell regularly for $20.00+. *Courtesy of Bill and Marlene Levin.* Floor models turn up far less often, and when offered are usually in the $150.00+ range.

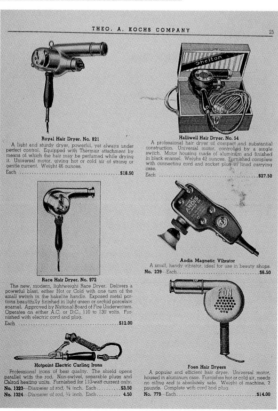

candescent light almost overnight. As soon as each shop had electricity become available, bare light bulbs lit the room. Of course, the bulbs were placed directly over the work area, and after 10 or 12 hours, the glare became too much for the barbers eyes. Green tinted, celluloid visors became popular and are seen repeatedly in Golden Years barbershop photos.

Prices for patron's eye protectors and barber's eye shields. To date, collector demand has been low and most dealers are almost never sure of the purpose for these items. The result has seen patron's eye protectors and barber's eye shields average $10.00 to $15.00. Expect this to change as new awareness of these unique items purpose becomes known.

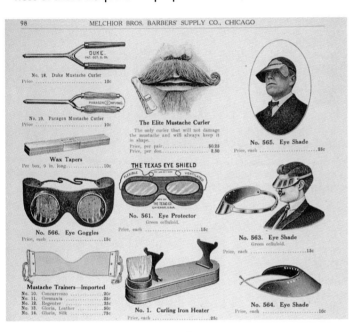

Backbar Sized Sterilizers

To better understand the thinking of just how important sterilization was during the Golden Years of barbering, take a minute now and read the above paragraph appearing under the little red devil on the Kochs catalog page. Just 30 years earlier, good barbershop hygiene meant only that your barber took a bath once a week.....*maybe*. By 1925, barbershop sanitation had reached a fever pitch. By far, the most new items to be found in any barber catalog of that time had to do with sanitation. Many of them had red cross or red star designations. Others had lettering or stenciling with words like "sterilizer" or "antiseptic." Nearly all of them shared the same background color: white! There was a variety of disinfecting liquids, sterilizing steamers, fumigants, formaldehyde, ultra-violet lights, individual bags for combs and razors, and containers of every description. All were designed to disinfect or sterilize. Air-tight cases of all sizes and materials were designed for formaldehyde vapor disinfecting. Larger ones could hold dozens of combs, razors, and scissors. Small, counter-top, combination sterilizers were designed to hold individual barbers tool sets. Opaline glasses and jars were designed specifically to hold combs, clipper blades, or scissors and razors. There was

Another simple remedy which we can recommend for the cure of Barber's Itch in the early stages"

Take the ashes from a good cigar, wet the finger tips with spital and make a kind of paste of the ashes and rub on the parts where the disease is first indicated.- Barber Instructor and Toilet Manual, 1904

Backbar Essentials

even a line of opaline waste paper vases. While a healthy interest in sanitation should have been encouraged, they went overboard in the 1920s. Because the medical community was quickly learning so much about sanitation, their warnings were sometimes alarmist in nature. State Barber Board agencies were springing up and adopting controls and guidelines never before heard of, and as we know now, sometimes unnecessary. Barbershops and beauty parlors were a reasonable target for the hype because of the personal nature of their service and the legitimate possibility of spreading disease. Skin and scalp diseases in particular. As the years have passed, barbershop sterilizing needs have moderated backward a great deal as when compared to 1925. As state agencies and barbers alike now understand, simple, regular, chemical cleaning eliminates most genuine sanitation concerns. Let's face it..... when was the last time you heard of a disease being transmitted down at Joe's Barber Shop?

THE Law decrees, the public prescribes, good-judgment advises, and conscience dictates — SHOP STERILIZATION.

Whether but one or all of these influences apply to you .... heed the need for SHOP STERILIZATION.

Adopt a system of shop hygiene and you are answering a public want, whether it is compulsory in your particular locality or not. Don't wait for the ominous club of the law to descend; there are penalties. Don't wait until an indignant public clamour rings in your ears; for, once aroused, the public is not easily quieted and you may find yourself bound, thereafter, by unreasonable limitations.

It's a moral obligation and bit of sensible foresight ... to act on your OWN initiative in the matter of shop sterilization.

Look through this catalog. You will find everything you need for shop hygiene. Then get in touch with your Kochs Dealer. Be sure you get KOCHS sterilizers. Look for the name:

Theo. A. Kochs Company
Chicago

Restored backbar sterilizer made by Erie City Manufacturing in 1911. 18" x 12" x 11." Two porcelain logo badges. Glass and wire-mesh shelves. Value as seen, $225.00+.

Early, oak backbar sterilizer made by Koken ca. 1910+. 12" x 12" x 8." Wood refinished and decal intact. Glass shelves. Value as seen, $125.00+.

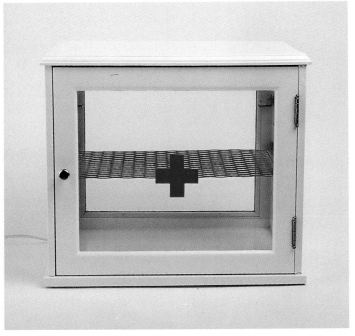

Restored backbar sterilizer ca.1930s. Manufacturer unknown. 14" x 12" x 9." Red cross repainted. Wire-mesh shelves. Value as seen $125.00+.

Lifetime Sterilizer brand "Protective Sanitary Service." Patented in 1934 and constructed of heavy Bakelite and stainless steel. The inner trays are both porcelain and glass with felt pads in the bottom to protect against chipping. Decals perfect. Unused condition as seen, $125.00+.

De Witt porcelain barbershop sterilizer ca. 1920+. Has compartments for razors, scissors, combs, and clippers. Unused condition. Value as seen, $150.00. Bottle of Ku-Rill germicidal liquid commonly used in backbar sterilizers. Value as seen with painted label and original contents, $45.00+.

Assorted comb sterilizers. **From left to right:** Frosted glass with stenciled descriptions and plated lid ca.1940+. $65.00+. Herpicide sterilizer in Bakelite with original lids ca.1920+. $125.00+. Jeris sterilizer with unique patterned glass and one-piece comb retriever and lid ca. 1950s. $35.00+. Herpicide disinfecting system with matching base ring and lid ca.1920+. $75.00+. Clear glass "Perfection" sterilizer with plated lid ca.1915+. $65.00+.

Miscellaneous sterilizers and antiseptic glassware. **From left to right:** Opaline razor-bath with stenciled description and hand painted star. Missing lid. $45.00+. Oster milk glass blade-bath with nickeled-lid. *Courtesy of Bill and Marlene Levin.* $50.00. Opaline razor-bath with stenciled description and nickeled-lid. $65.00. Hand decorated opaline antiseptic jar with nickeled-lid. *Courtesy of Bill and Marlene Levin.* $85.00+.

Backbar Essentials

Sanitary paper waste containers for the backbar. **Left:** Opaline glass with stenciled letters, hand trimmed star, and original lid. $175.00. **Right:** Opaline glass with lid. Seen in 1932 Kochs barber supply catalog, $125.00.

Prices for towel urns and paper vases. Pottery vases are regularly seen for less than $100.00 but can be influenced to higher values determined by highly collectible pottery designers or manufacturers. Pottery urns are seen at $200.00+ but are subject to the same considerations as the vases and could range higher. Paper vases made of glass range from $125.00+ for opaline models to more than $1,000.00+ for some rare art-glass examples in perfect condition.

Towel Urns And Paper Vases

For most of the Golden Years era, it was popular for better furnished barbershops to have paper waste vases and towel urns. They were often available in matching sets. The smaller of the two was for the backbar counter and it received soiled headrest paper. That was the paper that came from a roll under the barber chair's headrest and was referred to as shaving paper. Each customer received a fresh piece to rest his head on while being shaved. Also placed into this waste container were disposable sanitary neck strips. The larger of the two-piece pottery set looked similar in size and appearance to an umbrella receptacle. It stood behind the chair, under the counter, and received soiled and wet towels that had been used for shaving and facial treatments. Pottery urns and vases came in a wide range of styles, coloration, and sizes although most urns were 16" to 20" tall. Most paper vases were 6" to 10" tall. Paper vases were also made in thinner and more delicate art-glass styles in the early Golden Years. They were about the same heights, but were smaller around and held less waste than pottery vases. Art-glass vases were also made in matching styles, but *only* as a compliment to art-glass barber bottles and *not* towel urns.

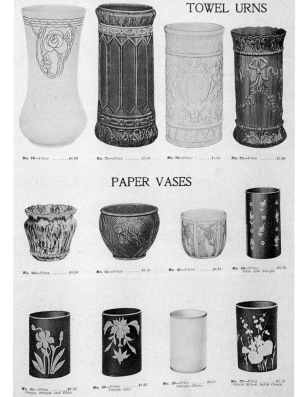

Backbar Accounting Methods

Not every barbershop had a mechanical cash register. Shop owners that didn't have that luxury needed to find practical alternatives to accurately account for the day's proceeds. Since most barbershop employees were paid on commission, it was equally important for them to keep their own records as well as the owner. One of the most popular methods was color-coded or numbered "checks." They were produced in brass, celluloid, wood fiber, cardboard, and rubber composition. They would accumulate throughout the day and be counted at closing time. Some sets of checks came in wooden boxes that were custom made to securely hold them. Better sets also had provisions for advertising signs attached to the tops or backs.

The twin check method has been in use continuously since about 1900. This is where a paper check pad has two identical numbers printed on a single sheet of perforated paper. As the barber finishes his patron, he tears off the bottom sheet and gives it to the patron who takes it to the register. The barber then tears the matching number off and pushes it down on his personal check-spindle as seen below. Each sheet is consecutively numbered. At the end of the day, both he and the boss can have an exact accounting of transactions.

Check punches were also found in every barbershop, even those with a cash register. They were used by the owner or cashier to validate one half of a twin check so that it couldn't mistakenly (or purposely) be used twice. Punches could also be used to identify individual barbers or transactions. They were available in a wide variety of punch-head configurations.

Prices for backbar accounting items. Complete sets of matching numbered checks in custom containers with original barbershop advertising are rare. As seen here, $350.00+. Barbershop, twin number, check pads with cast-iron based spindle, $15.00+. Koken, nickel plated, barbershop check stub holders are rare. Re-plated like new as seen here, $150.00+. Generically produced check punches if dated in 1800s, $45.00+. Dated 1900 to 1925, $20.00. If undated, $15.00.

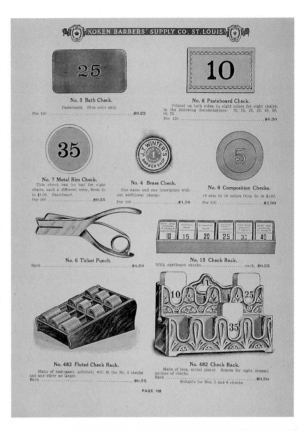

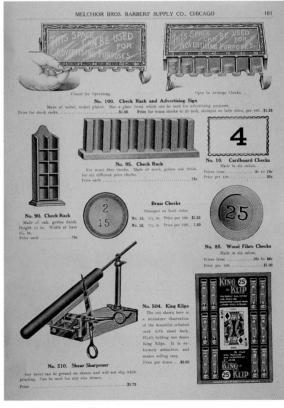

Miscellaneous Backbar Items

The following items seen here come under the miscellaneous category in old time barbershops. In keeping with the heading of this chapter, all of the following articles could be found on the barber's backbar. Most are standard flea market items and were generically produced, although all were seen advertised for sale in various barbershop supply catalogs during the Golden Years.

Prices for mirrors. Pre-1900 models were usually made of hardwood frames with beveled glass mirrors. Some were coated with an ebony finish. Average 6" to 8" plain mirror in good condition with original glass, $25.00. Celluloid handled plain mirrors, 6" to 8" in good condition, $15.00. **Tool cases.** Wooden, compartmented boxes for backbar tool storage or traveling. In oak as seen, $75.00+ without tools. Leather, straight razor pockets (also called "rolls") are usually found in brittle or tattered condition. If in good condition, a bare, six loop, leather pocket/roll could bring $20.00+. **Backbar hand lotions.** Clear glass backbar sized bottle of barber's favorite Hinds Hand Lotion from about 1910, $65.00+. Jergens lotion with contents from late 1930s, $20.00+. **Colgate shaving powder tin.** Unusual 2.5" x 5" backbar sized for mixing mug soap instead of using soap cakes. $20.00+. **Towel holder grips.** Pair of matching nickel plated towel holders as seen in 1891 Koken catalog. Mint, no rust, $35.00 for pair. **Oil cans.** These "pocket" oilers were usually no taller than 3" but were indispensable for oiling scissors, clippers, vibrating massagers, and all other barbershop tools with moving parts. They appeared in every full sized barber supply catalog known. As seen, from .50 cents to $15.00+ at flea markets.

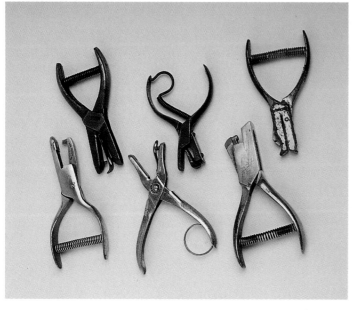

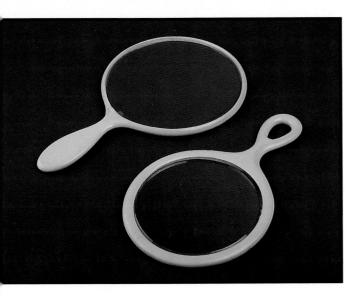

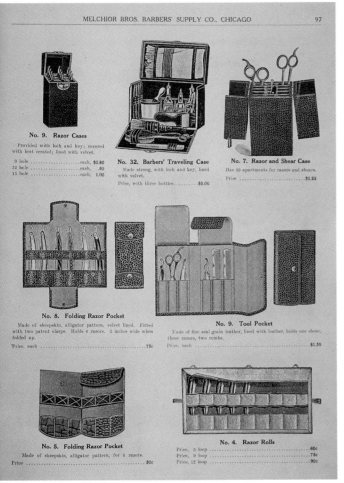

No. 9. Razor Cases

Provided with lock and key; covered with best ceratol; lined with velvet.

9 hole ....each, $0.80
12 hole ....each, .90
15 hole ....each, 1.00

No. 32. Barbers' Traveling Case

Made strong, with lock and key, lined with velvet.

Price, with three bottles.........$5.00

No. 7. Razor and Shear Case

Has 20 apartments for razors and shears.

Price $1.25

No. 8. Folding Razor Pocket

Made of sheepskin, alligator pattern, velvet lined. Fitted with two patent clasps. Holds 6 razors. 3 inches wide when folded up.

Price, each 75c

No. 9. Tool Pocket

Made of fine seal grain leather, lined with leather, holds one shear, three razors, two combs.

Price, each $1.50

No. 5. Folding Razor Pocket

Made of sheepskin, alligator pattern, for 6 razors.

Price 80c

No. 4. Razor Rolls

Price, 6 loop 60c
Price, 9 loop 75c
Price, 12 loop 90c

Backbar Essentials

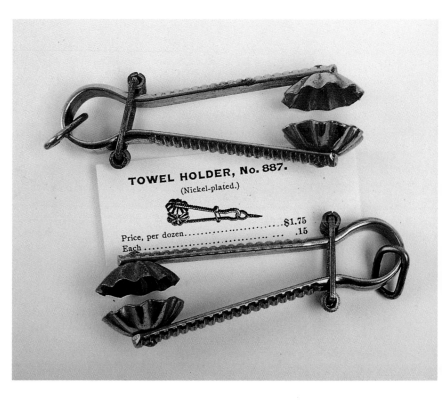

Chapter 4

Ancillary Services

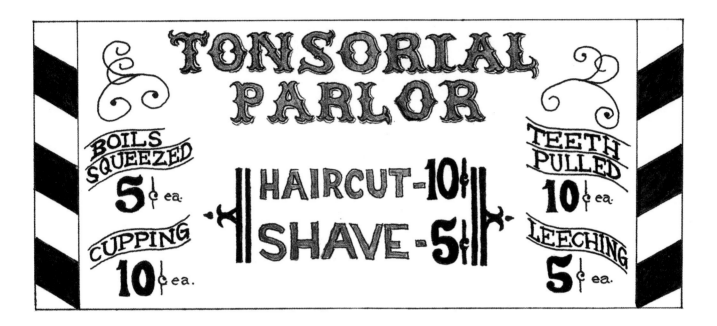

The services that were most often provided by barbers over the years have been haircuts and shaves. However, in the long history of barbering, there have been some interesting ancillary services performed as well. Some of those services seem bizarre by contemporary standards. For example, from the eleventh to the seventeenth century, barbers were legally sanctioned to do medical blood-letting, also known as phlebotomy or drawing blood from the body. Barbers also performed most of the battlefield amputations in the early campaigns. When it was popular, bloodletting was believed to be beneficial to a person's health by allowing some "bad" blood to be drained from the body. New blood was then produced which presumably restored their health. The barber used a scalpel, or fleam, to "breath" the vein and blood would flow from the small incision into a basin. When it was decided that enough blood had been drained, the barber applied pressure to the incision and stopped the bleeding. Hopefully, the person would feel better or at least *believe* that he did.

Barbers also practiced cupping and leeching. Cupping was performed by using a flame to super-heat a small flint-glass cup on the inside. The cup was then placed on the skin directly over the afflicted area, such as a sore wrist. As the outer layer of glass began to quickly cool down, (while the inside remained hot) suction was created that gorged the blood and skin into a balloon shape inside of the cup. It was believed that by drawing bad blood away from the problem area (though the blood remained in the body) the customers complaint would be relieved.

Leeching was the practice of placing live blood-sucking worms on the skin and allowing them to gorge themselves with the persons blood. It is not clear if barbers turned to leeching as an alternative when they were forbidden to continue venous bloodletting in the mid-18th century. We do know however, that leeching by barbers became very popular in the 19th century. The logic of this practice was not unlike that of phlebotomy which was to remove the so-called bad blood. While venous bloodletting was considered more of a general procedure for all sorts of internal maladies *including dementia,* leeching was usually viewed as more of a "local" treatment. I'm sure it would have been great for tennis elbow or carpal tunnel syndrome! Special, blown-glass leech bowls and other containers were made to hold the slimy creatures. Of all the unusual health remedies that barbers were involved in centuries ago, perhaps it was leeching that had the most merit. Current medical researchers have identified properties in leeches that have amazing medicinal qualities. They produce an especially strong anticoagulant that is being cloned to break down clots in the brains of stroke victims. They also have proven to be effective in the healing process of burns and reattachment of severed body parts. Leeches seldom leave scars and are also painless since they produce their own anesthetic as they work. Currently, leeches are being domestically farmed in Wales and are sold worldwide to various health care providers.

Instruments for blood-letting. **Left:** early 1800s, multi-width blades hinged to fold into brass shield. 2.75" long. $150.00+. **Right:** spring-loaded, brass-encased fleam from late 1700s. 2" long. Original leather covered wooden case. Mint. $250.00+.

Left: Bleeding/shaving bowls were made of decorated china, pottery, and various metals. Barbers preferred metal because of the durability factor. Prices can range from $200.00 to $750.00+ depending on decoration, age, and condition. Bowl seen here is brass with nickel plating. ca. 1850+. $300.00+.

Examples of mid-1800s surgical-edged lancets used to incise a vein. Made by J. Rodgers & Sons with handles in rosewood and ebony. As the need for these instruments was becoming obsolete, similar tools continued to be made and were marketed as ink-erasers until after 1900. Values as seen here. **Top:** mint condition, $60.00+. **Bottom:** some metal pitting, $20.00+.

"Cupping" glassware used for gorging blood away from afflicted areas of the body. **Left:** most recent style featuring bulb-squeeze as opposed to heat induced vacuum suction. As the practice of cupping was becoming obsolete near the end of the 1800s, these were marketed as beneficial for "facial" treatments performed by barbers. Value as seen with original rubber bulb intact, $45.00+. **Center:** ca. 1840 hand-blown cup with applied lip and ground pontil scar. Individually as seen, $50.00+. **Right:** ca. 1860 molded cups. Set of three as seen, $100.00+.

Blown-glass, pedestal, leach supply jar, ca. 1800-1830. 10.5" tall. New muslin and leather tie (as originals) to show how leeches were kept from crawling out of the container. As seen with small rim chip. $650.00+.

Tooth pulling instruments. **Top:** mid-1800s wooden-handled dental "key." $150.00+. **Bottom:** late-1800s ergonomically shaped dental tool for tooth removal. $25.00+.

Another unlikely service that barbers provided was tooth pulling. It was popular for them to do this through the middle ages and into the 1800s. By 1900, tooth pulling by barbers had become rare, and then mostly in rural areas. There is no historical evidence to suggest that barbers, at any point in time, rivaled dentists. Barbers were not known to repair or restore teeth. They just yanked them out! Drawings from the 1800s show that at least some barbers used the same pulling instruments as dentists. These dental instruments were generically available and were not marketed specifically to American barbers. We have, however, seen tooth-pulling instruments sold alongside of barbering equipment in a German catalog from the 1880s.

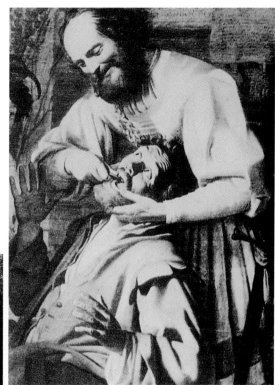

The barber-surgeon. Painting by Honshort. *Originally hung in The National Gallery, Brussels, Belgium.*

The Barber-Surgeon Dentist. Painting by Jan Steen. *Originally hung in the National Museum, Hague, Holland.*

Ancillary Services

Wig making was another service that barbers provided. As history clearly indicates, wig making dates back to ancient Egyptian times when plaited human hair pieces covered heads that were completely shaved. The longest period of wig popularity was from the mid-1600s until just after the turn of the nineteenth century. It was Louis XIV of France who rekindled the interest in wigs for men with his enormous powdered white hairpieces. Charles II of England who had been in exile in France, also began to wear powdered wigs during his stay there. When Charles finally returned to England, his wig was viewed as a statement of prestige by his countrymen. Perukes, or periwigs as they were also called, were soon being used by most of the English hierarchy. They were liberally sprinkled with baking flour to make them white. In fact, many homes of that period had a small closet just for powdering. That was the original of today's "powder room." Before long, barbers were making powdered wigs for gentlemen everywhere. This eventually included elite Americans. After the plague in England, there was concern that human hair wigs would fall from popularity. Many people feared that diseased hair would be removed from dead plague victims in order to make wigs. These concerns were put to rest and wigs continued to grow, not only in popularity, but in size too. By the beginning of the 18th century they covered the shoulders like a shawl and hung below the waist in the back. Conversely, by 1850 wigs had become much smaller. That was mainly for practical considerations such as how hot and cumbersome they had become. The newer and smaller wig styles were variations of the American Colonial peruke. Those powdered wigs used arrangements of curls and bows. Many had pigtails. This long time source of income to peruke making barbers ended rather quickly at the end of the 18th century. It was French philosopher Rousseau who protested that "the poor must go without bread because we must have powder for our hair." His voice as a French revolutionist was heard around the world. Before long, liberal sympathizers in both Europe and America had stopped wearing wigs as a matter of principle. This led to a new development. After nearly two and one half centuries of ornamental wigs, bald men at the beginning of the 19th century quickly discovered that they *still preferred* to have their pate covered one way or another. Toupees that were intended to replicate *only* the natural hairline became popular for bald men. About the same time, women's wigs and related "ornamental" hairpieces were all the rage. Men's toupees and women's ornamental hair demands launched a cottage industry that saw those products produced mainly by specialists. Barbers began referring their balding customers to the specialists much like today.

Illustration on the left shows large shawl-like wigs that covered the shoulders which were popular prior to 1850. Illustration on right shows example of post-1850 styles which were much more abbreviated and often gathered by fabric bows.

Example of oversized, powdered "periwig" popular in the 1700s.
Copper engraving by Phillip Killian.

18th century, colored, copper engraving by Debucourt entitled "Gentleman At His Toilet." Gentleman is seated in his "powder room" holding a bag in front of his face to guard against the powder which a servant is applying to his hair.

Finding wigs like we have described from colonial times or earlier is a nearly impossible feat. While museums may have a few disintegrating examples, they certainly are not collectible. The best remaining documentation of early wig makers is from the Victorian period and comes in the form of trade cards. We picture some here because of their relevance to the significant history of earlier wig making by barbers.

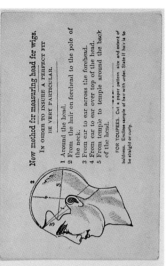

Trade/business cards of mid-to-late 1800s Victorian wig makers. Average value as seen, $20.00+.

By the time the Golden Years were approaching in the late 1800s, most of the above services that had been provided by barbers were already committed to history books. Advances in medicine, understanding of sanitation, and changing values in society all contributed to their demise. Barbers, who throughout history seemed to be entrepreneurial, were still looking for income from more than just haircuts and shaves. Many also lanced boils, dug out impacted ear wax, (with specially designed ear spoons) and removed blackheads. Others did nit-picking, (removal of lice and their eggs using special combs) provided eye rinses, and applied hangover treatments. More mainstream services provided in the Golden Years were as follows: in-grown hair removal; regular or steam facial treatments; manual or electric massage for the head, face, or shoulders; hair and mustache curling; nose and ear hair removal; hair and beard dyeing; shampooing; hair

singeing (hair burning with flaming candles); wig cleaning and dyeing; eyebrow arching; razor honing; and, a host of other "treatments" with lotions, potions, and tonics. Some of the more popular were egg shampoo, Florida water, Boncilla, sea foam, (dry shampoo) and hot oil. Electric violet-ray machines allegedly restored "health and vigor" to the hair giving hope to balding men. We will now take a look at some of the articles used in providing the above services.

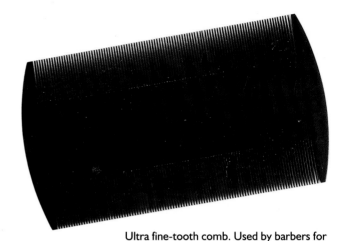

Ultra fine-tooth comb. Used by barbers for combing lice and their eggs (nits) from patron's hair. Secondary use was to comb ash residue from hair that had been singed (burned) by the barber. Hard rubber. 3.5" long. $10.00+.

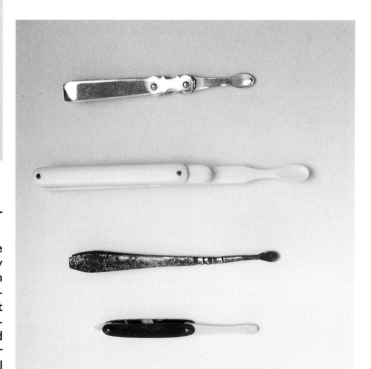

Ear spoons used by barbers to remove a patron's built-up earwax during the golden years. **From top to bottom.** Nickel plated combination ear spoon and tweezers from Koken barber supply, $20.00. Solid ivory folding ear spoon, $45.00+. Combination ear spoon and tweezers from Kochs barber supply, $20.00. European, Tortoise celluloid folding ear spoon, $35.00+.

Ancillary Services

1800s Victorian trade cards of hair and whisker dyes sold and applied by barbers. **Left:** Buckingham's "before and after" card. 3' x 4". $15.00+. **Right:** Hill's hair and whisker dye. 2.75" x 5". $20.00+.

Rare grouping of Murine eye wash barbershop promotion ca. 1910. Includes original advertising fold-out sent to barbershops, and both the applicator and refill bottles with mint paper labels. Group value as seen, $275.00+.

Trade card advertising Noonan's "Morning After Rub" applied by your barber. Shows barber at work and has related poem appearing on the reverse side of card. Said to be beneficial for headaches and/or tired feet. Barbers rubbed it on their hung-over patron's heads, and on their own sore feet. Unusual, 2" x 3.5" 1920s trade card. $35.00+.

When you wake on the gar-
ment-littered floor,
The morning after the night
before,
And see, no matter which way
you toss,
The grinning features of R E
Morse
And your dark, brown mouth
tastes just about
Like a Chinese family moving
out;
When you swear for a drink
you'd cut each vice,
And you find your pockets are
shy the price,
And the clink of the ice in the
pitcher tall
To your ear, is the sweetest
tune of all—
You're sobering up, by G——.
you're sobering up.

—MORNING AFTER RUB—

Barbershop "singeing-tapers" used for the service of burning patron's hair. This questionable practice was popular from between the 1890s and the 1930s. Noted barber school "professor" F.W. Creasy once said, "singeing the hair has been a custom among barbers for many years; but if he were to be asked why he did it, I doubt that there are many who could answer it, other than give some vague explanation." Average value for undamaged boxes with bright graphics and original taper-candle contents, $20.00+. Also pictured is a generic flame snuffer for extinguishing and freshening the wicks of taper-candles. $10.00+. Taper-candles in round lithographed tins are valued at $65.00+.

The Arnold Massage Vibrator patented in 1902. Wooden-handled example of dry-cell battery powered machine. (notice individual electric feed wires which got plugged into battery.) $75.00+.

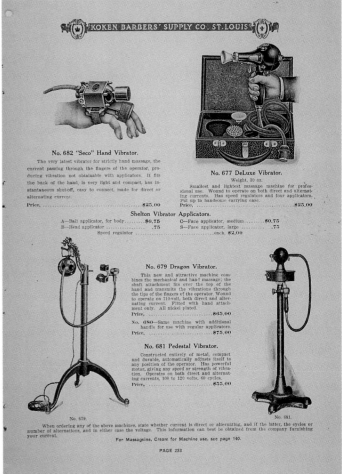

Barbershop hand-cranked neck and shoulder massagers. Hollow fruitwood bodies with eccentric-balanced gear mechanisms. Originally imported from Japan and seen in the USA during the early 1900s. Crank massagers remain rare when found intact and in working condition as seen. Each, $200.00+.

121

Ancillary Services

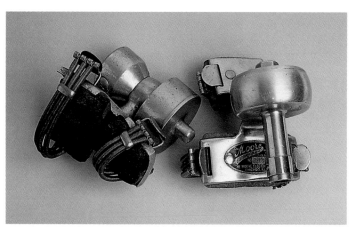

Examples of cable-driven, hand-held electric massagers. ca. 1910. Unusual when found with original foam-rubber hand padding and in operable condition. Model on the left made by the Race Company. Model on the right, Moore Company. Each, (without cable-drives) $60.00+.

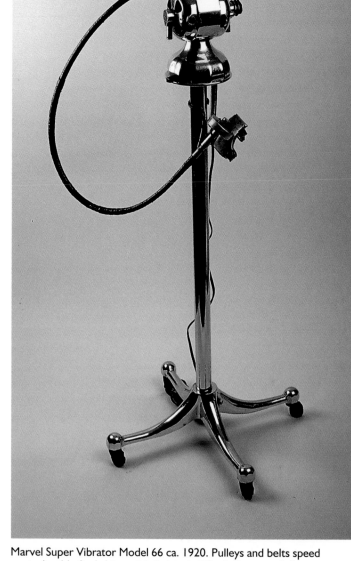

Marvel Super Vibrator Model 66 ca. 1920. Pulleys and belts speed control, cable final-drive, nickel plated, 44" tall. Runs good. As seen, $250.00+.

Electric vibrator made by the Shelton Company in 1906. Fabric-over-wood carrying case with burgundy pleated-silk lining. All attachments and original directions included. Works perfectly and appears unused. $75.00.

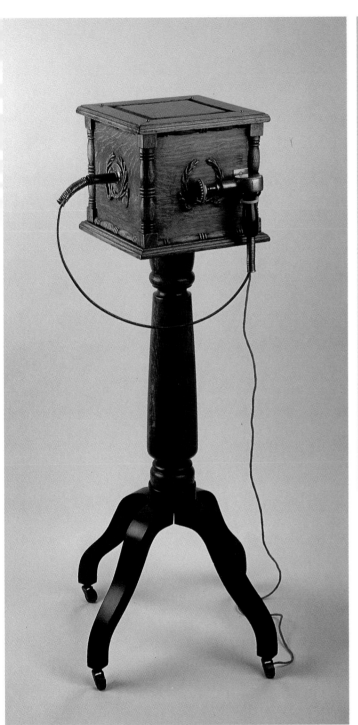

A.C. or D.C. electric barbershop vibrator in oak cabinet with carvings and Victorian influenced base design. Rolls on wooden castors. Massive motor and cable-drive works are dated 1895. Believed to be one of the first "pedestal" vibrators. Restored and running as-new. Rare in this presentation. $750.00+.

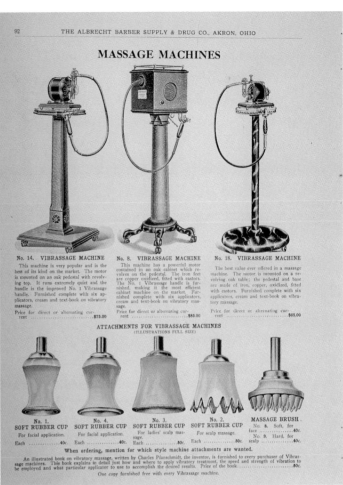

MASSAGE MACHINES

No. 14. VIBRASSAGE MACHINE
This machine is very popular and is the best of its kind on the market. The motor is mounted on an oak pedestal with revolving top. It runs extremely quiet and the handle is the improved No. 1 Vibrassage handle. Furnished complete with six applicators, cream and text-book on vibratory massage.
Price for direct or alternating current $75.00

No. 8. VIBRASSAGE MACHINE
This machine has a powerful motor contained in an oak cabinet which revolves on the pedestal. The iron feet are copper oxidized, fitted with castors. The No. 1 Vibrassage handle is furnished, making it the most efficient cabinet machine on the market. Furnished complete with six applicators, cream and text-book on vibratory massage.
Price for direct or alternating current $85.00

No. 18. VIBRASSAGE MACHINE
The best value ever offered in a massage machine. The motor is mounted on a revolving oak table; the pedestal and base are made of iron, copper, oxidized, fitted with castors. Furnished complete with six applicators, cream and text-book on vibratory massage.
Price for direct or alternating current $65.00

ATTACHMENTS FOR VIBRASSAGE MACHINES
(ILLUSTRATIONS FULL SIZE)

No. 1.
SOFT RUBBER CUP
For facial application.
Each .... 40c.

No. 4.
SOFT RUBBER CUP
For facial application.
Each .... 40c.

No. 3.
SOFT RUBBER CUP
For ladies' scalp massage.
Each .... 50c.

No. 2.
SOFT RUBBER CUP
For scalp massage.
Each .... 50c.

MASSAGE BRUSH
No. 8. Soft, for face .... 40c.
No. 9. Hard, for scalp .... 40c.

When ordering, mention for which style machine attachments are wanted.

An illustrated book on vibratory massage, written by Charles Planschmidt, the inventor, is furnished to every purchaser of Vibrassage machines. This book explains in detail just how and where to apply vibratory treatment, the speed and strength of vibration to be employed and what particular applicator to use to accomplish the desired results. Price of the book .... 50c.
One copy furnished free with every Vibrassage machine.

Wahl "Hand-E" model electric vibrator. Early 1930s. Inset photo shows barber demonstrating machine. Complete with all attachments and instructions. Unused condition. Runs perfectly. $50.00+.

Ancillary Services

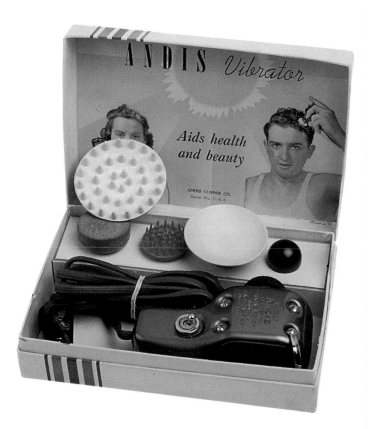

Andis electric vibrator as seen in Kochs barber supply catalogs. Late 1930s. Complete with all attachments and instructions. Unused condition. Runs perfectly. $40.00+.

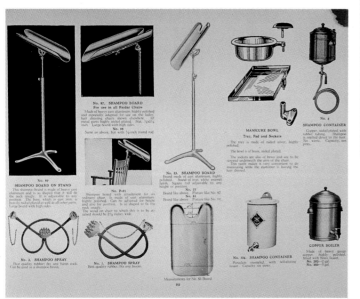

1925 Paidar barber supply catalog page showing various shampoo articles including shampoo boards which allowed more comfort. With "boards," the customer could remain seated and reclined in the barber chair. This position not only spared him the inconvenience of moving, but it allowed his face to stay dry through the shampoo process. The soapy water ran down the aluminum tray and into the sink. Value on shampoo boards: $75.00 to $125.00+ depending on condition.

Example of a "twisted-wire" shampoo stool as seen in most barbershop catalogs from the 1890s until the 1920s. They averaged 22" in height to be used with lavatory sinks that averaged 35" high. Shampoo stools were necessary before shampoo boards or neck-scalloped sinks were available to recline the patron *rearward*. Originally, the patron sat on a shampoo stool and leaned *forward* into the sink. Examples before 1920 were copper-oxidized finished with a leather seat as seen here. After 1920, many were nickel plated and had synthetic seat coverings. As seen, $50.00+.

While barber suppliers all had house-brands of shampoo soaps available, Packers Tar Soap was a favorite of many barbers. It came self-contained in a lithograph decorated tin and early advertising touted it as "an astonishing remedy for baldness, dandruff, and diseases of the scalp." **Soap:** for one tin with contents and bright lithograph intact, $15.00+. **Trade card:** as seen here, $22.00+.

Cremex brand shampoo "vaše" ca. 1920s. Cobalt blue and curved at the neck. Has finger grooves for better control with soapy hands. Rare presentation of a shampoo barber bottle. $225.00+.

Wildroot produced a very popular shampoo soap for decades. "Taroleum" was a favorite of many barbers and was produced by mixing crude oil, pine tar, and soap. **From left to right:** pre 1920 clear bottle with Wildroot Taroleum in raised glass and Wildroot embossed bottle-tube, $35.00+. Painted label stand bottles like these were popular for about 30 years from the 1930s on. $30.00+. Opaline glass bottle with hand painted "Crude Oil" which was barbers slang for Wildroot Taroleum Shampoo. ca.1925. Rare in this presentation, $150.00+.

Ancillary Services

Shampoo brushes as seen offered in barber supply catalogs in the late 1800s. Both have very stiff natural bristles and are set in ivory. 7" long. Each, $35.00+.

Hand carved bamboo shampoo "combs." Barbershop catalogs offered these items from the late 1800s into the 1920s. They were all approximately 2" in diameter but were made in different comb lengths to accommodate different hair thicknesses. Individually, $45.00+.

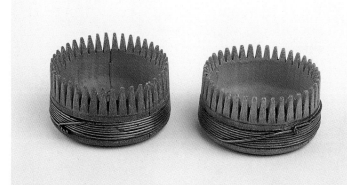

Rarely found matched set of bamboo shampoo combs. Copper bound to prevent splitting which was common from repeated wetting and drying. 2" diameter. The pair as seen, $125.00+.

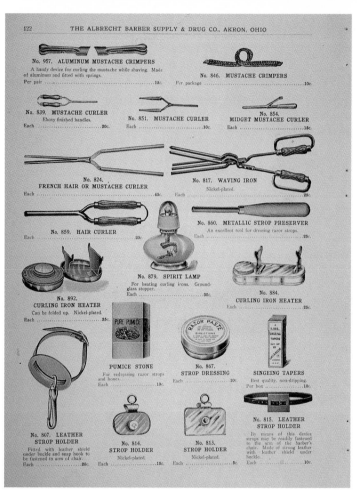

1910 Allbrecht catalog page showing a variety of curling iron heaters and mustache curlers and crimpers.

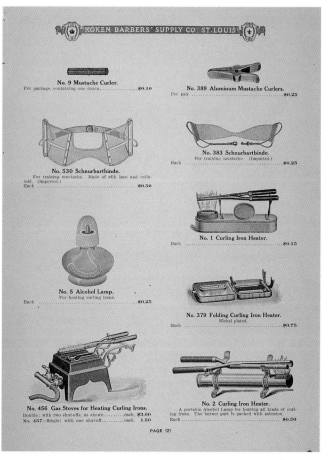

1910 Koken catalog page showing variety of curling iron heaters and mustache training devices.

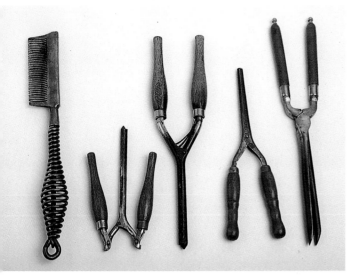

Curling iron variety. **From left to right:** copper pressing iron used for helping to straighten kinky hair, $20.00+. Folding, wooden handle iron, $15.00+. Large wooden handle iron, $12.00+. Small wooden handle iron, $10.00+. Professional model iron with burl-wood handles and brass fittings. The wooden heat guards spun on the metal frames allowing the barber to more efficiently work with the iron. $25.00+.

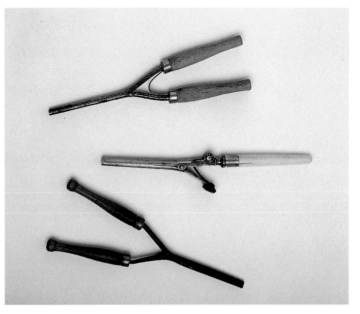

Mustache curling iron variety. **From top to bottom:** early, oak handles with center spring, $15.00+. Ivory handled, $50.00+. Oak handled model shows heavy wear with wood scorching and metal pitting, $8.00+.

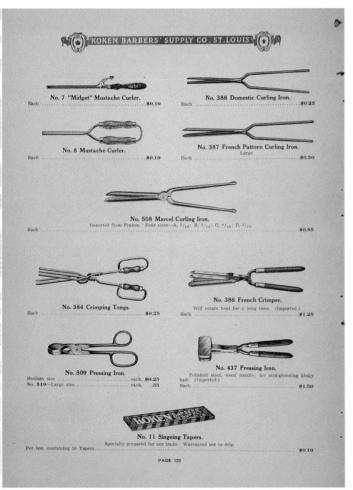

Koken catalog page with curling and pressing iron varieties.

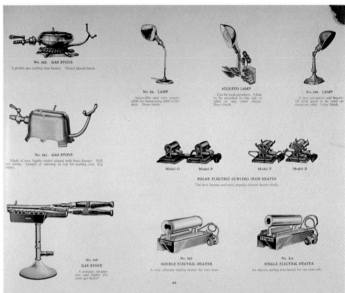

1925 Paidar catalog page showing a variety of curling iron heaters.

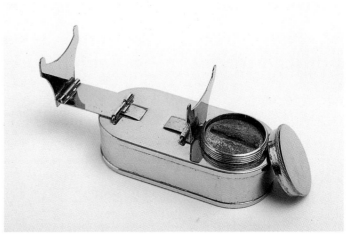

Alcohol burning curling iron heater ca. 1900. Heavy nickel plating over brass. Mint unused condition. $50.00+.

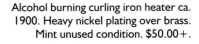

Ancillary Services

Gas-fired curling irons ca. 1890s-1910. Nickel plated steel bodies, copper burners, and brass petcocks. **Left:** figural turtle design. Rarely found with all of the original nickel plating intact because of extreme heat during use. As seen, $75.00. **Right:** Standard design gas heater with nickel plating found in unused condition. As seen, $60.00. *Note that this particular model is currently being reproduced in aluminum.*

Generic brilliantine bottles ranging from the 1890s to 1930s. **From left to right:** Cut glass, 4.5" tall, $60.00. Williams brand, 3.5" tall, $25.00. Rear, basket weave as seen in *Barber Bottles by R. Holiner, p.91.* 5.5" tall. $125.00+. Front, Tip Top brand with original contents, 3.5" tall **$25.00.** Pale amber glass, 3.75" tall. $45.00+. Blown glass, cracked-ice style, 5.25" tall, $150.00+.

Electric curling irons. **Top:** Oster brand heater as seen in various barber catalogs in the 1920s and 30s. Aluminum tube housing accepted irons in either end. On-off switch in cord. Works. As seen, $35.00+. **Bottom:** Wooden handled electric iron by General Electric. Originally supplied with two-prong plug or screw-in-socket type. Works. As seen, $20.00.

Brilliantine Bottles. These art-glass bottles were made specifically to dispense brilliantine, which was a petroleum based liquid intended to impart sheen to hair. They were so small (rarely over 5" tall) because brilliantine was dispensed in drops, not squirts. A little bit went a long way. Although there were large numbers of generic brilliantine containers made, the hand painted bottles seen here were sold only through barber supply catalogs and often matched other art-glass barber bottles. Brilliantine bottles are rare when compared to full-sized refillable barber bottles but remain a relative bargain in the $150.00 to $225.00+ range depending on condition and decoration. *Those seen here are courtesy of Tony Gugliotti.*

Hand decorated art-glass style pomade jars. These sat on barber's backbars and were made to be refilled with pomade which was a favorite hair "slicker" similar to Vaseline. Lids were usually brass or aluminum. Each, $75.00+. *Courtesy of Tony Gugliotti.*

China pomade dish originally from Dublin Ireland. Pre 1900. 4" wide by .75" deep. $35.00+.

Art-glass, refillable pomade container. Hand decorated green glass. $75.00.

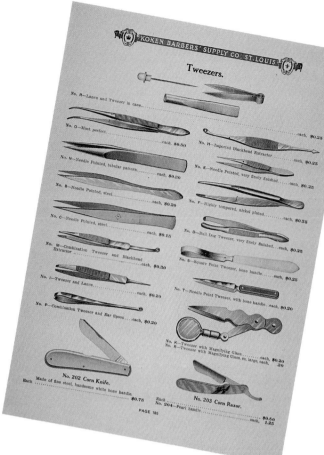

Assorted tweezers, diggers, and poppers as seen on pages from the 1910 Koken, and the 1910 Allbrecht catalogs. Barbers used these instruments for a number of services including lancing boils, removing blackheads, removing in-grown hairs, tweezing ear hair, and facial treatments.

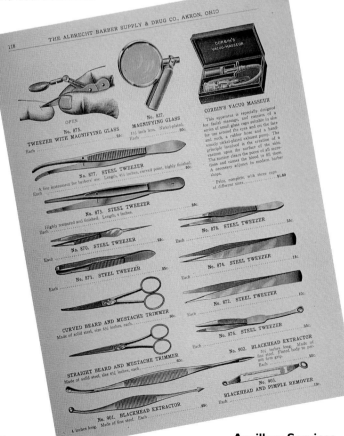

Ancillary Services

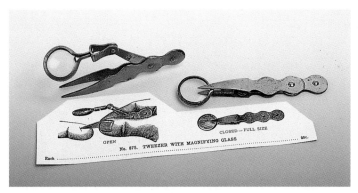

Unique tweezers allowed magnified inspection of the target. Nickel plated and folds to protect the glass when not in use. In condition as seen with no rusting, $20.00+.

Backbar sized containers of cold cream used for facial treatments. **From left to right:** tin-lithograph of Lilly's brand ca. 1920s, with contents, $25.00+. Clear glass Jeris brand. Lithograph lid with contents, $20.00+. Milk glass container, Daggett and Ramsdell brand with contents, $15.00+.

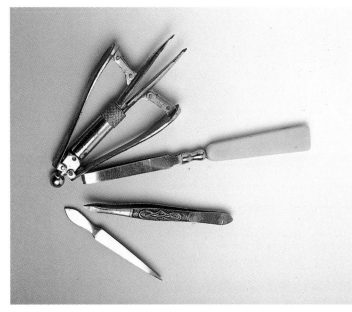

Assorted instruments. **From top to bottom:** marketed to barbers by the Segal Company as a "nose and ear hair puller." By squeezing the sides, the tweezers would snap back which supposedly was a better way of hair removal. $20.00+. Ivory celluloid handled, flat-nose tweezers, $8.00. Fancy design pincer tweezers as seen in the 1891 Koken barber catalog, $15.00+. Ordinary pincer tweezers as seen in various barbershop catalogs, $5.00.

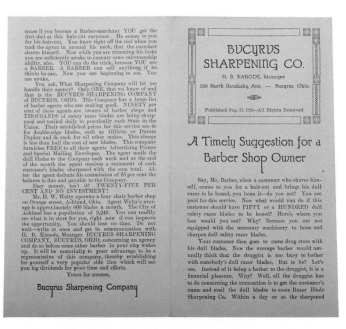

Another service that barbers supplied was the sharpening of customers safety razor blades. Barbers concluded that if customers were going to shave at home anyway, then it would help recoup income if they could encourage the customer to bring in his dull razor blades to be sharpened. After all, barbers had been charging customers to hone their straight razors for years. The pamphlet seen here is an original offer from the Bucyrus Company offering the barbers to become middlemen in a safety blade sharpening scheme. Interesting reading and good collectible paper. $25.00+.

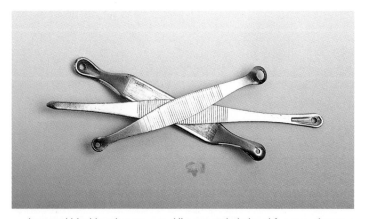

Assorted blackhead removers. All were nickel plated for easy cleaning and sterilizing. It is sometimes difficult to determine age with these instruments because there was hardly any change in their manufacturing designs throughout barbering's golden years. Average $2.00 to $3.00+ each.

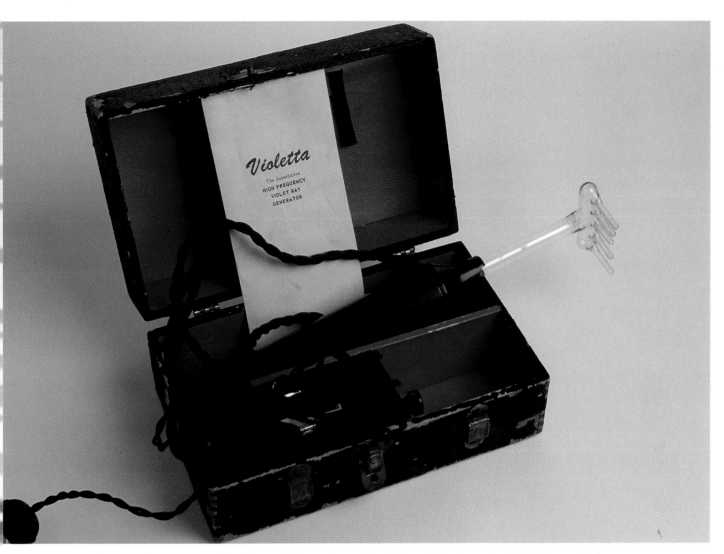

Violetta brand, violet-ray machine. Electrical device that used sealed, wand-like glass tubes filled with gas. When started, they had an eerie purple glow that appeared in the glass tube. When contacting the skin or hair, a spark would leap from the tip of the glass. Their main use in the barbershop was for the prevention of "falling" hair. Some manufacturer's claims guaranteed "new" hair with regular use. Their benefit remains dubious, *at best*, and they are usually sold under the "quack medicine" category. Many barber supply catalogs offered violet-ray machines during the height of their popularity from the teens into the 1930s. $60.00 to $125.00+ if operable and complete including "comb" attachment.

The hair, naturally parting in the middle and falling on either side, indicates womanly refinement, purity, and delicacy. When the hair extends and lies on the forehead in rings, it indicates a frank, open, and genial nature. The light-haired races are the thinkers, the poets, and the artists of the world.
Dark brown hair combines the two and the most desirable.
To sum up:
Black hair indicates physical strength.
White hair, mental vigor.
Red hair, a fiery temperment, passion, and devotion.
Wavy hair, a pliable, yielding, accommodating disposition.
Straight, stuck up hair, stubbornness and fidelity.
Very smooth, coarse-lying hair is "Oily Gammon." -Bridgeford's Revised Edition, 1904

Ancillary Services

Chapter 5
Amenities

There were a number of things that keep the old-time barbershop experience so well remembered. It wasn't *just* the barber's standard services. Golden year's advertising and written articles tell us of certain amenities that were, often times, just as important to the experience as the hair removal process itself. After reviewing this chapter, it should become clear why plenty of fellows were content to "while away time" at the barbershop.

Cigar Advertising

One of the first subjects to come to mind was the widespread availability of cigars and other tobacco products in barbershops. Tobacco was much more accepted from a societal standpoint than it is today. A good cigar was synonymous with a "shave and a haircut." Photographs from the Golden Years clearly indicate that barbers had a wide range of 5 cent stogies available. So prevalent was this practice, that barber supply catalogs sold a selection of cigar display cases for decades. Barbers were even known to occasionally offer a free cigar in hopes of increasing business by luring a customer from the competition. Very often, shops that sold cigars had colorful signs or other advertising that hung from the ceilings and walls. These advertising pieces are highly collectible themselves and are usually found at advertising or country store antique shows. This is not to suggest that cigar signs were intended solely for barbershops. They were quite generic and may have been seen anywhere. They were important to barbershop history simply because cigars and related advertising were seen in so many shops. Cigar and tobacco advertising signs usually have bright graphics and they can make an attractive, authentic addition to your barbershop display.

Spittoons and Cuspidors

Chewing tobacco and ground tobacco were also sold in many shops. The users of these products had an especially favored barbershop amenity. *The spittoon!* Barbershop patrons were encouraged to "have a chew" and they were put at ease by the convenient placement of cuspidors or spittoons. Their need to spit tobacco juice inside of the shop was always graciously accommodated. The difference between spittoons and cuspidors sometimes seemed to be a matter of semantics. Some barber supply catalogs referred to both types as cuspidors. Some others referred to both types as spittoons. However, in most catalogs, the tall, pinched-waist, one-piece designs were usually marketed as cuspidors. The low, two-piece, models were usually called spittoons. Whatever you choose to call them, they were produced in unlimited styles and materials and they stand in a collectible category of their own. The most popular cuspidors or spittoons that were actually used in barbershops during the early Golden Years were tall brass, self-righting types. In the mid-to-late Golden Years, wood fiber and white porcelain models were favored. Durable, practical, and easily cleaned seemed to be the main criteria for a good barbershop spittoon. One-piece pottery spittoons were not often seen in barbershops because they didn't come apart for thorough cleaning. They also broke easily if accidentally kicked. Some of the fine hotel shops (where presentation was more important than practicality) did use gold decorated china cuspidors. Incidentally, it wasn't only men who chewed and spit. Plenty of women used ground tobacco products. It is just that they would spit more discreetly. "Proper" ladies used spitting cups that were miniature versions of their full sized spittoon counterparts. They were tiny enough to be carried with personal belongings. Ladies "cups" were the perfect alternative to the socially unacceptable public spitting by a women.

Top: Tin-lithograph cigar sign. 8" x 14". As seen with small bare spot on lower-left, $125.00+. **Bottom:** Enameled red, white, and blue "door-push" sign. 3" x 14". Unused as seen, $45.00+.

Variety of heavy cardboard, hanging cigar signs. **From left to right:** "Hambone", 7.25" diameter, $45.00+. Herco Cigars, 4" x 7", $10.00+. Canadian Club, 7.25" diameter, $10.00+. *Note: the recent wave of cigar's popularity has seen some early advertising signs become reproduced. Check closely and ask the dealer.*

Opposite page: Black and white photo ca. 1915. This candid pose by the barbers and their cronies reveal tobacco products (mostly cigars) being enjoyed by seven out of eight of them. 5" x 7" photograph, $20.00.

Representative sampling of "cuspidors" as seen in an early Koken catalog. Notice the absence of china or pottery materials when marketed to barbers.

133

Amenities

There are plenty of reproduction cuspidors and spittoons out there. Often times, not even the dealer is aware that they are offering a fake. Reproductions are almost always made with very thin brass. Your first tip should be how light they are. A real one is moderate to very heavy for its size. The genuine article always has some evident wear and considerable oxidizing *inside*. Real cuspidors also have weighted bottoms that cause them to upright automatically if tipped over. Some reproductions have a piece of lead weight in the bottom but are slow to right themselves, if at all. Many reproductions have embossed letters that say things like "5 cent cigar," "Redskin Chewing Tobacco," "Santa Fe Railroad," etc. The best of these reproductions are actually very nicely done and are quite functional. While they may suit your display tastes, they have no appreciable value. Remember, if it looks *too* good to be old, it probably isn't. Many dealers charge nearly as much for reproductions as an original is worth. It would pay to spend a few more dollars and have the real thing.

Prices for brass cuspidors or spittoons are influenced primarily by condition. When found, many are dented and nicked due to the relative softness of the metal. Some collectors who find an excellent example have it polished and lacquered for lasting no-maintenance beauty. This can add nearly $50.00 to the purchase price. Examples seen here are in excellent condition (very minor wear) and have not been lacquered. **From left to right:** 1880+. Tall, pinched-waist, brass design. Self-righting. 12" high. $75.00+. Low, heavy brass, two-piece design. 1900+. 4.5" x 9". $45.00+. Unusual hammered-copper design. 1870+. 9" x 9". $100.00+.

From left to right: 1930s+. Porcelain-over-tin, one-piece design. 5" x 8". $15.00+. Porcelain-over-tin, two-piece design. 1920s+. 4" x 9". $20.00.

Three types of cuspidor material, other then brass, that were used by barbershops. **From left to right:** 1890+. Wood-fiber, two-piece model. 5" x 10". $35.00+. China (sometimes seen in swank hotels) model from the Ben Franklin Hotel in Philadelphia. Has dull-gold hand decorations which date it to pre-1891. 4.5" x 7". Appears unused, $150.00+. Cast iron with porcelain lip liner. 1890+. 5.5" x 8". Some small rim chips. $20.00+.

Baths

During the early portion of the Golden Years, from the 1880s until about 1920, baths were available in many barbershops. This amenity was a source of welcome comfort to many travelers. Horse drawn or rail transportation was typical in those times and both were *very* dusty. The absence of paved roads and air conditioning highlighted that problem. Other folks appreciated public baths because good plumbing and fixtures had not yet become a standard convenience in all private homes. Of the barbershops that did offer baths, most were located near transient areas, like the town rail station or stagecoach stop. Sometimes these same shops, especially if located in a hotel, also offered clothes laundry and pressing services. It is interesting to note that the barber supply catalogs from the last two decades of the 1800s show a wide variety of bathtubs, body brushes, signs, bathing soap, and other accessories. By the 1920s, some of the same companies offered no bathing or related equipment *at all*. This fact parallels societies progress, in general, with regard to plumbing conveniences after the turn of the 20th century.

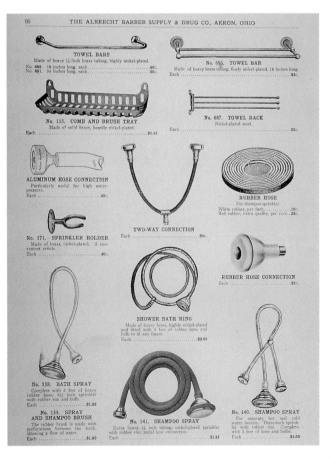

Galvanized tin bath tub ca. 1900. Upright seating position *just* holds a man for a limited bath. *Courtesy of Bill and Marlene Levin.* $125.00+.

Examples of barbershop bathing supplies from an early 1900s Allbrecht catalog.

Opposite page, bottom right: Example of a modern reproduction display piece. 9.5" x 11". $20.00. If, as seen here, with professional polishing and lacquer coating, $70.00.

Amenities

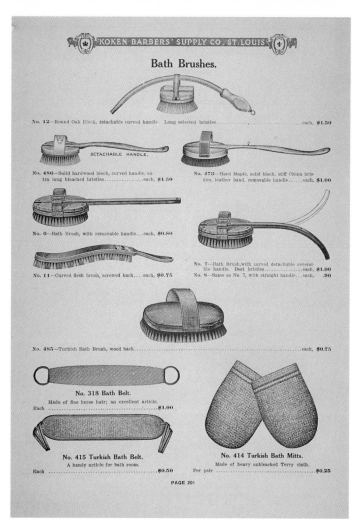

Barbershop bathing-brush assortment as seen in an early 1900s Koken catalog.

Reading Material

The waiting room reading material in most barbershops was so much of an attraction, that plenty of men were actually quite content to wait their turn to be "next." We need to remember that life had a much slower pace during the Golden Years and few people were in the big hurry that we all seem to be in today. The most popular periodicals seen in barbershops back then were the *Police Gazette* and various barbershop "journals." Many editions featured a pretty girl on the cover. The inside pages carried a corresponding article about her. These cover photos were considered risqué for the times and plenty of barbers put them up and out of reach so "little Jimmy" couldn't see them. Coverage of the big sporting news was assured and there were short stories written specifically to appeal to men. Detective stories seemed to be a particular fascination. Most of the magazines had a full page of jokes along with plenty of advertising that pitched masculine targeted products such as: shoe cleats, whiskey "still" recipes, police whistles and keys, exotic girlie "art," rupture trusses, poker "tricks and schemes," etcetera. Often times, a customer who was to be next in the barber chair passed on the opportunity so he could finish reading the latest issue of the *Police Gazette*.

Representative copies of *The International Police Gazette* which was undoubtedly the most popular barbershop reading material during the golden years. The examples seen here are the early, large (11" x 15.5") format. In later years they became smaller. **Left:** December 20, 1910 issue featuring Dorothy Dalton and inside story on Middleweight boxers from Mike Donovan to Mike O'Dowd. Complete magazine in excellent condition, $40.00+. **Right:** June 6, 1925 issue with "a modern stage beauty who brings up visions of the lovely Cleopatra." The inside story is titled "The Real John L. Sullivan." $35.00+.

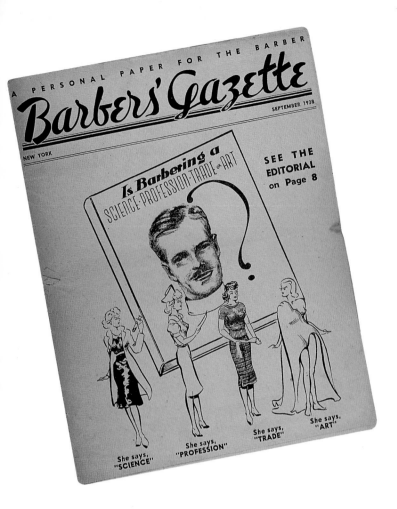

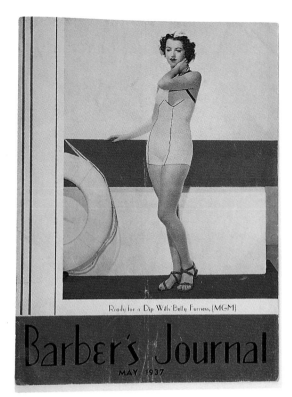

The most popular barbershop periodical to compete with the *Police Gazette* in the late golden years was the *Barbers Journal*. It was larger than other barbers journals at 9" x 12" and was far more comprehensive with an average of 40 pages. Front covers always featured a movie star such as MGM's Betty Furness seen here. Inside stories and ads were masculine slanted. If found complete and in good condition, $30.00+.

Copy of September 1938 *Barbers' Gazette*. This periodical was supposedly for barbershop entertainment but it was actually a thinly-veiled, manufacturer and jobber's advertising book. It had cover material that was masculine in nature and some jokes with barbers' "inside" information. It was rarely more than 8 pages in an 8" x 11" format. Scarce because of extremely poor quality paper that quickly crumbled with age. As seen, $45.00+.

F. W. Fitch's "house" periodical for barbershops. *The Square Deal* magazine was a very slick propaganda vehicle not only for the Fitch line of hair-care products, but for Mr. Fitch's personal philosophy such as changing the barber's title to "Dermatician." It was also loaded with anecdotal and masculine appealing articles. Distribution was mainly in the 1920s and it had a 7" x 10" format. Scarce. $35.00+.

Amenities

Porter Service

This amenity wasn't available in all barbershops, but it was very popular in metropolitan areas and was nearly always found in better hotels. Porters had a real function in a busy shop and were appreciated by all. By job description, they had a number of responsibilities. An average day at work for a porter went something like this: upon arrival at the barbershop, he would first see that the gas-fired towel steamers got lit so they were heated by the time customers arrived. He then made sure that each barber's station was supplied with all the daily essentials including clean capes and towels. The sidewalk in front of the shop had to be swept and the front door and window glass was cleaned when there was time. When a customer was finished and had climbed from the barber chair, the porter would offer to brush off all loose hair using a whisk. If the customer arrived wearing a hat and coat, the porter would use soft brushes to take the dust off of them too. When the freshly cut hair began to accumulate at the barbers feet, the porter would get it swept up. All brass and nickel surfaces were to be polished as time permitted but looking glasses got polished daily. That was necessary for the prevention of nicotine build-up resulting from heavy tobacco use. The bathroom needed to be kept tidy and fresh. Ashtrays were emptied regularly and spittoons were emptied and rinsed before leaving for the evening. All through the day, and in between these other duties, the porter was expected to chat with the customers in a patronizing way. Conversation subjects for porters were similar to those of barbers including the weather, sports, family, or the stock market. The hallmark of a good porter was to insure that every customer left the barbershop feeling special. Sort of like today's concierge. Occupational porters were not to be confused with the "boot-black" man. There may have been crossover duties in some cases, but porters were salaried employees as opposed to the shoe and boot polishers who worked on commission. Porters were often considered as business confidants by "boss" barbers who relied on their congeniality to please customers. Barber supply catalogs all had a variety of porters supplies and accessories throughout the Golden Years.

This early engraving is considered to be the best example of a porter's presence in an "upper-crust" barbershop. It appeared in *The Graphic Periodical* on April 16, 1870 and was from Phalon's Barber Saloon in New York city which was the forerunner of grand hotel barbershops during the golden years. The following is an excerpt from the accompanying story and is copied verbatim. *"You pass into the hands of an attendant, who forthwith commences, with surprising zeal, to whisk his little clothes-brush rapidly over your coat and trousers-which done, in a twinkling he seizes your hat and rubs it up till it assumes a mirror-like polish. The attendant who performs this is a squat, burly, self-consequent darkey, whose short jacket and too limited trousers, and endeavors to reach the shoulder of the gaunt customer for the moment under his care, give him an appearance amusing enough. He is doubtless, too, a loquacious body, indulging in very sage prognostications of the weather, and even-if you show a disposition to listen to his talk-entertaining you with his views on the political prospects and the "state of gold."* Engraving is 11" x 14". Excellent condition, $75.00+ unframed.

Pages from the 1910 Koken catalog
showing various porter's supplies.

Assorted brushes used by Porters including clothes brushes and
whisks. Also appearing are curved-back brushes that appear like dining
table crumb-sweepers but are proportionately larger and are
described in barber catalogs as Derby hat brushes. Whisks and clothes
brushes are common flea market items at less than $5.00. Derby hat
brushes are few and far between and are valued at $20.00+.

Porter's cap as advertised in numerous barber supply catalogs. As
seen, $75.00+.

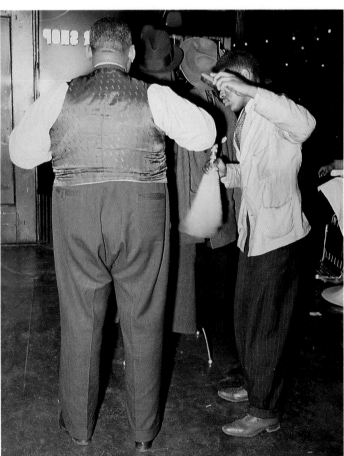

Black and white copied photo from 1941 shows porter at work in a
barbershop on the Southside of Chicago. 8" x 10". *Courtesy of the
Library of Congress.* $35.00+.

Amenities

Shoeshines

Far more barbershops had a "boot-black" than a porter. This fact had a direct link to the cultural situation of the employing shop. While shops with porters were normally serving the more upscale patron of the times, getting a "shine" was a desirable amenity in *any* barbershop. The demand for the service was bolstered by the fact that there were no canvas sneakers during the Golden Years. *Everybody wore leather footwear!* The main function of the barbershop's shoeshine man was obvious. They provided a unique opportunity for a fellow to accomplish three things while waiting for his haircut and shave: enjoy a cigar, peruse some spicy reading material, and get his boots polished simultaneously. A good shine-man was often busy even if the barbers were not. It was common for men to just drop in for his services. Photographs suggest that occasionally the shoe-shine man would do some other menial tasks around the barbershop. This would have been logical if he wasn't busy and if there wasn't a salaried porter employed. However, their main interest was to stay busy by providing shoe and boot care for commissions and tips. In today's world, with the relatively low earning capacity from shining shoes, (which again, is influenced by *many* millions of sneaker wearers) very few people get involved in providing this service. During the less pretentious Golden Years, many fellows proudly made careers out of this work. Shoe-shine men certainly added one more dimension to the Golden Years barbershop experience.

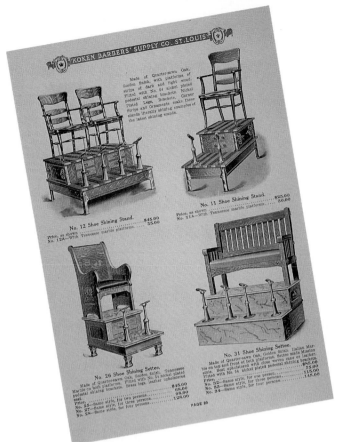

Cardboard, barbershop window sign. 7" x 11". Light-reflective paint. Unused. $35.00+.

Koken catalog pages show a wide variety of shoe-shine equipment that was available at the beginning of the 1900s.

Portable stand with "V-point" could be used to shines patron's shoes while they were seated in the barber chair. Models that were made prior to 1925 were usually black or copper-oxidized. As seen, $125.00+.

Manicuring

During the early portion of the Golden Years in the late 1800s, barbershop manicuring was a luxury reserved for the well-to-do class. As time passed, the service became more desired by routine business and professional men. We're not suggesting that every backwater town in the country had barbershops with a manicurist on staff. The service was found only in the better shops. By the mid-1920s, it had become a very popular amenity that was available in many shops having a white collar clientele. The manicurists were always female and the barbers made no bones about hiring the best looking women they could find. This was often as much of a lure as the barbers' "artistry." There are a number of sketches from the 1920s and 30s that portray a customer getting a haircut, smoking a cigar, and having a manicure. It seemed to be the ultimate "big-shot" perk of those times. The girls were able to work on the customers anywhere in the shop since the manicure tables were rolled around on castors. Many customers wanted to read and get a shine while they were waiting for an open barber chair. That kept their hands tied up, so some men had their manicure done while they sat in the barber chair being shaved or trimmed. In this instance, the manicurists had strict orders from the barbers to *never* be in the way. It was also understood that they should time the manicure in a way that it would be completed *before* the barber got done. The barbers didn't want anything to keep them from calling "who's next please" just as soon as possible.

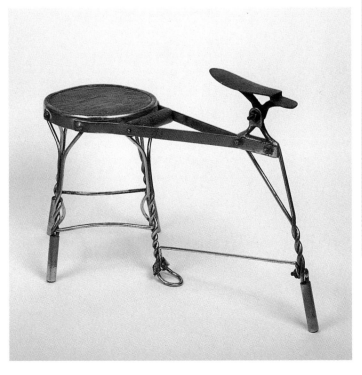

Portable shine stand in twisted-wire presentation. This example has had a complete professional restoration to like-new condition and includes the original accompanying "boot-black's" stool. As seen, $750.00+. Unrestored examples (without accompanying stool) can be found in the $350.00 range in fair condition. Rust and pitting are the big factors with this metal framed furniture.

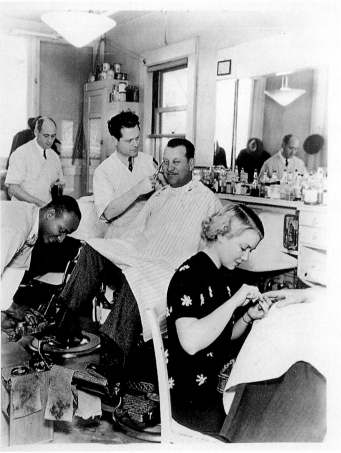

The ultimate barbershop "perk" of the 1920s and 30s. Haircut, shoe-shine, *and a manicure!* 8" x 10" black and white copied photo from late 1930s. *Courtesy of Cleveland State University Libraries.* $50.00+.

Portable shine stand with "V-point" and plated with nickel which dates it to after 1925. With some plating missing as seen, $75.00+.

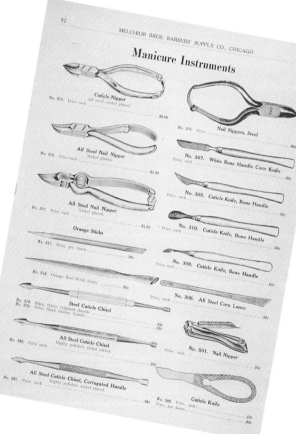

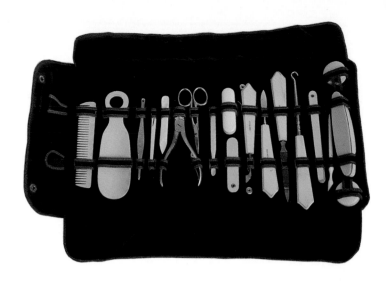

Purple, velvet-lined "roll-up" manicuring kit from the early 1900s. This high quality set is complete and appears to have never been used. As seen, $60.00+.

THE MANICURIST

She is "a clip," and 'tis her plan
To flatter every silly man;
  Her manner's bland,
  She holds his hand
And "trims him" every time she can!

COPYRIGHT, 1905 BY R. HILL

Postcard dated 1907 is titled "The Manicurist" and has a poem that seems appropriate. Excellent condition card, $15.00+.

Catalog pages from the Koken and Melchoir Companies show a variety of manicure equipment that was available to barbershops before 1910.

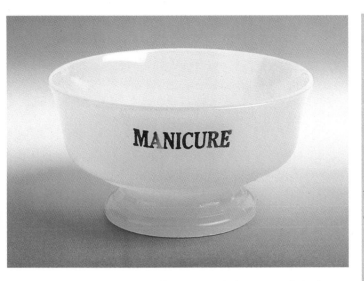

Opaline-glass manicure bowl. Made to match the same style barber bottles which were popular in the post-1920 era. Stenciled letters. As seen, $20.00+.

Catalog page from the Koken barber supply in 1910 showing manicure bowls, mini-tables, and attachments to hook directly to *wooden* barber chairs.

Examples of portable manicure tables to be used in the waiting area or at the barber chair. Some had a light source, others did not. Purpose-built manicure tables that were offered in barbers catalogs had the manufacturers badge on the front or rear. **Left:** Kochs brand, lighted wooden table. Small size, 29" high, 23" wide. 1930s. In excellent condition and with sterilizer decal intact, $75.00+. **Right:** Paidar brand, unlit walnut table. Large size, 30" high, 32" wide. 1930s. In excellent condition and with sterilizer decal intact, $100.00+. The manicure sign appearing on this table is foil-under-glass and measures 4.5" x 12". Dated 1936. In unused condition, $45.00+.

Amenities

Chapter 6
The Supply Closet and Textiles

In chapter one, we learned how barbershop essentials became plentiful in the early Golden Years, and also, how easy it would have been to stock a good supply of them. Catalogs had the goods and improved delivery services brought them to your door. Another development that helped to insure well stocked supply closets was traveling salesmen. Many large barber supply companies utilized a mobile sales force once the newly invented automobile became available. Traveling salesmen could easily carry a representative sampling of the company's goods right in their cars. They had fairly large territories and postcards were mailed to the barbers in advance which announced what day and time the salesman would arrive. The Koken company's post cards showed actual pictures of the particular salesman that would be calling.

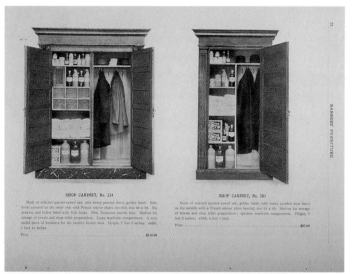

Barbershop supply cabinets as seen in an Albrecht catalog from 1911. If found in good condition with an original Albrecht logo intact, either of these oak cabinets would be valued at $1,200.00 to $1,500.00+.

Top right and bottom right: Front-side views of actual postcards mailed by the Koken Barbers' Supply Company to announce the arrival of their traveling salesmen. **Left:** Koken "hustler" James Pairo's actual photograph is seen as the driver of an artist-drawn automobile. Mailed on April 28, 1908, he indicates that he'll be calling on the First National Bank Barbershop during the week of July 10, 1908. Rare. $50.00+. **Right:** This postcard shows all 14 of the Northern Ohio regional "trade makers" for the Koken Company. Number 5, Don Williams indicates he'll be visiting Hendershot's Barbershop in Toledo on July 20, 1908. Rare. $50.00+.

When a barber ordered a razor, clipper, or scissors from a catalog, he knew pretty much what to expect without seeing it in advance. On the other hand, with an artist decorated mug, art glass backbar bottle, or electric massager, nothing could have been better than to have somebody actually demonstrating the real thing. This was especially true with barbershop textiles which are fabric-based and begged to be touched in order to experience the quality or softness. During all but the very end of the Golden Years, barbershop shaving was a huge part of the business and because of that, natural fiber towels were purchased in large quantities. Barbers wanted the most durable and comfortable fabrics for their patrons. Seeing the product in advance was the preferred method of selecting their towels. Traveling salesmen were also responsible for widely expanding the demand of stylish wearing apparel for barbers. Nothing was more effective in making sales then allowing a barber to try on a coat or vest he admired. After all, there was a large mirror already in place and the salesman's sample *always* looked better then what the barber was wearing before the fitting. Is it any wonder that supply company salesmen kept the barber's closets so well stocked?

Bulk supply containers took plenty of closet space and they held a variety of products. The most prevalent were large tins or glass bottles containing tonics. Smaller, backbar sized bottles were refilled from them. Also taking their share of room were bulk towels, cartons of paper headrest rolls, boxes of Sanek or similar type neck strips, packages of soap cakes, and large soap powder cans which were used to refill backbar-sized dispensers.

While textiles and bulk supplies were seen in virtually every Golden Years barbershop, few of the original containers still exist *at any price*. It would be nice if there was better availability of those items because many are colorful and interesting. All would make a nice addition to an old-time barbershop display. The reason they are so scarce is an inherent problem: fabrics were made with cotton, linen, or similar material. As you might expect, they were used until they were worn out. At that point, barbers threw them away and bought a new supply. Worn out is worn out! They simply weren't thought of as things to keep. Similarly, metal and glass bulk containers, along with cardboard boxes, were discarded when empty. Why keep them? There are a number of collectibles in today's market that are considered "ephemera." Simply stated, that means after an item's initial use, it would be disposed of. Collectors of ephemera are plentiful and some dealers specialize in articles that were never meant to be saved.

The items in this chapter are some of the most elusive to find. More than likely, it will only be advanced barbershop collectors who have an interest in buying them. Even if you do not fit that category, just being aware of these items is interesting and will expand your knowledge of barbershop collectibles. It will also give you something else to keep your eyes open for as you go antique hunting. Just what you need, right?.......*more "stuff" to find!* Actually, it is good that there is not a big demand for these items because there simply would not be enough to go around. Barbershop apparel, miscellaneous fabric items, and bulk containers produced before 1920 are *beyond* scarce. They *will* command handsome prices from interested buyers. Conversely, if you should find one of these items at a market or show, it *could* be a relative bargain. It's the old supply and demand principle. Since there may not have been much interest previously, a dealer might let one of these items go quite reasonably. Expect this to change if more collectors begin to add these already scarce articles to their displays. The best hunting tips for bulk supplies are country store or advertising shows. For anything fabric related, textile or antique clothing shows will be your best bet. Dealers of ephemera are certainly worth checking with too.

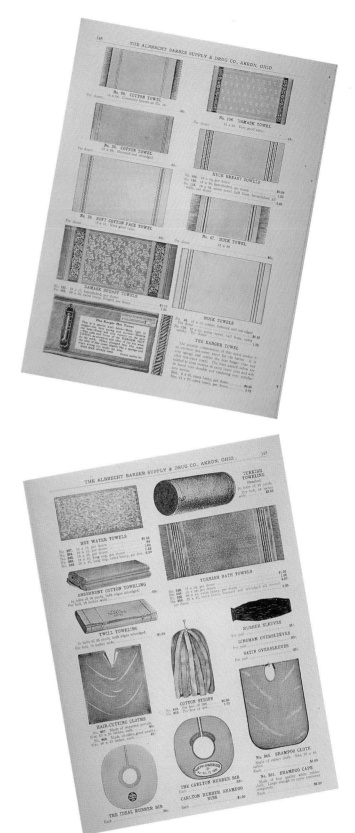

Catalog pages from the Albrecht Barber Supply Company showing large variety of towels and capes. Barbers utilized different grades of towel fabrics for different purposes including neck towels, breast (top layer) towels, bath towels, and water towels (steamed to prep the face for shaving.) Damask breast towels (colored and pattern-woven) were very attractive and much heavier than other towels. As a result, they were more likely to survive the years and turn up occasionally with textile dealers in the $5.00 to $10.00+ range.

The Supply Closet and Textiles

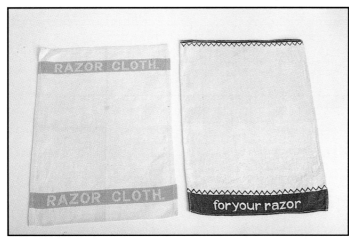

Fine, 400-count, Irish linen, razor wipes. This was a delicate but absorbent fabric for the barber to final-dry his razor with after use. Each of these scarce wipes are approximately 8" x 10" and valued at $25.00+.

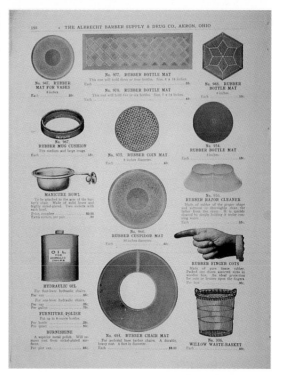

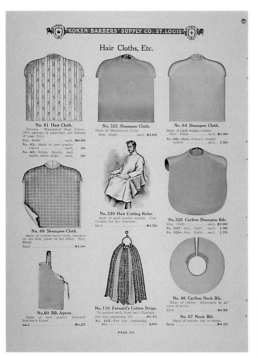

Above and right: Variety of rubber textiles from the Melchior and Albrecht Barber Supply Companies. These barbershop items include mats to be placed under mugs, bottles, waste vases, coins, cuspidors, and barber chairs. Backbar mats were valuable for saving broken glassware and chair mats for easing the barbers' sore feet. Miscellaneous rubber items included bath scrubs, finger cots (barbers still make good use of them,) and massage cup bulbs. Mats are scarce and will bring from $20.00+ for a good condition bottle, cuspidor, or mug mat, to $100.00+ for a good condition chair mat.

Above and right: Koken Barbers' Supply textile variety. Many of these were treated to repel water. Notice the forearm "over sleeves" which were Gingham material to be worn while haircutting, and rubber material over sleeves for shampooing. Original over sleeves in representative condition, $50.00+ per pair. Rubber shampoo bibs or hair cloths intact and in patterns as seen here, $35.00+.

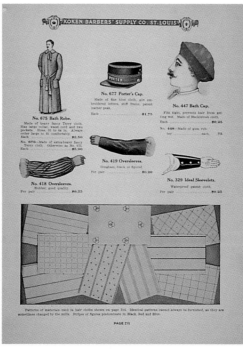

Catalog pages from the Melchior and Albrecht Barber Supply Companies showing a representative variety of barbers apparel in 1910. They ranged from vest to tunic length. Collars went from open lapels to cadet style. Favorite material for the times was "Drill." The standard field color was white but many jackets also had stripes of red or black. If found in representative condition, any of the jackets seen here, $150.00+.

Colgate bulk-pack from the late golden years. Unopened as seen, $35.00+. Display sign for soap cakes dated 1921 on the metal holder, $20.00+.

1908 Melchior Barber Supply catalog page showing typical examples of bulk, shaving mug soap cakes. Also seen are bulk boxes of soap powder. Early soap cakes in bulk-packs with contents as seen here, $45.00+ each. Powder boxes with contents as seen here, $75.00 each.

The Supply Closet and Textiles

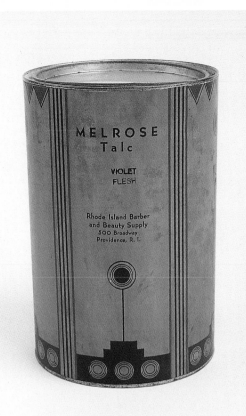

Melrose brand, cardboard talcum canister. 9" high 5.5" wide and holding 3 pounds of flesh-colored talcum powder. Deco style graphics. With contents as seen $60.00+.

Below: Page from the Koken Barbers' Supply catalog showing various sharpening instruments for barber's tools. The grinding wheel type seen here were often referred to as "botch" grinders by barbers because of their poor results. The type seen at the bottom the page were thought to give better results because of improved "jigs" and operator control.

Above and right: Examples of bulk soap powder in cardboard canisters. These average 9" tall and 5" diameter and hold 2 pounds of powder. Notice the Williams brand can which has directions in both English and Italian. These were popular with the large influx of immigrant Italian barbers after 1910. With contents and in condition as seen, $50.00+.

Bench mounted "botch" grinder from the late golden years. The fine-grinding wheel on these models was beveled and split which supposedly required no jig. Sharpening results were marginal. Although used by barbers, they were also sold generically for knife sharpening. As seen, $15.00+.

Barbershop "botch" style grinders, both of which clamp to the edge of a backbar. **Top:** Koken "Firefly" model. Reduction gear with chain drive. Works. In condition as seen, $150.00+. **Bottom:** Early direct-drive model. Works. Stamped Koken Barber Supply. $125.00+.

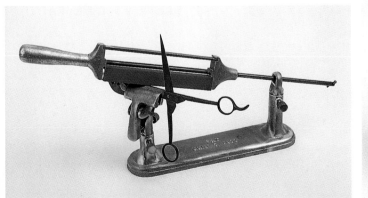

This design of scissors sharpener was popular after 1900. It featured a reversible honing stone with coarse and medium surfaces. It also had a corrugating file. Most importantly, it came with a jig that securely held the scissors in place for better sharpening results. As seen, $45.00+.

Barbers needed two things in the course of putting an edge on a razor: stone-oil for the hone, and antiseptic for the occasional finger cuts that went along with straight razor handling. **Left:** Pike brand "STONE OIL." 7" tall with screw-cap opening. 1920s. With perfect graphics and contents as seen, $30.00+. **Right:** Mosso's brand antiseptic. Popular with barbers for two reasons: it was a good treatment for minor razor cuts and it also relieved sore feet. 4" tall. With perfect graphics and contents as seen, $15.00+.

The Supply Closet and Textiles

Barber supply company bulk-bottles for tonic or concentrated ingredients. All have cork-top openings and raised glass lettering. **From left to right:** Koken Company, St. Louis. Square shape, 9.75" tall. $100.00+. Buckeye Barber Supply, Dayton Ohio. 10.5" tall, 150.00+. Koken Barber Supply, St. Louis. Amber colored, 10.5" tall. $135.00+. Kochs Barber Supply, Chicago. 9.75" tall. $100.00+.

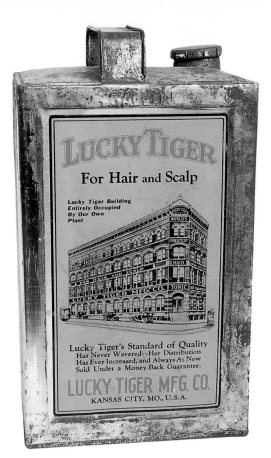

Lucky Tiger brand, one gallon lithograph-tin. 4" x 6" x 11". Cork opening with cap. Some rusting and lithographic loss on one side and rear. As seen $85.00+. Much more if perfect.

Wildroot brand, half gallon lithograph tin. 3.5" x 5" x 8". Cork opening. Lithographs are about 95% clear. $135.00+

1.5 gallon Koken Barber Supply bottle. 6" diameter, 14.5" tall, paper labeled. Has wax-sealed cork and contains original contents of Ambrosial Hair Tonic concentrate. Excellent label graphics. Rare. $225.00+.

Noxema brand, bulk shaving cream. 5" x 7" cobalt colored glass jar holding 4 pounds. Has raised glass letters and paper label. As seen, $75.00+.

Bulk, glass containers of Witch Hazel for refilling backbar bottles. Dickinson's brand was widely held as the barbers' favorite. However, Rexall's brand was readily available at the drugstore *and* for a lesser price. I have personally heard stories from barbers who worked in the 1920s and 30s about secretly pouring Rexall's product into empty Dickinson's bottles. This was so the customers wouldn't think their barber was giving them anything less than the best as he refilled his backbar bottles. **Left:** Rexall's bottle with original contents and slightly stained graphics, $15.00. **Right:** Dickinson's bottle with perfect label graphics, $20.00.

Assorted backbar-sized shaving creams produced for generic distribution but favored by many barbers. Brands seen here include: Molle, Burma-Shave, Barbasol, Noxema, Palmolive, Spark'l, and Krank's. These turn up fairly often at flea markets for $5.00 to $20.00+ depending on scarcity and also how ornate the glass molding and graphics are.

The Supply Closet and Textiles

Jeris brand, bulk tonic bottle for refilling backbar bottles. With original cap and bright paper label showing some rough edges, $25.00.

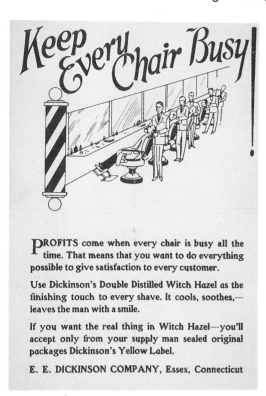

Original fold-up advertisement for Dickinson's Witch Hazel which was direct-mailed to barbershops. One side shows the colorful Dickinson's graphics and Postal cover. When opened, the reverse side was intended to be displayed in the shop. 8.5" x 11" and frameable. $35.00+.

Bulk boxes of headrest rolls. Made to be held in the base of the barber chair headrest and dispensed so that each customer had a fresh piece to lay his head on. Most barbers also tore off a small piece to be laid on the patron's chest. It was then used to wipe soap from the barber's razor as he proceeded with the shave. **Left:** Parasilk paper rolls from the Taverna Barber Supply, St. Paul, Minnesota. New-old-stock with contents of twelve rolls and great graphics, $175.00+. **Right:** Marcal brand paper rolls. New-old-stock with contents of twelve rolls and good graphics, $150.00+. **Note:** These prices are currently influenced by the fact that *single* rolls are in demand for $15.00+ each. They are hunted by owners of antique barber chairs who wish to place *original, old,* headrest paper in their chairs.

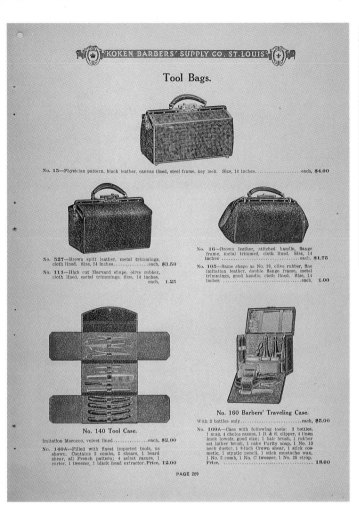

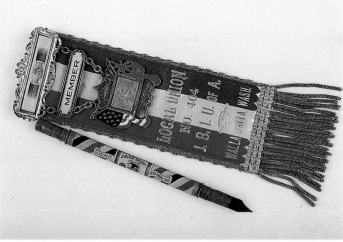

Union items were found in many barber's closets. Convention delegate's badge from Walla Walla, Washington. Never used, in original envelope, $65.00+. Union graphics on combination ink pen and pencil, $35.00+.

Barbers' tool bags could be found in the closet at most barbershops. Throughout the golden years, barbers routinely made house calls for favored patrons who couldn't get to the shop. The bags seen on the top of this Koken catalog page were generically made and were also sold to doctors. They can be found from $50.00 to $85.00 in good condition. The two styles at the bottom of the page are purpose-built for barbers. They would range from $75.00 to $125.00+ in good condition.

Gift from hand clipper salesmen. Barber's stickpin with miniature Brown and Sharpe hand clipper in gold. As seen in original presentation, $60.00+.

Rubber door-mat advertising Wildroot Cream-Oil Tonic. 14" x 20" Black with white letters. In representative condition as seen here, $75.00. *Courtesy of Tony Gugliotti.*

The Supply Closet and Textiles

Chapter 7

Retail Products

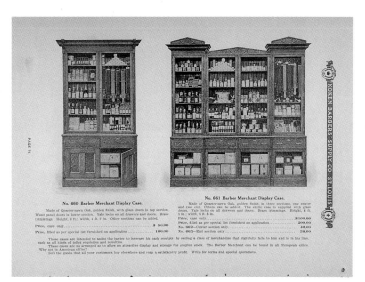

Koken barbershop catalog page from 1910 shows retail display cases in quarter-sawn oak. If either were found in representative condition and with the original Koken logo badge, the case on the **left** would bring $1,000.00 to $1,500.00+. The case on the **right**, $2,500.00+.

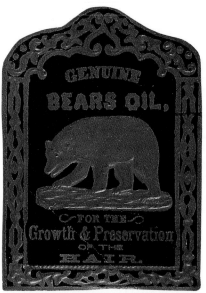

Gold embossed label typical of late-1800s hair products. 2" x 3" and believed to be unused. Scarce label as seen here, $20.00+.

Handwritten druggists prescriptions for hair preparations, mid-1800s. Each as seen, $20.00+.

There was a large number of retail hair care products available to be sold in barbershops by the mid-1800s. In fact, the first patent for a hair preparation was issued in 1847 and by 1900, more than 800 additional brands had been registered. It wasn't only hair tonics that were being sold in barbershops, but a good variety of other grooming and shaving needs like talcum, pomade, brilliantine, and in the later Golden Years, safety razor blades. Of all the retail items that barbers offered, bottled hair "remedies" and "cures" were the best sellers. These retail product bottles are not to be confused with professional, refillable, barber bottles such as the art-glass or opaline types previously discussed in chapter three. Retail tonic bottles are much smaller and were usually rectangular in shape. Most had cork stoppers and were clear glass, cobalt blue, or amber colored. They are identifiable by raised glass lettering although some, especially in the middle Golden Years, also had paper labels. Most barbershop showcases were loaded with them, but they were rarely seen on the backbar.

Prior to the boom in commercial bottling of retail hair care products, druggists wrote legitimate prescriptions for scalp and hair problems. They also wrote prescriptions for toilet water and hair dye. However, the publics fascination with commercial "hair remedies" grew so rapidly in those early years, that by 1860 they had become a mushrooming retail phenomenon and were no longer thought of as prescriptive.

Most early patented hair tonics were formulated and bottled by independent druggists and "chemists." *Legitimate or otherwise.* There were also plenty of barbers who sought patents and trade marks and it wasn't unusual for them to sometimes bestow themselves with such grandiose titles as "Professor" or "Doctor," although few had any academic credentials. They were simply entrepreneurs who were taking advantage of lax, or non-existent, regulatory agencies and the public's clamoring for all kinds of hair and scalp products. Barbers really had it made during the early portion of the Golden Years because they could stir up batches of readily available tonic recipes quite easily. Their motive, of course, was to dispense 5 and 10 cent squirt applications on haircut patrons. It was *far* more profitable than selling their tonics in retail bottles.

Many hair remedies sold prior to 1906 are now considered to have been "quack" cures. Few were truly effective and often times they actually worsened the public's hair and scalp problems. Their formulas called for high concentrations of sulfur, lead, and what we now know to be poisonous, wood alcohol. The public wanted, *badly*, to believe that the concoctions worked because there were *real* scalp and hair problems in those times. Conditions commonly referred to as "barbers itch" and "scald head" were prevalent. With both, the scalp was itchy, flaking, and sometimes infected. In hindsight, we have learned that the sufferers of those complaints didn't need quack preparations nearly as much as they needed more frequent bathing and less lice infestation. However, in the publics zeal to "restore health" to their hair, they continued to buy anything that sounded good. For **general hair health** you could have chosen from the following: Hair Cocoaine, Invigorator, Hair Elixir, Auxiliator, Hair Tea, Quinine Tonic, Hair Drops, Sea Foam, etceteras. For **shampooing, curling, and conditioning,** there was: Capillaris, Cleansing Balm, Kathairon, Grand's Greasejuice, Dandrifuge, Curleykew, Hair Wash, West Indian Curler, Egg Shampoo, Brilliantine, Vegetable Balsam, etceteras. For **hair loss and baldness** a fellow could choose from an endless supply including the following: Hair Recouperative, 4 Day Restorer, Hair Rejuvenator, Hope For The Bald, Hair Fertilizer, Salvation For Hair, Hair Food, Practical Hair Grower, and Hair Reviver. Some scalp conditions were due to **insects or infection** and called for stronger concoctions like: Mexican Hair Tonic And Nit Killer, Anti-Parasitine, Human Mange Medicine, Herpicide, Danderine, Tricopherous, Pasteur's Germicide, and Scalpine. If you wanted to change your **hair coloring**, you could have: Glosso, Lightning Dye, Colour Restorer, Golden Hair Dressing, Electric Dye, Hair Shader, Hair Stain, No Gray Hair, Colorator, and Hair Transformer. And, for those who wished to **eliminate hair,** (go figure) it is a safe bet that these products probably worked: Skookum's Hair Death, Silent Shaver, Hair Eradicator, Anti-Hairine, Barber In A Bottle, and (no kidding) Butcher's Hair Destroyer!

Typical "bald cure" advertisements seen during the late 1800s. **Top:** 4" x 6" print advertisement, $10.00+. **Bottom:** Rare serial numbered "insurance" handbill for assuring no further hair loss with the use of this product. 5.5" x 9" double-sided. In condition as seen, $45.00+.

Retail Products

The time frame that these products were offered in was about a fifty year period of the proverbial "dog chasing his tail." Often, when a person used the above listed "tonics," his "barbers itch" was actually perpetuated by the harmful ingredients the product contained. Certainly, the users would have felt *something* going on after applying things like "Human Mange Medicine," to their scalps but, **was it really beneficial?** Frequent and unnatural hair loss was also a big problem in barbering's early Golden Years. I wonder how often it was a direct result of wood alcohol poisoning or some other harmful tonic ingredient? At any rate, and not coincidentally I suspect, there was an abundance of "bald cures" available. Of course, we now understand that many of the ingredients in old hair remedies were caustic, poisonous, and definitely harmful. In 1906, the American Food and Drug Act (FDA) enacted legislation that aimed to insure everyone's health by eliminating harmful substances from all commercial products. It was perfect timing for the good of the hair care product industry: the public had become accustomed to purchasing a whole variety of hair and scalp preparations and now the FDA would insure that they weren't harmful. The manufacturers *did* have to stop making wild claims and guarantees about their products, but they continued to prosper with tonics that had simply become better for the hair. Today, hair care products are a billion dollar industry.

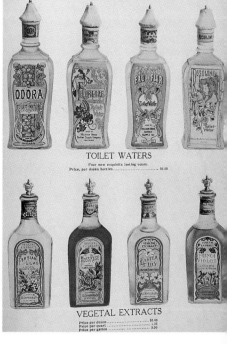

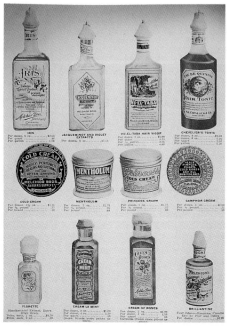

Sampling of barber catalog retail products from 1898 to 1910. Few of these products are found as seen here with bright graphics. In representative condition, most would be valued at $35.00+.

Old photographs show us that barbers sometimes sold an eclectic variety of retail items, but most often the products were hair, scalp, shaving, or tobacco related. After their customers switched to shaving at home with safety razors, barbers figured to recoup some of their lost income one way or another. They knew that the men had to buy blades for their safety razors so barbers began to sell them. In talks with some of the old timers, they lament that it went against their pride to concede *anything* to the notion of a former customer shaving at home with a safety razor. However, selling replacement blades brought needed cash. Some barbers would even take in safety razor blades for sharpening along with straight razors. The actual benefit of "renewing" safety razor blades was always somewhat suspect but nevertheless it produced additional income for barbers while it was popular.

Collecting retail hair care bottles is easy and they are found in a broad price spectrum which is influenced by age, condition, and rarity. Many are less than $10.00. Others could be several hundred dollars. There are plenty of them to be found at flea markets and bottle specialty shows. While they make a nice display empty, or with colored water, they invite even more interest if shown with original advertising. Advertising trade cards are collectible in their own right and are easily found at antique paper or advertising shows.

Matched set, Penslar Tonic bottle and advertising sign. 1930s. Rarely seen backbar-sized bottle in green glass standing 9.25" tall. $125.00+. Advertising sign is heavy cardboard measuring 14" x 22". Bright, clean, graphics. $85.00+.

Variety of pre-1900 retail hair-care products. All are easily identified with raised glass lettering. Prices are for bottles in condition as seen. **Rear, left to right:** Newbro's Herpicide. 6" tall, $5.00+. Burnett's Cocoaine. 7" tall, $60.00+. Hay's Hair Health, amber color. 6.5" tall, $12.00+. **Front, left to right:** Barker's Hirsutis. 7" tall, $20.00+. J.B. Williams. 6.25" tall, $10.00+.

Matched set, Dr. Lynas Hair Grower bottle and sign. Late-1800s. 3.25" jar has original label completely intact with bright graphics. $45.00+. Cardboard sign measures 7" 13". Unused condition. $45.00.

Retail Products

Seven Sutherland Sisters Hair Grower and copied advertisement. Early 1900s. Embossed bottle is 6" tall. $15.00+.

Danderine Hair Tonic and corresponding advertising pamphlet. Tonic bottle stands 6.25" tall and shows edge-wear on label. From post-1900 period after company moved to Chicago from West Virginia. $22.00+. Pamphlet is 23 pages of usage tips for product. From pre-1900 period before company moved to Chicago. $20.00+.

Matched set, Barry's Trichopherous bald remedy and trade card. Late-1800s. Bottle is 6.25" tall. $12.00+. Trade card measures 3" x 5.25". Bright graphics. $15.00+.

Matched set, Lyon's Kathairon bald cure and trade card. Late 1800s. Embossed bottle is 6" tall. $15.00+. Trade card is scarce. 3" x 5". Bright graphics, $45.00+.

Set of Hall's Vegetable Sicilian Hair Renewer and trade card. Late-1800s. Honey-amber bottle is 8" tall with paper label intact. $45.00+. Very common trade card is 3.5" x 5". Bright graphics. $12.00+.

Retail Products

Matching set of Parker's Hair Balsam bottle and trade card. Late 1800s. Deep amber bottle is 7" tall. $15.00+. Trade card measures 3" x 4.5". Bright graphics. $15.00+.

Left: Glover's Sarcoptic Mange Medicine for animals *and humans!* Unused, boxed, and directions for use on both species. 1920s. $20.00+. **Right:** Glos-so Hair Dye Compound. Unused, boxed, and directions for use. 1920s. $25.00+.

Matched set, Murray & Lanman Florida water bottle and trade card. Late 1800s. Bottle stands 9" tall. $20.00+. Trade card measures 3" x 4.5". Bright graphics. $12.00+.

Opposite page, bottom: Several different talcum powders that retailed in golden years barber shops. **Left to right:** Mennen's Borated Talcum in lithographed 4" tin. Late 1800s. Graphics are dark and rate at 75%. Original contents. $20.00+. Early trade card for 1800s Mennen's talc measures 3" x 4.25". Bright graphics. $22.00+. Colgate talc for men. 1940s. $5.00+. Mennen's talc for men. 1930s. $8.00+.

Matched set, Pinaud's Lotion bottle and trade card. Late 1800s. Embossed bottle stands 6.5" tall. $12.00+. Trade card measures 3" x 4.5" and is dated 1882. Bright graphics. $22.00+.

Retail Products

Assorted retail Pomade products. **Left to right:** Vaseline brand. 1920s. Unused, boxed, 2.5" tall. $20.00+. Matching Vaseline trade card $20.00. Royal Crown Pomade. 1930s. Cardboard containers. Original contents. $15.00+. Herolin Pomade. Square, tin container. $15.00+. Stacomb Pomade. Milk glass container. 1920s. $18.00+.

Tripoli brand, cardboard comb display. 1920s. 9" x 11". As seen $50.00+.

Rare set of Dr. LaFieu's Mustache Vigor and accompanying advertising pamphlet. 1870s+. Envelope with mustache growing powder has never been opened. 12 page pamphlet is all testimonials from 1879 to 1883 of men who claim luxuriant mustache growth after using the powders. $85.00+.

OK Comb Cleaner cardboard display with original contents. 1930s+. Bright graphics. As seen, $45.00+.

Wooden, Gillette safety razor counter display. 13" x 17". Front decal perfect. $75.00. Price is influenced by safety razor collectors who purchase these for displays.

Examples of safety razor blade display cards seen in many barbershops 1930+. This unused variety all call attention to the barbershop in some way on their graphics. Blade displays range from $30.00 to $75.00+ if complete and undamaged.

Retail Products

Chapter 8

Barbershop Signs

San Antonio, Texas barbershop, 1939. This candid photograph elevates the importance of exterior barbershop signs to new heights! *Courtesy of the Library of Congress.* Value, $35.00+.

Signs are a colorful and interesting segment of barbershop collectibles. While they are collectible entirely on their own, few other antiques can enhance a barbershop display so graphically. They are made from a variety of material including: porcelainized steel, cardboard, tin, celluloid, wood, paper, plastic, and etched glass. The letters and artwork on wooden exterior signs were painted by hand. Lithography was widely used for some of the more colorful interior signs. Ink presses with hand-set type printed out the majority of the shop's interior text signs such as price menus or hours of operation. Porcelain signs have letters or artwork that is baked into the material. It seems that barbershop signs fit into four main categories: exterior business, interior retail, interior services, and window and door glass signs. Barbershop signs of all types turn up regularly at advertising shows. Recent specialty auctions have realized record prices for good barbershop signs.

BARBERS

These are actual barbershop signs that were offered for sale in the 1920s. Now, all we have to do is *find them*. Happy hunting!

Exterior Business Signs

Exterior business signs were usually affixed directly to a buildings facade. When a barber went into business, he hired the local sign painter to personalize such an existing sign. If the barber went out of business or moved to a new location, the sign remained in place and the incoming business had it repainted for themselves. Because of this, there are few hand-painted, exterior, barbershop signs remaining. When they do surface, they are not always desirable because of deterioration. The most popular exterior signs during the Golden Years, and also to collectors now, are those that were sold through barber supply outlets. Most of them are porcelain over steel and they remain very attractive. Very often, they have the same striped design as their barber pole counterparts and are just as brightly colored. Some two-sided signs are formed at a 90 degree angle at one end which serves as a built-in mounting bracket. They allowed people passing in both directions to read the sign simultaneously. Other signs are curved into half-round shapes. Once those were mounted to a flush surface, they projected from the wall, but only half as far as a traditional round pole. However, the purpose was served because pedestrians and motorists could see them from a distance as they approached the shop. Along with great longevity, another plus was the fact that porcelain pole-signs required no maintenance as with an electrified, spinning barber pole. Many barbers used both types for added impact. The most frequently seen porcelain signs are those that are two-sided and have an outer border of red, white, and blue stripes with the words "Barber Shop" appearing in the center. More unusual, are porcelain signs advertising specific services such as bobbing or shampooing. Always desirable, are porcelain half-round poles, especially early models with stars on them. Many porcelain signs were produced generically and sold through barber supply companies. One of the better known early manufacturers was the Bob White Company of Milwaukee, Wisconsin. In later years, the Marvy Company also produced many porcelain signs. The colors occasionally have some loss of brightness if exposed for many years to direct sunlight. This is expected to some degree and doesn't necessarily devalue the sign. Porcelain signs that have been dropped, or struck hard enough to chip portions off the surface, will be worth less than fully intact examples.

There were also exterior signs that were given to the barbers to help promote their businesses. They were usually made of tin and had embossed or painted messages. Hair tonic manufacturers like Brylcream, Jeris, and Wildroot made these attractive signs available for free. Some were generic appearing and made no mention of a barber shop. Others, not only advertised the tonic, but prominently stated "Barber Shop" as well. They were intended to be used as exterior signs.

Perhaps the most rare of all barbershop exterior signs are glass examples. Custom made stained glass signs are at the top of the heap. They are beautiful to view, and when intact, are *expensive*. Most were commissioned to be made for the particular shop where they were to hang. Some were intended to match the equally rare stained glass pole tops described in chapter two. Grand hotel shops with other lavish furnishings were often the buyers of those finest quality signs.

Another type of glass sign had surface painted letters and sometimes hung from a metal bracket. However, to prevent breakage, they were usually flush-mounted against the building. Custom glass signs were nearly all personalized with the name of the particular shop or street address. The last example of an exterior glass sign are the ones that had lettering and artwork etched into the glass. Gold leaf often filled the etched letters for a rich look. These remain rare, especially if they are etched with additional artwork such as razors or scissors.

Porcelain flange sign. 12" x 24" double-sided. Bright color, minor edge chip. $150.00+.

Porcelain, half-round sign. Dates to 1928. 9.5" x 48". Bright color, minor chip. $275.00+.

Barbershop Signs

Porcelain, half-round sign. Dates to 1931. 14" x 24". Some fading to color. Has original iron mounting bracket. Unusual lightning bolt patterned stripes. Made by Kochs. $300.00+.

Porcelain, double-sided flange sign. Separate advertisements on each side. Noonan's Barber Supply, Boston. 12" x 16.5". Bright graphics, minor edge chips. $300.00+.

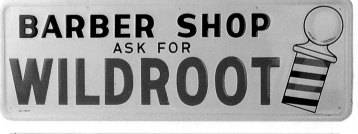

Porcelain flange sign. 12" x 24" double-sided. Some fading and minor chips. Unusual hair bobbing sign. ca.1925. As seen, $300.00+.

Right two: Painted tin Wildroot advertising signs from the 1950s. The combination of thin metal and spray paint left these signs subject to premature rusting. Exterior barbershop sign measures 14" x 40". Value in condition as seen with no rust, $200.00+. General use Wildroot sign measures 10" x 28". Value in condition as seen with no rust, $150.00+.

Exterior glass globes that hung from a suspended light fixture. **Left:** 10" diameter, milk glass globe with hand painted lettering intact. *Courtesy of Tony Gugliotti.* $75.00 to $125.00. **Right:** Kochs Barber Supply manufactured light fixture. Original wall bracket and 17" double pane glass. Canteen style. Complete professional restoration to "as new" condition. *Courtesy of Bill Wright.* Valued by owner at $1,200.00.

Historically significant etched glass sign from 1925 when hair tonic magnate, F. W. Fitch, attempted (unsuccessfully) to have barbers professional title changed to "Dermatician." Letters and art work are etched and filled with gold leaf. 10" x 30". *Courtesy of Mike and Mary Sparks.* $500.00+. Front page cover of the *Square Deal* periodical (Fitch's supply house advertising magazine) shows F.W. welcoming all "Dermaticians" to town for a National Convention. Inside propaganda story on the importance of shedding the "Barber" title. 7" x 10", 24 pages. $35.00+.

Interior Retail Signs

Interior retail signs were given to barbershops by manufacturers of tonics and other personal grooming needs. Most of these signs are cardboard and can be quite colorful depending on how they have aged and their original quality. Signs that hung in barbershops are often darkened from exposure to nicotine and light. The finest examples of cardboard signs are those that have letters and artwork which have been die-cut or embossed. The problem with thin grade cardboard signs is that they become brittle with age. It is always advisable to frame them if they are in danger of cracking apart. Framing will not effect the value of a brittle sign, but having one split apart sure will. Better grade interior signs are made from tin which may be embossed and stiffened with cardboard backing. They are more durable than plain cardboard and are generally found in better condition as a result. Tin sign graphics were often produced by lithography. This process produced signs with a high-contrast color but which could sometimes crack with age. A tin sign is usually more attractive than a cardboard sign with the same age and exposure.

Early in the Golden Years the quality of signs was mediocre. As advances in printing capabilities evolved, so did the quality of signs. The middle of the Golden Years, from about 1890 to 1930, saw the widest range of expensive to produce, tin-lithograph signs. After that period when manufacturing's cost-efficiency became an issue, cardboard material became the clear choice for interior signs. However, the overall quality of cardboard signs had improved allowing them to be, not only more durable then earlier signs, but more brightly colored as well.

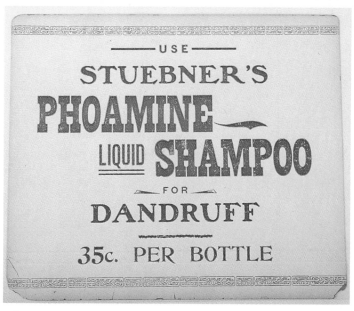

Cardboard sign for Stuebner's Foamine Shampoo. 10" x 12". ca.1915. Rough edges but shows well. $50.00+.

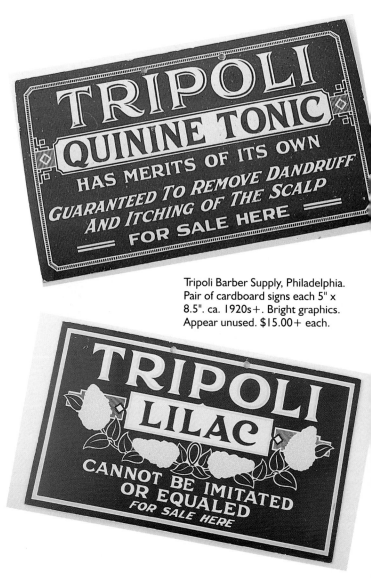

Tripoli Barber Supply, Philadelphia. Pair of cardboard signs each 5" x 8.5". ca. 1920s+. Bright graphics. Appear unused. $15.00+ each.

Mennen's talcum card-stock sign. 9.5" x 12.5". ca. 1890s stone-lithograph. Bright color. $75.00.

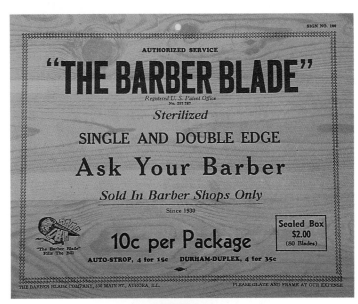

Noonan's Barber Supply, Boston. Deco inspired ca. 1930s cardboard sign measuring 4.25" x 9.5". Appears unused. $20.00+.

Advertising thermometer made of molded plastic and cardboard. ca. 1940s+. Ed. Pinaud's Lilac Vegetal. Works. 9.5" x 28". $125.00+.

Thin cardboard sign (not a decal) for Rayette dandruff lotion. ca. 1940s+. 5" x 18.5". Appears unused. $60.00+.

Examples of safety razor blade advertising seen in barbershops. **Top:** 8" x 10" cardboard sign for Barber Blades. Dates to 1932, appears unused. $25.00. **Bottom:** 14" x 19" die-cut, cardboard sign for Treet Blades. Bright graphics but minor soiling. $75.00+.

Barbershop Signs

Lithographed tin sign for "Vigorator" which was a Canadian Company that also distributed to the USA. 5" x 9" with 95% of lithograph intact. ca. 1895+. As seen with graphics darkened from age, $50.00.

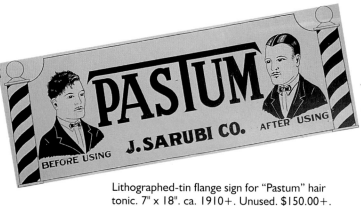

Lithographed-tin flange sign for "Pastum" hair tonic. 7" x 18". ca. 1910+. Unused. $150.00+.

Examples of signs made expressly for barbershops which state the price of an application of tonic. **Note:** prices for tonic application averaged 40% to 50% of the price of a haircut and included a leisurely rubbing-in. These ca. 1910+ signs are the most desired type by current barbershop collectors. Very scarce category. **Top:** 8.25" x 11" heavy cardboard sign for Klondike Head Rub. Embossed tonic bottle with gold foil cap. Die cut letters. Minor water spot lower right corner. $200.00+. **Bottom:** Pinaud's application sign. Custom made in pen-and-ink on thin paper. 9" x 14". Paper has turned yellow from age but two-color graphics are perfect. One of a kind paper sign. $75.00+.

Examples of tonic application price signs that have a mechanical wheel with adjustable prices. ca. 1910s+. They allowed price flexibility between competing shops. As a result, the companies who provided the free signs to barbershops ultimately sold more tonic. **Left:** Pinaud's "price wheel" sign. 6" x 8", dates to 1921. Celluloid covered graphics and cardboard back. Rare. $225.00+. **Right:** Crusella's Rhum Quinquina "price wheel" sign. 8" x 9.25". Varnish coated bright graphics. Rare. $250.00+.

Lithographed-tin one-sided sign for "Daisy" hair tonic. ca. 1910+. 9" x 9.75". Unused as seen, $150.00+.

Lithographed-tin, one-sided sign for "Dandro Solvent" hair tonic. ca. 1900+. 9.25" x 13.5". $175.00+.

Barbershop Signs

Two types of nationally organized barber union signs. **Upper:** Associated Master Barbers. Lithographed-tin that is debossed and self-framed. 6" x 15". ca.1925+. Unused condition as seen, $125.00+. **Lower:** Journeymen's union self-framed lithographed-tin. 7.5" x 9.5". ca. 1915+. Near mint condition. $100.00+. Note: these signs were also produced with celluloid coated cardboard in later years and would be valued at $75.00 in mint condition.

Scarce D-Drops Scalp Tonic decal for door or mirror glass. 5" x 6". Some darkening from age although unused. $25.00+.

Window, Mirror, And Door Signs

Window, mirror, and door signs are those that have been made expressly for applications on glass. Decals, adhesive transfers, "will return by," and "hold-to-light" were the usual variety. Decals and adhesive backed transfers that advertised hair products were given to the barbers for display in the front window or on the backbar mirrors. Because of their extreme thinness, not many of these fragile examples remain even though they may have been unused. Another obvious factor in their rarity is that, once they were peeled from their delivery sheet, they were applied to glass. After their useful advertising duration in the window, they were scraped off into shreds of waste paper.

Scarce decal advertising Stephan's tonic to be placed on a door or mirror glass. 6" x 12.5". Unused with bright graphics. $35.00+.

Fitch brand shampoo sign with barbershops hours of operation. To be applied on an interior door or window and read from outside. 8" x 8" clear plastic background. Unused. $20.00+.

Above, Top right, and right: Mechanical clock signs for barbershops which hung on the inside of a closed shop to inform when the barber would return. **Sappy's Barbershop:** 11" x 11" cardboard dated 1929. Like new condition. Scarce black related item. $75.00+. **Correct-Way Tonic:** 7" x 7" cardboard. Unused. $20.00+. **Brylcream:** Highly detailed, heavy cardboard sign. Has clocks for leaving and returning times. Sliding "open" and "closed" window. 9" x 12". $65.00+.

Barbershop Signs

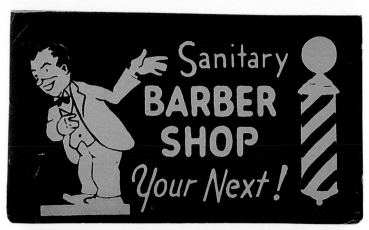

Scarce examples of unused hold-to-light signs ca. 1925. Black fields with pink graphics which appear to be lit when held in front of a light source. All measure 8" x 14" and are each valued at $50.00+. Note misspelling on "You're Next" sign.

Many old-time businesses closed for lunch and a sign was hung in the window that stated the proprietor would return by a specific time. Some had the face of a clock printed on the sign and there were hour and minute hands that moved. These could be placed at the appropriate settings. Others simply stated "will return at" a designated time. While there are generic door signs, the ones intended specifically for barbershops are marked accordingly. Usually, they will have been provided by a hair product company and are imprinted with a corresponding advertisement or the barber's name. Most early door signs were made with heavy cardboard although in the later Golden Years, plastic became the favorite because of better longevity.

Hold-to-light barber shop signs are among the most interesting. These are cardboard signs that nearly always had a black

field with letters or artwork in a high-contrast color. The letters would appear to glow brightly when placed in front of a light source. Their purpose was to serve as a low cost window sign that appeared to be lighted but without the expense of electricity. They would often be placed in a window transom over the shop's doorway where they could best pick up the shops interior lights. To understand their value better, you must first recall that it wasn't unusual for barbers to work ten to twelve hours per day. Many of those hours were after dark. Hold-to-light signs were a good deal since they were inexpensive for the barbers to purchase and they remained highly visible day or night. If they had a downfall, it was that they were made of cardboard and were subject to deterioration from condensation on the inside of the windows. To find one with good clean graphics and no water damage is unusual. If you suspect that you have found one and want to be sure, simply hold it over your head facing a light. If it is a real hold-to-light sign, the letters will appear to be glowing. These barbershop signs are scarce and are priced accordingly.

Interior Service Signs

Interior service signs was used primarily to communicate a barbershop's hours of operation and the services that were available. Price menus make up the majority of those signs. Cardboard was the material of choice because prices changed frequently and the menus didn't have to last too long. They listed all of the shops services and corresponding fees. Some were personalized with the name of the barbershop or they had other information that could include an address, phone number, or date. The more information on the sign, the higher the current value. Price menus are among the most difficult of all barbershop signs to find. They were custom made for each shop because it was rare for any two shops to offer exactly the same list of services. Since no shop *needed* more than one menu, often times , only *one* was printed. There were no generic pre-priced menus although some product manufacturers provided menus that allowed the barber to "fill in the blanks." These were often molded plastic and weren't seen before 1950. Each time that the barber raised his prices, the outdated menus became irrelevant and were discarded. Good early menus are rare and expensive but they compliment a barbershop display in a way guaranteed to invite conversation. When reading the menus at our museum the guests invariably ask, *"What the heck is hair singeing?"*

Hours of operation sometimes appeared on menus but they were usually printed on a separate sign. In many cases, barbershop hours' signs were printed at the expense of the local barbers' union who then distributed them to all of the union shops in town. The union was especially "strong" in the mid-to late Golden Years and most barbers belonged. It was not unusual to get a visit from a union representative who made sure the signs stayed hung, and further, that you *abided* by what was written on them. It was also not unusual for a barber who acted a little too independently of the union to find his front window mysteriously broken. Can you imagine that?

Occaisionally, a barber chose to have interior signs custom made which told of "specials" that were available. Since they were usually intended to announce a new service or something of an incidental nature, sign makers used material not much thicker than writing paper. These signs were designed to be used for an interim period. Once the message had been adequately conveyed, they were thrown away. If they didn't get thrown away by some miracle, most of them (like the previously discussed decal signs) have deteriorated to some degree because of their extreme thinness. Professionally made paper signs for barbershop interiors are rare today, especially if they were made during the Golden Years period.

Associated Master Barbers
Chapter 922

Starting Wednesday Dec. 12, 1945

WILL BE CLOSED ALL DAY

WEDNESDAY

Shop Hours

CLOSED all day Wednesday

Cardboard interior signs concerning Wednesday closing. This practice became popular as WORLD WAR II was ending. **Top:** Historically significant sign announcing the practice of all union shops closing on Wednesday. 11" x 14" cardboard. Some water staining. Dated 1945. Rare. $75.00. **Bottom:** Small, 6" x 9" generic sign for Wednesday closing. Unused. $10.00+.

HAIR CUTTING
25¢

Rare set of hand-lettered barbershop signs ca. 1920s. Each sign is 11" x 14" and painted in three colors. **Haircut 25 cents sign:** Top right corner damage but shows good overall. $100.00+. **Children's Haircut 25 cents sign:** Slight corner damage but shows excellent overall. $135.00+.

CHILDREN'S HAIR CUT 25¢

Barbershop Signs

Hair Cut	=	=	35 Cents
Shave		=	15 Cents
Tonic	=	=	15 Cents
Hair Line	=	=	30 Cents
Shampoo		=	25 Cents
Egg Shampoo		=	35 Cents
Ladies' Shampoo		=	75 Cents
Bera Lotion		=	5 Cents
Massage	=	=	35 Cents
Hair Singe		=	30 Cents
Razors Honed		=	35 Cents
Razors Reground		=	$1.00

"IT PAYS TO LOOK WELL"

Hair Cut	25¢
Shampoo	25¢
Singe	25¢
Shave	25¢
Massage	25¢
Boncilla 25¢ Extra	
Steam	25¢

PRICE LIST

Hair Cut	$ .50
Shave	.25
Singe	.25
Shampoo	.35 .50 .60
Massage	.35 .75
Tonics	.20 .25
Razor Honing	.50
Witch Hazel or Menthol Steam	.10
Ladies Neck Clipped	.10
Toilet Water	.05
Hair Lined	.15
Hair Cut or Shave at Home	1.00

J. N. McCabe
PAINTED POST, N. Y.

Cardboard price menus ca. 1900 to 1930s. Prices for barbers' services varied from place to place much like today. For this reason, it is difficult to trace each sign's precise decade of origin. However, the menus seen here all exhibit services offered that are consistent with the above time period. The range for these rare and highly desirable barbershop signs (exclusively from the golden years) is from $100.00 to $300.00 depending on condition. Newer signs, from after WORLD WAR II, are still desirable but are valued proportionately less.

SANITARY
BARBER
SHOP
P TO DATE
SERVICE

Rare set of five matching paper signs.
Crudely printed and self-framed. These
signs each measure 8" x 14.5" and hung in
an upstate New York barbershop ca.
1920. Some yellowing due to age but
overall excellent condition. $350.00+.

LADIES'
HAIR
BOBBING
OUR
SPECIALTY

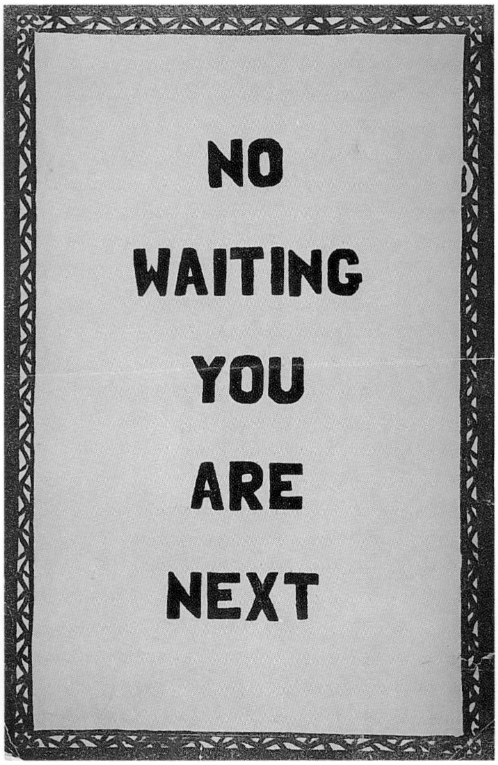

NO
WAITING
YOU
ARE
NEXT

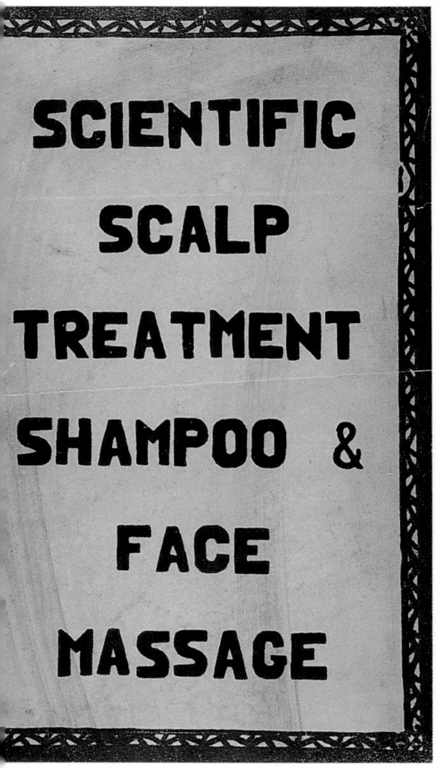

SCIENTIFIC
SCALP
TREATMENT
SHAMPOO &
FACE
MASSAGE

SPECIAL
ATTENTION
GIVEN TO
CHILDREN'S
HAIR CUTS

There are a few types of miscellaneous barbershop advertising items that we would be remiss not to mention. The first are "Good For" tokens. Many business owners during barbering's Golden Years purchased rolls of coin-appearing tokens which were stamped with the shop name and service offered on one side. The flip side usually had a number (5 or 10) stamped into the center. This number indicated how much of a discount one could expect to receive if redeeming the token at the time of service. Some other tokens were redeemable for a cigar, bath, or other barbershop amenity. They were stamped in a variety of metals including: aluminum, bronze, brass, steel, and copper. They were also available in rubber fiber and the proverbial "wooden nickel." Barbers utilized these "good for" tokens in several ways. As they strolled about town, they could offer the tokens to prospective customers or they could try to lure back an old customer with a discount. They could also give a hand-full to a valued employee as an incentive to help him build his own clientele within the shop. The time that tokens were *most* handy, was after a customer had been accidentally cut by the razor or scissors. In this instance, a barber might offer two tokens, as opposed to the usual one. While you may believe that 5 or 10 cents was not much of a lure, you must remember that during the height of "Good For" tokens popularity, a shave or haircut was only 15 or 20 cents! These tokens were *worthwhile*.

Electrotypes were another important part of barbershop advertising. They were small examples of generically produced advertising layouts. They could be purchased through the barber suppliers and were relatively inexpensive. Once a barber had an Electrotype in his possession, he could take it to nearly any printer and get professional custom work. He could have his business cards, bill heads, and letterheads all personalized with quality results. The Electrotype could be used repeatedly as long as the barbershop's basic information did not change.

The last subject of barbershop signs and advertising is one that I personally believe has been distorted somewhat. I'm referring to the large wooden or metal models of barber's razors or scissors. When found, they are nearly always offered as "trade signs." I have personally had dealers tell me that these pieces were made expressly to indicate that "shaving was available in a barber shop." They supposedly "hung outside or were displayed in the window." I have often seen other trade signs that *did* hang outside businesses and there is much photographic evidence to back that up. In the hundreds of actual barbershop photographs that I have researched, (including many exterior shots) I have yet to see an oversized razor hanging out front. Only barber poles. It was common knowledge that *all barbers shaved and cut hair.* There may have been some shops to be found with a huge razor out front, but I feel pretty confident that most of the so-called razor "trade signs" we see for sale today are little more than folk-art or fantasy pieces. Especially if they are not *really* oversized. Most of them are wooden or tin and are rarely made to perfect scale. When you *do* see one that is made in *heavy* metal and is in perfect scale, it is usually a razor manufacturer's production model as those seen in chapter three. Model razors remain rare and can cost thousands of dollars in today's market. They were not, however, intended to be barbershop trade signs. Even if my observation holds water, fantasy or folk-art razors and scissors that have been well made are still in demand. They often bring high prices regardless of their origins.

"Good For" token advertising used by barbers throughout the golden years. They were made from brass, copper, aluminum, steel, wood, and fiber composition. One side had the barbershop's name, the other had a number designation (usually 5 cents) "good for" a discount. They currently range in price from $10.00 to $50.00+ depending on condition and volume of information on each token.

Encased cents as those appearing here are not to be confused with early "good for" trade tokens. Encased cents are copper pennies wedged into a ring of aluminum with stamped advertising. They were popular ca. 1950. Average value, $1.00 to $3.00+.

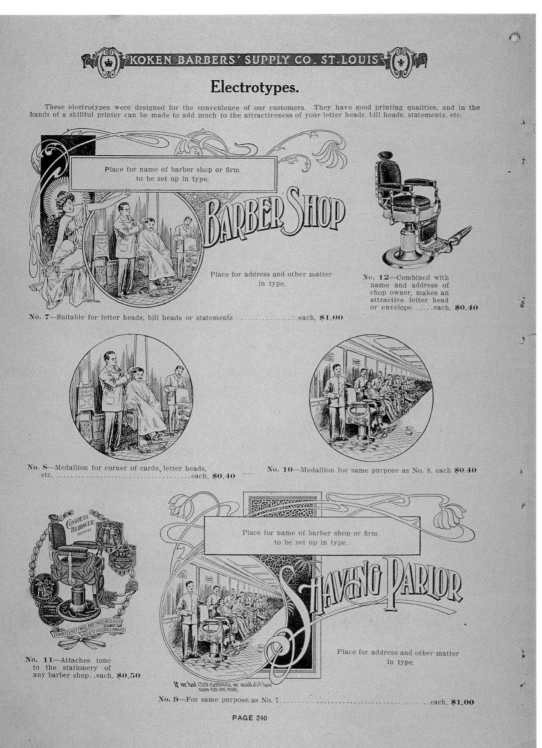

Variety of Electrotypes (printing plates) sold by the Koken Barber Supply Company to be personalized by the barber's local printer. If found today in good condition, any of those seen here would be valued at $50.00+.

Barber "trade sign" or fantasy piece. Carved wood, scaled, straight razor replica. Measures 4' long when opened. Paint scratched but in overall excellent condition. $250.00+.

Barbershop Signs

Chapter 9

Paper

Barbershop related antique paper is interesting, colorful, and best of all, it is still plentiful. Now that there is a growing awareness about the decline of barbering in general, any related paper from the Golden Years is receiving increased interest. It is invaluable for documenting locations, prices, individuals, dates, products, and events pertaining to barbershop history. Prices for good early paper is going up and the logic is simple. Any occupation in decline gets an increased number of enthusiasts who want to document the history. There is no better way than with antique paper. We spoke earlier in chapter one about the undeniable value of catalogs and photographs in helping to document our current day antiques. While those two areas of paper collecting are the ultimate defining resource, other subjects remain that are, not only informative, but strikingly visual as well. There was no color photography during the early Golden Years but there certainly were color illustrations and printing on nearly everything else. Some of the most graphic and popular barbershop paper collectibles are: post cards, trade cards, ink blotters, business cards, labels, greeting cards, magazine covers, sheet music, matchbooks, and photographs. Others that are less colorful but which provide even more written history are: state issued licenses, letter and bill heads, barbershop books, woodcut art prints, news stories, and advertisements. There is obviously a wealth of information to be gleaned from these paper subjects.

Perhaps the best part of collecting antique paper is that when you've learned all you can from it, you can display it in many functional ways. Magazine covers, advertisements, and early sheet music, in particular, make great conversational wall decorations. When framed nicely, they can compliment any casual room's decor. Nice antique frames for them can be found at flea markets and they are usually reasonably priced. The standard size you will use for the above items is 11"x14," but always measure to be sure. Matting, if desired, will need to be custom cut. Nothing can beat these colorful images when hung with a barbershop display. Many current day barbershops and salons around the world are basing entire decorating schemes around these early framed images and related antiques.

Some collectors of antique paper care more about quantity and diversity than about decorative wall hangings. Those collectors usually gravitate to post cards, trade cards, and business cards. There seems to be a never ending variety to choose from with each new one being more interesting than the last. With post cards alone, there are more than 700 documented *different* barber scenes falling into ten defined categories. As with trade and business cards, postcards may be framed in groupings for wall hanging or kept in photo albums. When kept the latter way, a huge collection can fit neatly into one album displayed on your coffee table. It is ready to share with guests at all times and you can dust a huge collection in two seconds flat! Try that with a one hundred piece shaving mug collection. Another good point about collecting paper, is that you will never have to miss a pre-planned "antiquing" day because of bad weather. To a true collecting buff, there is not much worse than anticipating a weekend hunt, only to awaken to rain falling on the window pane. Unlike most antique flea markets, which are usually outdoors, paper shows are exclusively indoors. They are always warm in the winter and cool in the summer. Many dealers have chairs for you to sit on when looking through their goods.

At paper shows, most dealers' goods are well displayed and you should be able to quickly tell if they might have something of interest to you. For instance, if you approach a booth that is wall to wall antique stock certificates, keep going. If, on the other hand, the next booth has old magazines and trade cards, you might want to take a look. Because of the flat, stackable shape of paper collectibles, it is nearly impossible for a dealer to show a clear offering of every piece in their inventory. If there is nothing catching your eye with a barbershop theme, ask. Paper dealers know every piece they have and can usually dig it right up. If it is something that they have left behind on that particular day, many dealers will take your name and address and mail the piece to you on "approval." That simply means when you receive the item in the mail, if you choose to buy it, you mail a check. If for any reason you don't want to buy it, simply pay the postage both ways and mail it back.

Either a briefcase or knapsack would be your best bet to take along when going shopping. Most paper collectibles, aside from large art works or cardboard signs, will fit into them and remain protected while browsing. Of the two, I prefer the knapsack for hands-free carrying. While on this subject, I would like to point out that paper dealers, more than others, appreciate shoppers who don't carry roomy bags that are open at the top. While we don't like to think of thievery by fellow antique hunters as a problem, it is. Paper dealers have inventories that include small flat objects that can instantly disappear into an open bag. These dealers also like you to let them know when you wish to compare paper that you've purchased elsewhere with theirs. In the case of postcards or trade cards in particular, there are many duplicates of exactly the same image still in circulation. There could be twenty dealers at the same show, all of whom are offering the same card in a broad condition range. Unfortunately, that scenario tempts an unscrupulous buyer. For example: some people have been known to "upgrade" a so-so item they may have purchased ten minutes ago, with an identical and *perfect* one now in front of them at another dealer's table. This "switching," which in reality is **theft**, can translate into a real dollar loss for paper dealers.

After you have made a purchase of antique paper, you should be aware that there are good ways to protect it from rapid deterioration thanks to modern technology. Paper often becomes brittle or discolored simply from aging. While you may find a print that seems to have retained brilliant color, it probably is because the image hasn't previously been exposed to the elements. Many good paper images gleaned from newspapers or periodicals have sat stacked on top of one another for decades. When you isolate them from the relative protection of the stack, they can sometimes go downhill quickly due to humidity and light. If you are going to keep them in albums, (great for postcards or similar articles) you can purchase acid-free, clear vinyl sleeves that are good for storage and display. It is a well known fact that acids, which exist in regular vinyl storage sleeves, can actually hasten paper's deterioration. Acid-free sleeves are available in every imaginable size with openings to accommodate anything from postage stamps to extra large art work. They may be had with, or without, three ring binder holes. All, are relatively inexpensive. If you are going to have your antique paper article framed, commercial framing stores also carry acid-free mats and supplies. They can provide frame glass that filters and minimizes light exposure. Complete "archival" quality frames done by a professional will cost a bit more than usual however, if you want to insure the continuing appreciation of your picture's beauty, not to mention value, you should consider it.

If you do decide to attend a paper show, they are advertised in most major antique publications. One of the best sources for show dates is the P.A.C. newspaper (Paper and Advertising Collector.) They can be contacted by writing to P.O. Box 500, Mt. Joy, PA 17552.

As with all antiques and collectibles, condition and obvious rarity of barbershop paper will influence the asking price. And also, like the others, some skilled haggling will influence the selling price. As we take a look at each sub-title, there will be corresponding price spectrums that are currently applicable.

Postcards

Postcards are probably the most commonly collected barbershop related paper. They were all intended to be sent through the mail and most of them were. Occasionally, a card will turn up that was never mailed. The condition of an unused card will generally be better than one that went through the postal system. However, if a card does have a postal cancellation mark and a written message, it is not considered a fault providing the card is not otherwise damaged. Having been a collector of barbershop post cards intermittently over about a ten year period, I have isolated more than 700 different cards with barbershop images. Post cards, in general, remain plentiful because even as they were being printed and mailed in those early years, they were simultaneously being collected. Since post card collecting has had alternating periods of popularity over the decades, they remain by the millions. As my personal collection of barbershop related postcards unfolded, I discovered that they were produced in approximately ten distinct categories plus one for miscellaneous. They are all barber themes as follows: comedy, military, lady barbers, black barbers, barber schools, animal barbers, real photo cards, historical shops, advertising, foreign barbers, and miscellaneous. **Prices for post cards** range from 50 cents to over $100.00 for an especially good, real photograph postcard of a barbershop in-

terior. If there was a price range for barbershop post cards from the Golden Years era, it would be between $1.00 and $20.00 with an average of $8.00. The following is a brief background on the hobby of postcard collecting in general. It will also enable you to date your cards.

Pioneer Era (1893-1898) This was the birth of picture postcards and took place in 1893 at the Columbian Exposition in Chicago. Many of these cards said "Souvenir of...." or "Greetings from...." They all have undivided backs and if the postage is listed, it will say 2 cents. They were very popular and led to the lasting future of postcards.

Private Mailing Card Era (1898-1901) On May 19, 1898, the U.S. government gave permission to private printers to produce postcards. They all were required to carry the inscription "Private Mailing Card" and can be identified accordingly.

Post Card Era (1901-1907) It was on December 24, 1901 that the U.S. government gave permission for the use of the words "post card" to be imprinted on the backs of what were formerly called private mailing cards. The first cards of the post card era had undivided backs and *only* the address was to appear on the back. The message, therefore, had to be written on the front (picture) side. For this reason, many of these early cards have writing on the face of them. This fault is more acceptable as they become more scarce and it won't *necessarily* devalue the card.

Divided Back Era (1907-1915) This was the peak period of post card collecting and hoarding. It lasted for approximately eight years and in that time, the postal service estimates that nearly 700 million postcards went through the mail. The divided back made it possible for both the message and the address to be written on the backside. Another identifying characteristic is that the front view normally filled the entire card with no white border.

White Border Era (1915-1930) It was during this period that post card collecting slowed down. Cards were no longer being imported from Europe and the U.S. printers tried to fill the void. They didn't do so well as the quality wasn't the same and often times, they were just reprinting the quality cards from the divided back era. These cards are easily recognized by the white border after which they were named.

Linen Era (1930-1945) As American printing technology improved, so did the post card quality. It became popular to use a high rag-content paper that appeared like linen. While these cards do play a role in helping define the changing American scene, they are most sought after for their comedy portrayals. Many collectors of Black Americana also find "linens" to be a good source.

Photochrome Era (1939 to present day) These are the cards that are still offered for sale in gift-shops. The full-color photographic image is reproduced as a half-tone on modern lithography presses. They receive their shiny look from a varnish overprint. The chrome era overlapped the early linen period.

Real photo Cards (1900 to present day) These cards are those that have an actual photograph on the face. They can sometimes be hard to date unless postmarked or identifiable by subject matter. The stamp box sometimes shows the printing process such as: AZO, EKC, KODAK, VELOX, and, KRUXO. These are often reproduced and must be checked carefully to avoid being duped, although most dealers will mark them accordingly.

Artist Signed. The artist's signature (may be full name or initials) is incorporated as part of the printed design. It does *not* mean that the card has been personally signed.

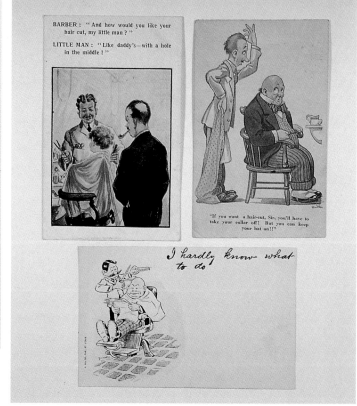

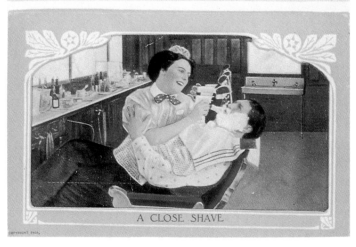

183

Barber Shop, Hotel Saint Paul, St. Paul, Minn.

HOTEL NORVAL BARBER SHOP, LIMA, OHIO. FRANK M. FOCKLER, PROPRIETOR.

THE O. K. BARBER SHOP, 217 N. 20TH STREET, BIRMINGHAM, ALA.
PICKARD & ERCKERT, PROP.

A CHINESE STREET BARBER, PEKING.

185

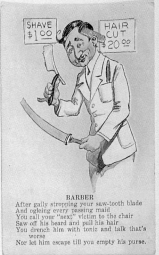

"SAY, JIMMY, HE'S LOOKING FOR 'EM WITH A LIGHTED TAPER."

BARBER
After gaily stropping your saw-tooth blade
And ogleing every passing maid
You call your "next" victim to the chair
Saw off his beard and pull his hair
You drench him with tonic and talk that's worse
Nor let him escape till you empty his purse.

Getting out of a bad scrape.

"Why does your dog always look so attentively when you shave anybody?"
"Well, you see, a little while ago I cut a piece of a man's ear off, and now he thinks he's going to have something every day!"

Magazine Covers

Most of the best known periodicals have had covers or centerfolds that were devoted to barbering or shaving. In fact, it almost seemed as though the public had a fascination with those images during barbering's Golden Years. As barbers have declined, so have their once newsworthy images. I know of only a handful of barbershop scenes that were printed on magazine covers since the late 1940s to the present. Prior to the 1940s however, barber scenes showed up regularly in such diverse publications as *Harper's Weekly, Judge, Colliers, The Country Gentleman*, and many others. The *Saturday Evening Post* featured a barbershop cover at regularly spaced intervals for 50 continuous years. Some of the best artists and cover illustrators of those times produced the original art works. Names like Leyendecker, Anderson, Dohanos, and Norman Rockwell were responsible for those graphic interpretations of the American barbershop. Magazine covers and centerfolds are some the best collectible paper that lend themselves to framing. A selection of barbering and shaving scenes go a long way in recalling the old barbershop experience.

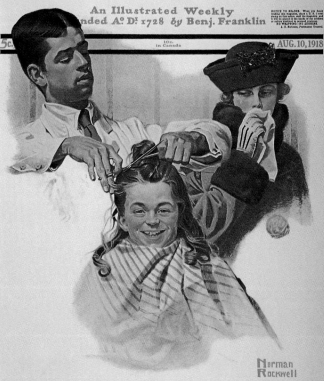

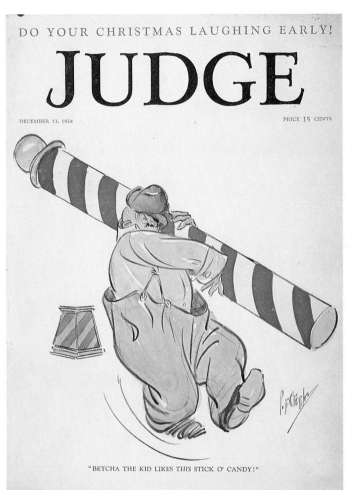

JUDGE

DECEMBER 13, 1924   PRICE 15 CENTS

"BETCHA THE KID LIKES *THIS* STICK O' CANDY!"

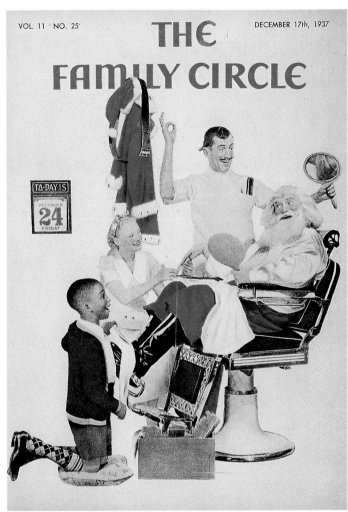

VOL. 11 NO. 25   DECEMBER 17th, 1937

THE FAMILY CIRCLE

TO-DAY IS
DECEMBER
24
FRIDAY

THE SATURDAY EVENING POST

An Illustrated Weekly
Founded A.D. 1728 by Benj. Franklin

MAY 10, 1930   5c. THE COPY
10c. in Canada

Ben Ames Williams—Almet Jenks   Marie, Grand Duchess of Russia
Margaret Culkin Banning—Marge   Thomas Beer—Anne Cameron

May 18, 1940   5c

norman rockwell

DOROTHY THOMPSON By JACK ALEXANDER

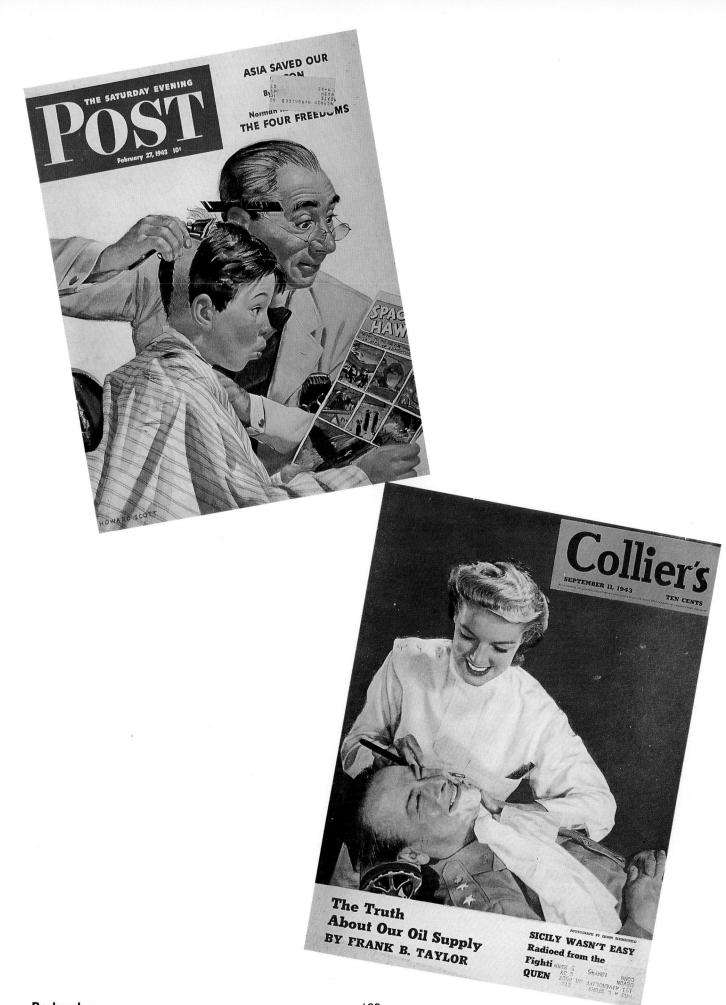

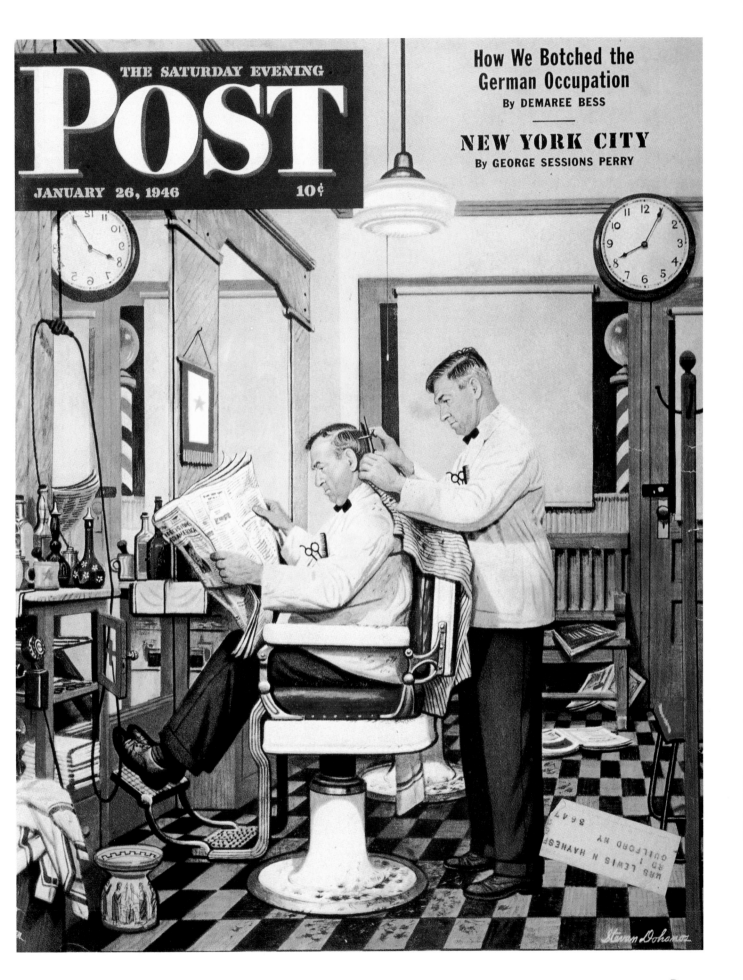

Paper

THE SATURDAY EVENING

POST

APRIL 29, 1950   15¢

I ESCAPED OVER THE ROOF OF THE WORLD
A U.S. Consul's Own Story of His Flight From the Reds

ranged from 1.75"x3" to 3.5"x5.5". Sometimes they were die-cut into shapes such as artists' palettes, or fans. In the 1890s, their size seemed to standardize into a stubby rectangular shape of approximately 2.75"x3.5". The 2"x3.5" size for business cards, as we know them today, began around 1920. Some of the most desirable business cards are those which came in sets. They would comprise from two to eight cards with matching text information, however, each card had a different color or scene. It is these sets that make gorgeous groupings to be framed and hung. There is a good availability of Golden Years barbershop business cards.

Business card value guide: The price range could be from $.50 cents for a card from the 1940s, to $40.00+ for an 1890s Victorian beauty. However, the average card made between 1870 and 1920 will average $15.00+.

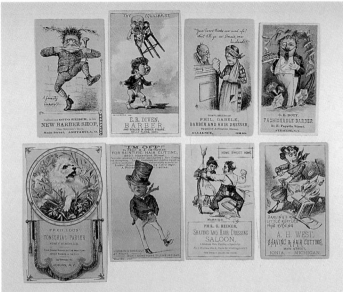

Magazine cover value guide: Current prices reflect age, rarity and condition. Another significant factor in pricing is that some collectors seek only certain artists. If you have found a barbering or shaving image cover and it seems overly priced, you may find that it is because of the buying public's interest in the artist. Not necessarily the subject matter. Average prices for excellent condition covers or centerfolds will begin at about $20.00. A recent paper show saw a 1918 *Saturday Evening Post* with a barbershop scene bring $95.00. Victorian Era prints and centerfolds in good condition range up to $150.00+.

Barbershop Business Cards

The notion of using barbershop business cards started during the mid-1800s. They continued to increase in popularity until they have become taken for granted today. The most collectible of them came from the late Victorian period. Cards from those years reflected the barbers' increasing pride in their businesses and each card seemed to try and out-do the competitors' cards. It was often a virtual creativity contest to see who could come up with the most clever business card. Some had poems or jokes. Others had photos and civic information and many were double-sided. They are an excellent source of barbering history during the Golden Years but they are valued more for their stunning, brightly colored graphics and ingenuity. Victorian business cards from prior to 1890 were either quite large or quite small. They

Sheet Music

It never ceases to amaze me when I find another different piece of barbershop sheet music. To date, I have been able to locate nearly 50 songs that were written by, or about, barbers. All are written for piano, voice, or both. Every one bears a cover with a colorful barbershop scene. While the latest of them (that I have found) was written more than 40 years ago, prior to that time there was obviously quite a variety during the Golden Years. The earliest piece that I have found is from the late 1800s and was written to be performed in music halls in England and America. American sheet music with barber subjects between 1900 and 1925 was mainly vaudeville or ragtime songs. Those particular cover illustrations are the most graphic and make exceptionally good wall decor when framed. I shouldn't neglect to tell you that the words to some of this music about barbers is hilarious and could still be played and sung if you chose.

Sheet music value guide: Some of these musical pieces are sought after because of the musical styles which were popular during the period they originated in. Others, because some people collect only certain performing artists. These factors, along with age and condition, determine the price scale which ranges from $10.00 to $60.00. Average piece of barbershop sheet music from the Golden Years era is $30.00.

Ink Blotters

Since plenty of you grew up in a ball-point pen writing world, you may ask "what is an ink blotter?" Prior to the invention of writing instruments as we currently know them, everybody wrote with pens that were continuously filled with fresh supplies of liquid ink from glass wells. The ink flowed out of a point called a "nib" as you wrote. Because it wasn't a perfect science, sometimes not enough ink came out, sometimes too much. At any rate, you occasionally needed to dry (blot) excess ink. Especially if you wanted to fold your letter into the envelope and you didn't want to wait for the wet ink to dry. Hence, the need for blotters. I don't know positively when fountain pens stopped being used in favor of the more convenient ball-points, but I do remember still having inkwells in my desk at school in 1950. Ironically enough, fountain pens are currently back on the market being sold as "luxury" writing instruments. Another example of progress through creative marketing! In all fairness, the new fountain ink pens write beautifully but they too can use a blotter. The early blotters that we refer to on these pages, have been a collectible paper subject for many years. Their availability is quite good con-

sidering that they were not originally meant to be saved. Advertising was their biggest advantage besides soaking up ink. The front of the blotter carried business information that made impression after impression with the user. Each time they picked up the blotter to use the ink-absorbent backside, they *had to look* at the advertisement on the front. Businesses of all kinds purchased blotters to give away to their customers. During the mid-to late Golden Years, barbershops across the country were no different. As a result, many interesting barbershop blotters remain to be found today.

Ink blotter value guide: Of all barbershop paper collectibles, blotters are some of the most affordable. Prices generally range from $5.00 to $15.00 with an average of $8.00+.

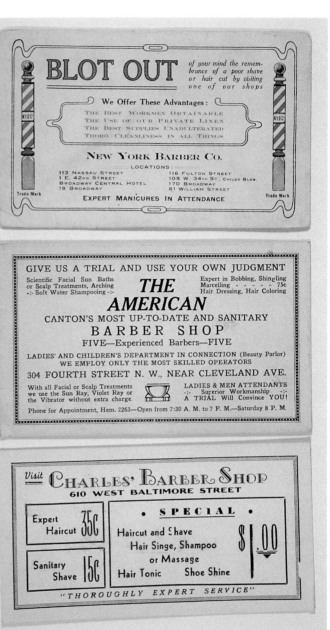

Trade Cards

The hobby of collecting trade cards has gotten bigger than ever lately. While it is true that people were saving them even as they were being printed in the late 1800s, like postcards, their popularity has see-sawed. They remain plentiful today and trade card auctions are bringing record prices for highly desirable items. Fortunately, cards that have barbershop graphics or images advertise general products in most cases. This keeps the prices fairly reasonable for the barber collector since some trade card subjects, such as clipper ships, bring astronomical prices. Probably the most interesting cards relating to barbershops are those that advertise shaving soap, toilet waters, and hair care products. Occasionally, a manufacturer of barber implements also issued a

trade card for his product. Often times, you may see a beautiful barbershop or shaving scene on the front, only to turn the card over and find a coffee advertisement. This was common for a business to put an unrelated, but attractive, scene on the front of their card. After all, the purpose of these cards was advertising and anything that would get the publics attention would do.

Trade card value guide: Because there are plenty of duplicates of the same card out there, *condition really counts*. It would never pay to purchase a card in poor condition unless it was rare. Because maybe not today, but soon, a better example *will* come along. Trade cards with barbershop or shaving scenes in excellent condition will cost between $5.00 to $60.00. The average will be $15.00+.

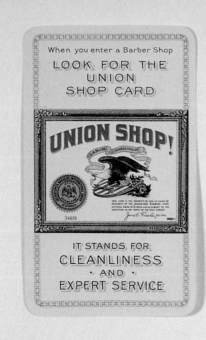

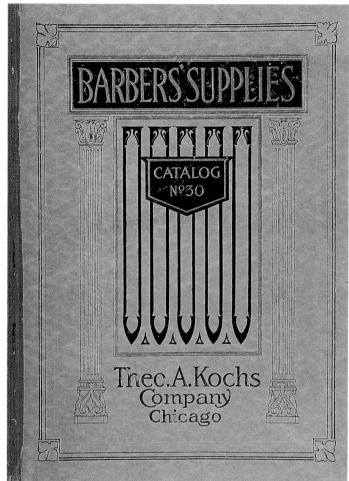

Catalogs and Photographs

As we discussed in the first chapter, and again in the introduction to this chapter, catalogs and photographs offer the most
factual and definitive reference to today's barbershop antiques
and collectibles. Catalogs show what items were produced and photos bring them to life. Catalogs have
been continuously printed and distributed by a large
number of barber supply concerns since the late
1800s. Some were only 10 or 12 pages. Others have
exceeded 300 pages. Most small and mid-sized companies printed catalogs that previewed their entire
line under one cover. Larger companies like Koken
or Kochs printed many specialty catalogs in addition to their "big book." The specialty catalogs
were for exclusive coverage of poles, chairs, sanitary equipment, or shoeshine equipment.

Catalog value guide: The problem with
finding catalogs today, is that most of them were
discarded each time a new one was sent to the
barbershop. Why would a barber want to keep
something that only showed last years styles
and had outdated prices? As you might expect,
good clean examples of late Victorian and early
1900s barber supply catalogs are indeed rare.
Prices for pre-1920 issues reflect that fact
with single catalogs climbing into the hundreds of dollars. Catalogs from the 1930s
and later average $75.00.

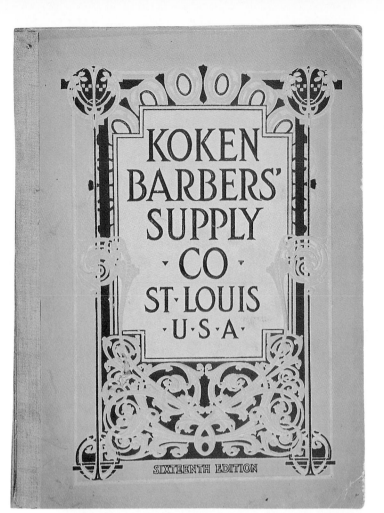

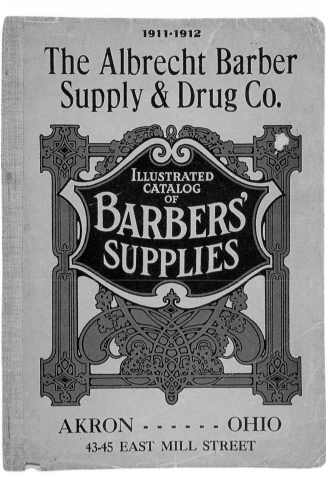

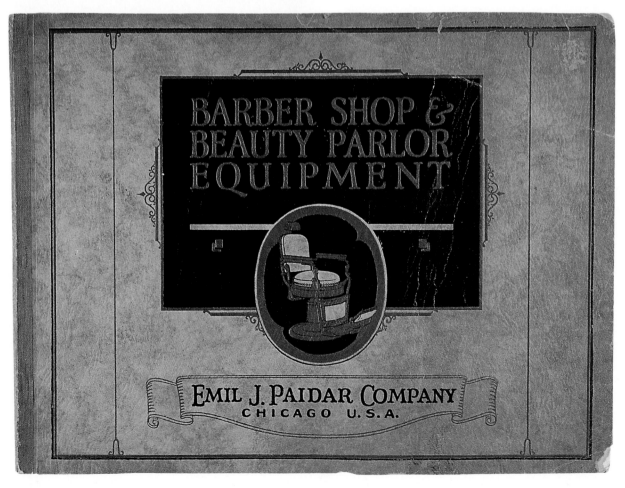

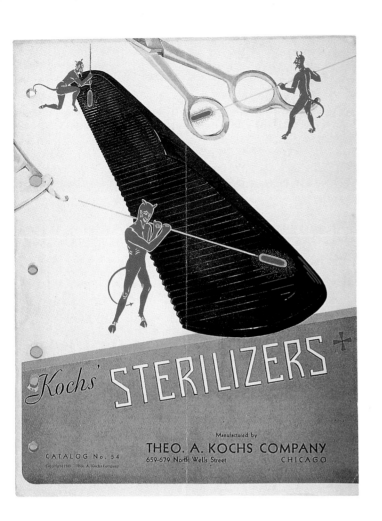

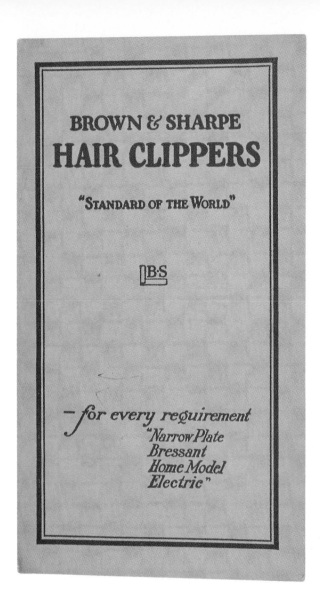

decorated shaving mugs. Especially desirable photos are those that depict women barbers, black barbers, and ancillary services being performed such as massage, bobbing, or manicuring. Also sought after are sets of photos from the same shop which have been taken in intervals and show chronology over the years.

Photograph value guide: Photos can be found at antique paper shows and auctions. Reproductions are showing up more often and with the latest technology can sometimes look better than the originals. The problem is that reproductions are worth far less. Check carefully. I have had reputable paper dealers try to sell me barbershop photos for top dollar that they *truly* believed were original.

Prices for original, early, barbershop photographs are based on size, clarity, and volume of detail. Pricing is very uneven from dealer to dealer because some of the above criteria is interpretive. That is to mean that what one person construes as good clarity and lots of details, will be viewed differently by another. For the sake of having a reference, lets look at an imaginary 8"x10" photo that was taken professionally in 1917. It has perfectly clear black and white contrast. There are three barbers with starched jackets and ties. One is giving a woman a bobbed cut. Another is giving a man a shave. And the third is selling a customer a cigar from an in-focus cigar case. In the background is a combination mug and barber bottle rack filled with personalized glassware. On the wall is a reverse running clock and an in-focus calendar reading December 1917. You can easily count nine identifiable items on the backbar's marble counter. On the far left is a man getting a shoeshine while perusing the *Police Gazette*. You...... have just entered barber photo nirvana! I have seen genuine photographs with *much less* detail sell for over $200.00. If it was a reproduction print of the same scene, it may be worth $35.00, and then only because of the buyers desire to own such a powerful image, *not* for antique value. If there was an average price for a professional quality, *well detailed*, 8"x10" barbershop photo taken before 1925, it would currently fall between $75.00 and $150.00. Possibly more if it was older. Less if it was newer.

Photographs that were taken during the Golden Years are considerably more plentiful than catalogs. That is due in no small way to the fact that, unlike catalogs which were intended to be discarded, photos were intended to be saved. And they were. They can be found at most paper shows and are usually mounted on a stiff cardboard backing. Photo sizes prior to 1930 are usually 8"x10", 5"x7", or 3"x5". Most of them were professionally taken since few people, barbers or otherwise, owned personal cameras during the early Golden Years. In order for photos to be desirable to today's collector, they should be clear and undamaged. Because of the limited photographic technology back then, many pictures have wash-out spots from unfavorable lighting situations. Of course, there were no color photos and all are black and white. Routine photos have the barber or barbers posed in an unsmiling stance next to their chair. Critics of these photos say if you've seen one, you've seen them all. While at first glance they *can* seem repetitive, closer examination will reveal many objects that document a variety of other barbershop antiques. The worth of these pictures increases if they show identifiable bottles or

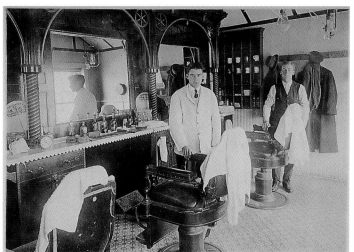

Paper

The "VIRGINIAN" 1916.
SANITARY TONSORIAL PARLOR
H.H. HOENRICH PROP. SARASOTA, FLA.

BATHS

Barbershop

Advertising

To date, most people who have been collecting barbershop related product advertising are advanced collectors. Their interests are with documenting a certain antique or product example that may be in their collection. Especially if it is a unique item that was marketed for only a short time. It is always interesting to find just about everything there is to know concerning an antiques original offering. With choice early advertising, this can easily be accomplished. Barbershop and personal grooming supplies were heavily marketed during the Golden Years. Shaving soap, razor, and tonic manufacturers all had huge ad budgets. Full page advertisements were frequently seen in national publications. While most of those early ads were in black and white, some ads were creatively illustrated in full color. The best of them were two-page centerfold spreads in rich color. A nicely framed grouping of razor and shaving soap ads makes perfect wall decor in a bath or masculine office setting. With collectors seeking to add more framed pieces to their collections, attractive advertisements are getting more attention. This is one area of collectibles where you needn't worry about condition. Paper advertisements are usually "mint" when found. Why? Because they are on interior pages of magazines and periodicals that have, in most cases, sat stacked in piles for years. They have been protected from discoloring, bending, tearing, and the weather. There is occasionally a slight darkening of the extreme outer edge. In most cases, it is undetectable.

Advertising value guide: Prices remain fairly low, even for perfect condition, full page, color ads. These bargains can regularly be found for between $5.00 and $15.00.

A happy Christmas reflection

BRYLCREEM
THE PERFECT HAIR DRESSING

KEEPS YOUR HAIR IN PERFECT CONDITION

THE LARGE BOTTLE WITH A SPECIAL BRYLCREEM PUMP MAKES AN IDEAL CHRISTMAS PRESENT . . . .

The County Perfumery Co., London, N.W.10

one for a quarter or fifty cents, you *will* feel compelled pick up everyone you come across thereafter!

Early examples can be identified by a noticeably wider match striking area. They also are printed on cardboard that appears dull compared to today's shiny, varnished surfaces. Many from the late 1920s and 1930s reflect the popular "deco" look of that time. As most of you know, during the early to mid-Golden Years, reading material that was sometimes considered risqué was popular in barbershop waiting areas. As society's values changed and more women were patronizing barbershops for bobbed haircuts, the risqué reading material was sometimes abandoned for more mainstream periodicals. However, barbers were still able to satisfy their male customers lust for the sight of a pretty girl, thanks to matchbooks. In the 1930s and 1940s, partially clothed or fully nude pictures of women were some of the most popular barbershop matchbooks. The barber only handed them to men who he knew would be receptive........and appreciative! Little Jimmy nor his mother were ever offered these matches so they were never offended. Hey, what can be said about the *fact* that for many years barbershops were mostly an adult, male experience? The "girlie" covers often came in sets with a number of different poses. Other popular sets included comedy sketches and animals. Also very desirable are covers that have a barbershop price menu or other pertinent information on the inside flap. There are two schools of thought concerning the cataloging and display of matchbooks. One is to leave the match sticks intact, and the other is to carefully open the staple and remove or "shuck" them. This certainly leaves the covers more flat and easier to put into vinyl sleeves. Some also argue that it reduces fire risk. Either way, barbershop matchbooks are historical, fun, and inexpensive to collect.

Matchbook value guide: Single books range from $.50 cents to $5.00+. Average books are $1.00 each. Matched groupings are proportionately higher.

Matchbook Covers

Collecting barbershop matchbook covers is just a microcosm of the larger and long standing hobby. General matchbook collectors sometimes have thousands of covers in many categories. One current matchbook organization alone has more than 6000 active members! The first match was invented in 1827 and book matches as we know them today first came about in 1892, although the striker was on the *inside* of the cover at that time. Just before 1900, manufacturers began to sell matchbooks with advertising on their covers to businesses. It was during this period that the striker was moved to the *outside* and the "close cover before striking" warning was added. For many years, matchbooks provided businesses with a form of "giveaway" advertising that was unrivaled. Barbershops, in particular, seemed to really embrace the concept. Perhaps, because of the fact that so many tobacco products were sold in early barbershops? I have personally located more than 600 of these tiny barbershop billboards and I'm sure that mine are only the tip of the iceberg. They have provided me with invaluable information about the changing barbershop scene from the 1920's and later. Information on services, prices, amenities, hours of operation, and how they varied across America's landscape for many years. The problem with barbershop matchbooks is that they are colorful, information laden, and *cheap!* So, what's the problem you ask? It is that once you buy

Paper

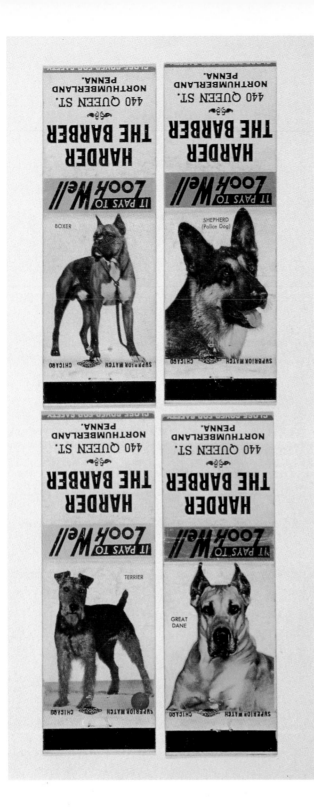

bershop illustrations were commissioned works done expressly for mass-reproduction prints which appeared on magazine covers or advertisements. Those originals probably still exist in art galleries somewhere or they may be privately held. If located, they would be considered investment grade original art and wouldn't really come under the barbershop collectibles umbrella. Interesting barbershop art that *is* both obtainable and beautiful exists from the late 1800s in the form of woodcut prints, pen and ink drawings, and stone or steel lithographs. Those images covered a broad variety of barbering and shaving scenes. Some of my personal favorites are works that were commissioned to appear in the *Judge* and *Puck* periodicals during the Victorian years. Most were political caricatures that used the barbershop setting as a vehicle for their stinging humor. Satirical art was often done in beautiful water colors. Many are full, two-page centerfolds which reflect public sentiment concerning the country's political atmosphere. When formally framed, certain pieces of this art are appropriate not only with a barbershop display, but in your library or office.

Art value guide: This a *very* subjective category from dealer to dealer and buyer to buyer. Because of that, you can expect to pay from as little as $20.00 for a single page, black and white scene, to $175.00 for an artist signed, color centerfold.

SOUTHERN SKETCHES—A GENTLEMAN OF COLOR.—From the Water-color Painting by T. W. Wood.—[See Page 629.]

Art

Generally speaking, art is a widely diverse subject. As art pertains to barbershop collectibles, it is much less complicated. Barbershop art could be construed as any picture with a barbershop scene that was originally generated by an artist. Most artists' bar-

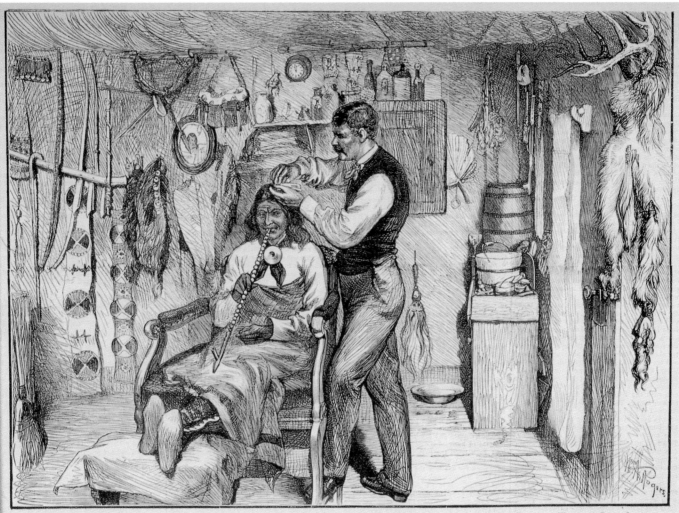

A BARBER'S SHOP AT STANDING ROCK, DAKOTA TERRITORY—AN INDIAN CHIEF HAVING HIS HAIR DRESSED.—[DRAWN BY WILLIAM A. ROGERS.]

Paper

UNCLE SAM'S SANITARY BARBER-SHOP. NEXT!

THE NATIONAL BARBER-SHOP.—"NEXT!"

Barbershop Books

Few books have actually been written by barbers. Those that I am aware of (aside from instructional texts) give plenty of factual reference to barbershops and their place in society during the times in which they were written. That span was between the early 1800s and early 1900s which does offer a decent 100+ year chronology of the business. However, the books also seem to be thinly-veiled opportunities for the barber/authors to share their personal philosophy on life in general. Are they interesting? Yes. Are they important to today's barbershop antique collector who is interested in research? Only minimally. The kick, more than likely, will be for an advanced collector who simply wants to own one or more of these *rare*, barber authored, books. They really do make a nice addition to any collector's library that contains a number of other books about barbershop collectibles.

More plentiful books about barbering, specifically in the Golden Years, are instructional texts. Individuals like Professor Bridgeford and A.B. Moler wrote instructional books for their own schools for years. The barbers' union also published a textbook that was a compilation of the best barbering methods. This book was very successful and was revised as needed to remain in print for more than three decades. You may suspect that instructional books only have value in teaching haircutting or shaving. Actually, I have found them to be a wealth of insider information about ancillary services, recipes for products, authoritative views on sanitation, mugs, bottles, razors, and more. *Quality* research. They're filled with information that eliminates things you may have been guessing about concerning your collectibles. Often times, textbooks unceremoniously debunk popular collector's tales.

Barbershop book value guide: When you come across one of these textbooks from the golden year period, you can expect to pay between $10.00 and $50.00 depending on age and volume of information. Books written by barbers, *other than* instructional, are difficult to find and can range up to $150.00+.

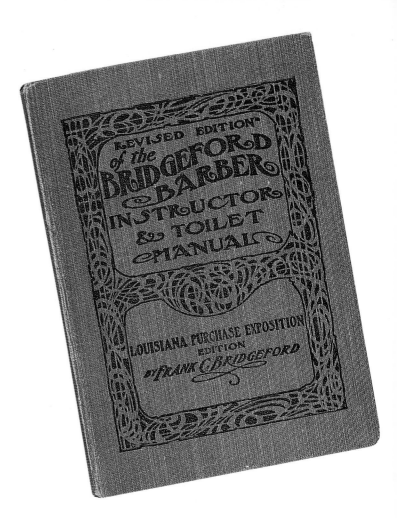

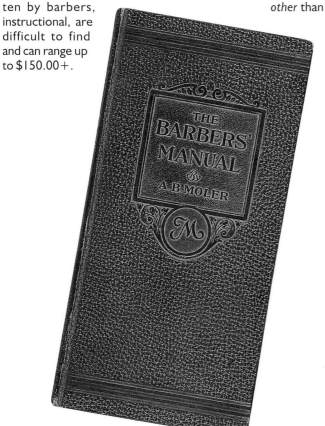

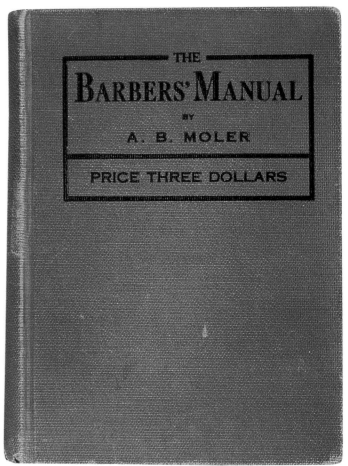

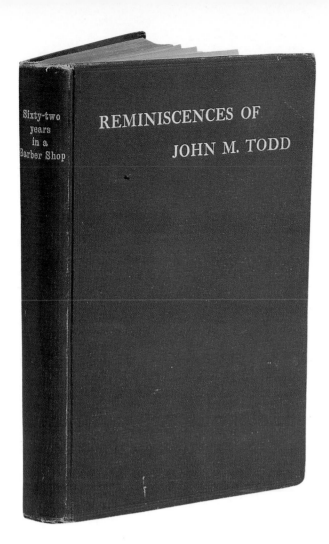

early golden year's bottles with the original labels are worth more than those without them. There are unscrupulous dealers who have applied a new/old label to *any* bottle they may have laying around and sell it as an original. Many people have been duped, especially if they don't know what the original bottle shape was. The rule of thumb here is "if a labeled bottle looks much too good to be true," it probably isn't. Ask questions!

Paper Labels

Label collecting is another hobby that has had a legion of enthusiasts for many years. That contributes to why they remain so available today. Labels pertaining specifically to barbershop collections, are those that represent hair, scalp, and after shave products. There is a nice variety of them from the mid-to late Golden Years period. Advances in printing processes saw labels being produced that had spectacular color and graphics. The best of them in the 1800s were embossed and some had foil embellishments. By today's standards they were very ornately done. Most labels from any period of the Golden Years are nearly always found in mint, unused condition. The reason being is that they were printer's over-runs and often times have sat in stacks since being printed. Apparently, there were buyers for these extra labels who kept them warehoused for years. Labels are easily stored in photo albums and look great in a framed wall grouping.

Paper label value guide: Over time, they have found their way to many paper dealers who regularly sell post-1920 paper labels from 50 cents to $2.00 each. Those made in the 1800s with a fancy Victorian influence, such as gold-embossed labels, can cost as much as $20.00+ but average $12.00. Labels for black hair and scalp products are post-1930 and average $5.00 to $8.00 each.

Note: This is an area of collectibles that has been known to produce some unethical dealing. As we discussed in chapter three,

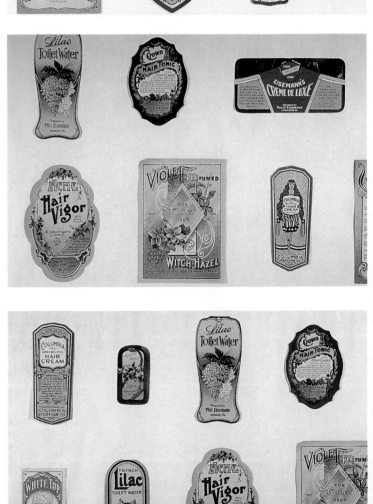

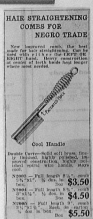

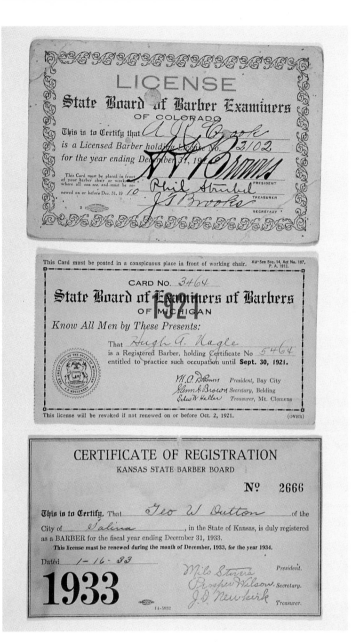

Miscellaneous Paper

These are pieces of old barbershop paper that don't fit into the main categories but are interesting enough be included here. Some, such as Golden Years barber licenses or billheads, go great with a display. Others, like barbershop greeting cards or jokes, are simply entertaining. Barbershop jokes from the Golden Years indicate that sometimes the old adage "the more things change, the more they stay the same" is true.

Miscellaneous paper value guide: The price range for good **license examples** begins at approximately $50.00 for one issued between 1900 and 1910. Each decade since would be about $10.00 lower so that a 1940s license should be worth about $10.00. Condition may influence this guideline. **Bill heads and letterheads** range from about $10.00 to $35.00+ for highly ornate Victorian era examples. **Stereo-view cards** average $7.00 to $10.00+. **Barbers wage books** were used to keep personal records of haircut and wage percentages. Lucky Tiger example seen here, $15.00+. **Greeting cards** seem to range between $10.00 to $35.00 depending on the detail and art work. Some cards values are influenced because of a certain designer's work that is highly desirable. **Barbershop jokes** are taken from pages of periodicals published during the Golden Years. They are rarely more than $20.00 and average $8.00 to $12.00 each.

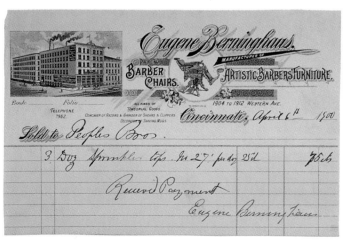

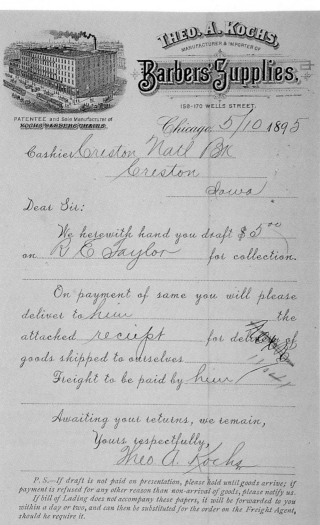

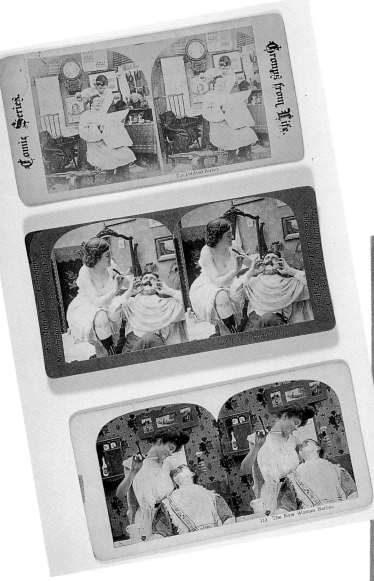

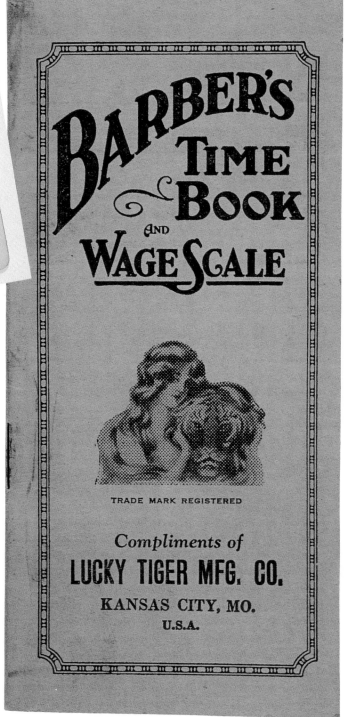

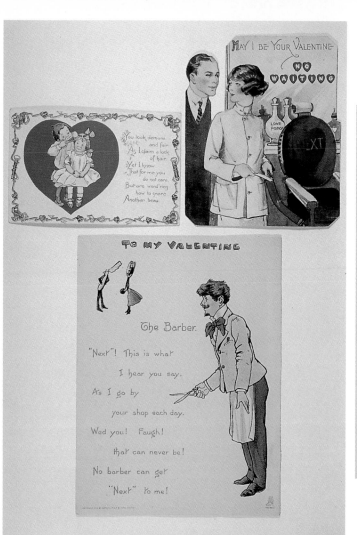

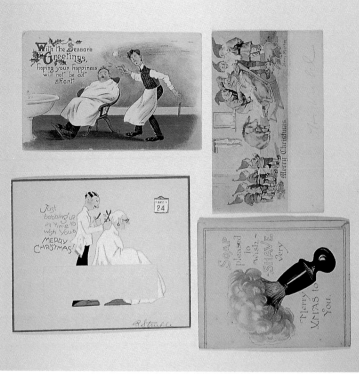

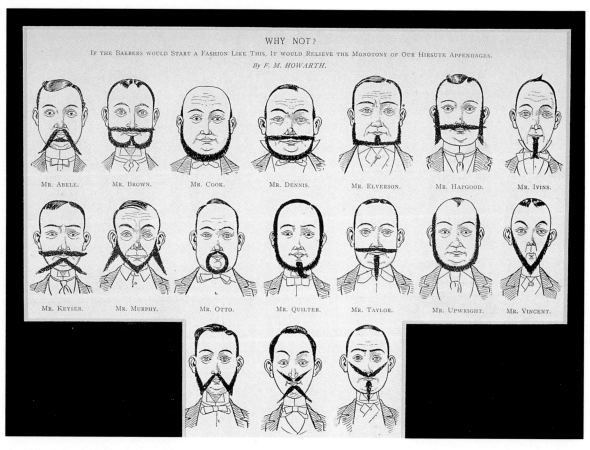

WHY NOT?

IF THE BARBERS WOULD START A FASHION LIKE THIS, IT WOULD RELIEVE THE MONOTONY OF OUR HIRSUTE APPENDAGES.

By F. M. HOWARTH.

MR. ABELE. MR. BROWN. MR. COOK. MR. DENNIS. MR. ELVERSON. MR. HAPGOOD. MR. IVINS.

MR. KEYSER. MR. MURPHY. MR. OTTO. MR. QUILTER. MR. TAYLOR. MR. UPWRIGHT. MR. VINCENT.

A BOTCH BARBER.

You dizzy little thing you, how like a bird you flutter,
You ought go to sweeping streets, and scraping out the gutter.
Then as to fixing up the hair, it makes your victims bluer
To think that such a poor sham should work as a shampooer.
You might succeed in cutting wood, but as for cutting hair.
The Kickapoo could do it much better in his lair.
Your razor is as dull as you, but viler is your breath,
While your tongue can talk a regiment of Turks to certain death.

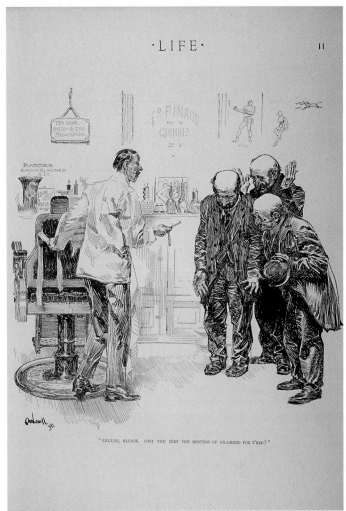

Chapter 10

Novelties

In debating whether to include barbershop related novelties in this book, it was pointed out to me that I had promised to write about "everything" under the barbershop umbrella. It may be true that I have unintentionally missed *something* along the way, but with so many neat novelties items out there, they couldn't be overlooked. It is apparent that the world's modern retail market is keenly aware of the publics fascination with barbershop nostalgia. New "old" barbershop items keep popping up. While most of them represent old style barber poles, there is also a wide variety of other articles. Our situation as collectors of antique barbershop items, (along with all of their corresponding novelties) is still not as bad as that of Coca Cola collectors. For example, it often seems as though that particular field has nearly as many new and reproduction collectibles as there are authentic antiques. While most collectors heartily agree that currently produced barbershop novelties can't begin to compare with their authentic collectibles, they will usually admit to having a few novelties lying around. How many of us have a ceramic barber pole or a new "old" shaving mug? How about a decorative sign that says something similar to: Haircuts 10 cents, Shaves a nickel? They may be recent, but these "go-alongs" to our hobby are harmless and only reinforce our dedication to barbershop collectibles. While some of the novelties pictured here do have age and are bonafide antiques, most have been manufactured in the last 25 years, and others *just last week*. In spite of how new some of them are, novelty barbershop collectibles are regularly traded along with legitimate antiques. Pick up a few of the best of them while they are cheap! *You know what will probably happen with this "stuff" one day!*

Left: Ceramic pole 17" tall. $10.00 flea market item. **Center:** Leaded glass crafted pole. *Courtesy of Len and Elaine Calinoff.* $50.00+. **Right:** Hallmark brand gift candle made in the late 1960s. $10.00 when new.

Whimsical barber pole is recently made and measures 7" x 32". Purchased for $12.00 in Lancaster, Pennsylvania Dutch gift shop.

Avon brand glass containers for men's after-shave products. Barber pole stands 6.75" tall. Shaving brush stands 5" tall. Both trade at flea-markets for $3.00 to $7.00.

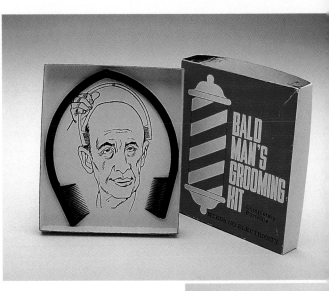

Cardboard boxed gag item believed to originate in the 1960s. Bald Man's Grooming Kit. Reveals a hinged, one-piece comb capable of grooming the few remaining hairs on each side of a bald man's head simultaneously. Flea market item seen for $15.00+.

Recently made ladies earrings and matching pin with barber pole motif. *Courtesy of Ed Jeffers' Barber Museum.* $10.00+.

Left: Cardboard boxed gag item dated 1939. Outside cover reads "New Shaving Kit." Inside reveals miniature pen-knife and a block of whittling wood with shavings. $20.00+ game collector's item. **Right:** Plastic coin bank dates to 1952. Coin is inserted at the top and spirals down the barber pole into bottom receptacle. *Courtesy of "Aunt" Hilda McMullen.* The value on this one is purely sentimental for me but it is a $20.00+ game collector's item.

Left: Souvenir ashtray from the State of Virginia ca. 1950. This cartoon scenario mimics one of the most repeated customer's greeting and barber's reply of all times. 5" diameter glazed-ceramic ashtray. $10.00+. **Right:** Plastic scale model of a Donnelly outdoor advertising billboard measuring 3.75" x 6.25". The model's billboard scene is actually a post card that slides out. The Donnelly Company strategically placed actual billboards with this message around the country to show the power of outdoor advertising. The response was overwhelming. It didn't hurt that the billboard's subject matter was one of the hottest counterculture issues of the 1960s. Scarce limited production plastic model, $25.00+. Postcard alone, $10.00+.

Parker Brothers Barber Pole game ca. 1900. Game challenges the players to flip the rings onto the pole. Rings and flipping squares are dyed, solid ivory. Felt mats are provided for better flipping results. Unused and complete. Rare. $100.00+.

Left: Limited production Burma-Shave nostalgic tin made by the American Safety Razor Company. 4" x 5" x 6". Unopened and containing original contents of a mug, brush, and soap. In condition as seen, $15.00+. **Right:** Limited production men's grooming kit by The Silver Crane Company dated 1990. 3" x 5" x 6". Shows *amazingly* detailed barbershop street scene in 1900. Unopened and containing original contents of a comb, shaving soap, 2 razors, shaving brush, and a towel. In condition as seen, $20.00+.

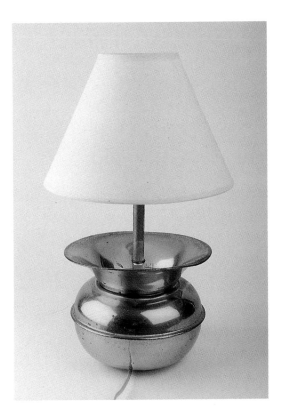

Fake spittoon lamp, U.L approved. 17" tall. Brass. Flea market item at $15.00+.

Enesco brand limited edition collectible gift titled *Shave And A Haircut....Ho! Ho!* Battery powered, mechanized, and lighted. 1993. Sold new for $125.00.

Novelties

Ceramic blade banks were often used by barbers for discarding Weck-type safety blades used in their shops. Barbers preferred banks that could be emptied when full. Home shavers preferred child-proof banks which had no opening to access the blades once they had been dropped in the top slot. Many banks were discarded when full which contributes to their general scarcity. Blade banks were produced in a large variety of figural styles. Their value range is wide at $15.00 to $175.00+ for rare editions. The average range, such as those pictured here, are valued between $20.00 and $50.00+. As with all glassware, chips or cracks will influence the price.

Shaving mugs of this type are often referred to as "fakes" by purist collectors. I believe that is a little harsh for most of the mugs seen here which date to the 1950s. Although they were certainly reproductions of original pre-1920s mugs when they were made, these 50s models are starting to get some age themselves. They obviously have no place with an "all original" mug collection, but they are very pretty (not to mention functional) novelties. They are suitable for a beginning collector. Some dealers try to pass them off as very old mugs but most who know what they are sell them in the $15.00 to $20.00+ range.

Novelties

Above and Opposite page: Modern prints of nostalgic barbershop scenes are good decorating items when framed. They are also inexpensive. Completely framed prints like George Wysocki's *Shaves and Haircuts* average $35.00+ for this 14" x 16" classic. 8.5" x 11" single-sheet reproductions like Norman Rockwell's *Barbershop Quartet* are on heavy stock ready for framing at less than $5.00.

Novelties

Closing

In reading over the book now that it is finished, I am happy to say that I am absolutely sure of my calling in life. That...... would be *haircutting!* While I have always admired great writers and have often wished that I could be one of them, I'm not. I'm a barber and happy about it. Besides, I set out to write an historically documented reference book, nothing more. I'm proud of the book mainly because it was honest work and I gave it my best.

My intent was to write a book that was the first to cover the *whole spectrum* of barbershop collectibles. Moreover, I wanted it to be presented from an occupational perspective. There have often been times when I have felt that collectors, in general, don't explore the history that serves up their treasures. To me, it almost seems greedy, or at least materialistic, for a collector to gather historical objects and not pay some homage to their origins. Especially if the antique subject stems from a fading occupation such as traditional barbering. For that reason, I hoped to put plenty of factual reference into the book along with the photography. Since most of the significant barbershop collectibles came exclusively from the Golden Years, I also thought it would be important to put the chronology of that particular period more clearly into focus. Of course, I hoped that the book would encourage new collectors and interest long standing "Barberiana" fans, as well. If I have met most of those objectives, then I will feel as though I've made a contribution to the pastime that has given me so much pleasure. Finally, and more than anything else, I was just plain hoping that the book would be *enjoyable* to you. If it has been, you can thank the people who encouraged me to get going with it.

When Peter and Nancy Schiffer came to my home and offered me a contract to do this book, I was beyond flattered.

Schiffer antique reference books are among the finest to be found. I went to sleep that night in a queen sized bed with a king sized ego. When I woke up the next morning and realized the significance of what might transpire, I didn't want to come out from under the covers. Figuratively speaking, I stayed under them for the next five months. In the interim, there were a couple of politely encouraging phone calls from Peter. Not pushy, just encouraging. My wife Joan, who is also my best friend, often reassured me that it would be just fine with her. This, in spite of the fact that she knew it would become the "year of the book" since I'm one of those nuts who can't pause from a project until it is finished. While I wanted badly to begin, my self confidence kept me slowed down. As the months passed, other friends in the antique world would occasionally urge me on. Finally, I called Peter and told him that I was ready to start. I'm darn glad that I did. While "book-building" is *really* hard work for me, the learning experience has made it very rewarding and definitely worthwhile. It's quite a heady experience for me, as a barber, to actually author a book that pertains to the history of my profession. Research suggests that there have only been three others previously. I'll bet that they all enjoyed their 15 minutes of fame as much as I am. So, while I am content that my book effort may never be counted as a literary "classic," you can rest assured it *will* stand as my personal "opus."

Please direct inquiries to: The Barbershop, 1959 Route 33, Hamilton Square, New Jersey 08690. If a reply is requested, please include a stamped, self-addressed envelope. E-mail to: Barbrpole@aol.com

Bibliography

Atlanta Constitution, The. May 25, 1913.

Augusta Herald, The. March 4, 1919.

Aurand, A. Monroe, *Curious Lore About Hair.* Harrisburg, Pennsylvania: The Aurand Press, 1938.

Barlow, Ronald S., *The Vanishing American Barbershop.* El Cajon, California: Windmill Publishing Co., 1993.

Bennion, Elizabeth, *Antique Medical Instruments.* New York, New York: Sotheby's Publications, 1979.

Bridgeford, Frank C., *The Bridgeford Barber Instructor Manual.* Kansas City, Missouri: Everitt Titus Co., 1904.

Chicago Tribune, The, November 28, 1896.

Creasy, F.W., *The Barber Salesman.* Oklahoma City, Oklahoma: Anderson Barber Supply, 1931.

Daily Inter Ocean, The. July, 1, 1895, July 7, 1895, July 14, 1895.

DeSilvis, J., *The Tonsorial Artist.* New York, New York: Mah' Studios, 1925.

De Zemler, Charles, *Once Over Lightly.* New York, New York: J.B. Williams Co., 1939.

Estep, Keith E., *The Shaving Mug And Barber Bottle Book.* Atglen, Pennsylvania: Schiffer Publishing Ltd., 1995.

Fadely, Don, *Hair Raising Stories.* USAF Academy, Colorado: Self-published, 1992.

Graphic, The. April 16, 1870.

Harper's Weekly. July 31, 1875, May 31, 1884.

Harper's Young People. April 29, 1890.

Harper's New Monthly. September, 1873.

Harper's Weekly. October 2, 1875, March 25, 1871.

Holiner, Richard *Collecting Barber Bottles.* Paducah, Kentucky: Collector Books, 1986

Hunter, Mic *The American Barbershop.* Mt. Horeb, Wisconsin: Face To Face Books, 1996.

Illustrated London News, The. March 9, 1861.

Judge. May, 1896.

Judge. November, 1904.

Judge. October, 1891.

Krumholz, Phillip L., *Value Guide For Barberiana And Shaving Collectibles.* Bartonville, Illinois: Ad Libs Publishing Co., 1988.

Krumholz, Phillip L., *Collector's Guide To American Razor Blades.* Bartonville, Illinois: Self-published, 1995.

Krumholz, Phillip L., *A History Of Shaving And Razors.* Bartonsville, Illinois: Ad Libs Publishing Co., 1987.

Krumholz, Phillip L., *The Complete Gillette Collector's Handbook.* Bartonville, Illinois: Self-published, 1992.

Leslies. January, 1858.

L-W Book Sales , *Barbershop Collectibles.* Gas City, Indiana: L-W Book Sales, 1996.

Macfadden, Bernard, *Hair Culture.* New York, New York: Macfadden Publications, 1924.

Mashburn, J. L., The Postcard Price Guide. Alexander, North Carolina: WorldComm Press, 1992.

Moler, A.B., *The Barbers Manual.* (three editions) St. Louis, Missouri: Moler Colleges, 1904, 1911, 1924.

New York Sun, The. September 17, 1899, January 28, 1901.

New York Herald, The. May 9, 1890, November 12, 1894.

Powell, Robert, Blake *Occupational and Fraternal Shaving Mugs Of The United States.* Hurst, Texas: Catalog Publications, 1978.

Puck. July, 1885.

Puck. September, 1880.

Rehder, Denny, *The Shampoo King, F.W. Fitch and his company.* Des Moines, Iowa: Waukon and Mississippi Press, 1981.

Ritchie, Roy and Stewart, Ron, *Standard Guide To Razors.* Paducah, Kentucky: Collector Books, 1995.

Rohrer, Prof. Joseph ,*Rohrer's Artistic Hair Bobbing.* New York, New York: Rohrer's Institute, 1924.

Standardized Textbook Of Barbering. Chicago, Illinois: Associated Master Barbers Of America, 1926.

Sunday Oregonian, The. February 7, 1909.

The Razor Anthology. Knoxville, Tennessee: Knife World Publications, 1995.

Todd, John M. *Sixty Two Years In A Barbershop.* Portland, Maine: John W. Roberts Co., 1906.

Washington Post, The. September 12, 1893.

Wilbur, Keith C., *Antique Medical Instruments.* Atglen, Pennsylvania: Schiffer Publishing Ltd., 1987

Woodbury, William A., *The Care Of The Hair And Scalp.* New York, New York: G.W. Dillingham Co., 1915.

Index

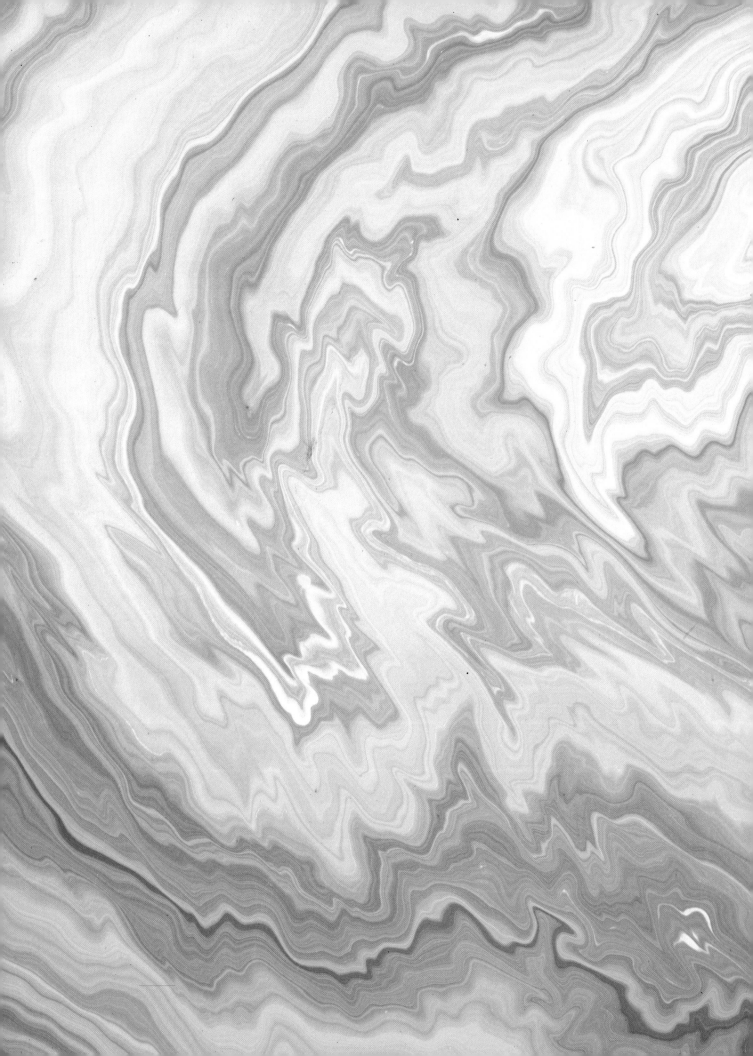